The Fireworks of
OSCAR WILDE

By the same author

Celtic Nationalism (with Hugh MacDiarmid,
Gwynfor Evans and Ioan Rhys)
The Sins of our Fathers: Roots of Conflict in Northern Ireland
The Mind of an Activist: James Connolly
P. G. Wodehouse: A Critical and Historical Essay
Burke and Hare
*The Quest for Sherlock Holmes: A Biographical Study of Arthur
Conan Doyle*
Éamon de Valera
Macaulay

as editor
Conor Cruise O'Brien Introduces Ireland
The Edinburgh Stories of Arthur Conan Doyle
A Claim of Right for Scotland

as co-editor
1916: The Easter Rising
James Connolly: Selected Political Writings
Scotland, Europe and the American Revolution
Ireland and America
Christmas Observed
Edinburgh: An Anthology

The Fireworks of
OSCAR WILDE

Selected, edited and introduced by
OWEN DUDLEY EDWARDS
★

with a Preface by
OSCAR WILDE

BARRIE & JENKINS
LONDON

First published in Great Britain in 1989 by
Barrie & Jenkins Ltd
289 Westbourne Grove, London WII 2QA

The extract from *The Aesthetic Adventure* by William Gaunt is printed by
permission of A. P. Watt on behalf of Michael Simone O'Reilly and
J. J. Reilly.
Where possible the texts (typographical corrections excepted) are
those finally passed by Oscar Wilde for the press.

British Library Cataloguing in Publication Data

Wilde, Oscar, *1854-1900*
    The fireworks of Oscar Wilde.
    I. Title II. Edwards, Owen Dudley
    828'.802

    ISBN 0-7126-2153-9

Typeset by SX Composing, Rayleigh, Essex
Printed in Great Britain by Richard Clay Ltd

Contents

For my Aunt
Elizabeth Wall

If, with the literate, I am
Impelled to try an epigram,
I never seek to take the credit;
We all assume that Oscar said it.
Dorothy Parker,
'A Pig's-Eye View of Literature: Oscar Wilde'

He left behind, as his essential contribution to literature, a large
repertoire of jokes which survive because of their sheer neatness,
and because of a certain intriguing uncertainty – which extends to
Wilde himself – as to whether they really mean anything.
George Orwell,
'*Lady Windermere's Fan* – a Commentary', BBC broadcast, 21 November 1943

PREFACE

The Remarkable Rocket

The King's son was going to be married, so there were general re-
joicings. He had waited a whole year for his bride, and at last she had
arrived. She was a Russian Princess, and had driven all the way from
Finland in a sledge drawn by six reindeer. The sledge was shaped like
a great golden swan, and between the swan's wings lay the little
Princess herself. Her long ermine cloak reached right down to her feet,
on her head was a tiny cap of silver tissue, and she was as pale as the
Snow Palace in which she had always lived. So pale was she that as
she drove through the streets all the people wondered. 'She is like a
white rose!' they cried, and they threw down flowers on her from the
balconies.

At the gate of the Castle the Prince was waiting to receiver he. He
had dreamy violet eyes, and his hair was like fine gold. When he saw
her he sank upon one knee, and kissed her hand.

'Your picture was beautiful,' he murmured, 'but you are more
beautiful than your picture,' and the little Princess blushed.

'She was like a white rose before,' said a young page to his neighbour, 'but she is like a red rose now'; and the whole Court was
delighted.

For the next three days everybody went about saying, 'White rose,
Red rose, Red rose, White rose' and the King gave orders that the
Page's salary was to be doubled. As he received no salary at all this
was not of much use to him, but it was considered a great honour, and
was duly published in the Court Gazette.

When the three days were over the marriage was celebrated. It was
a magnificent ceremony, and the bride and bridegroom walked hand
in hand under a canopy of purple velvet embroidered with little pearls.
Then there was a State Banquet, which lasted for five hours. The
Prince and Princess sat at the top of the Great Hall and drank out of a
cup of clear crystal. Only true lovers could drink out of this cup, for if
false lips touched it, it grew grey and dull and cloudy.

'It is quite clear that they love each other,' said the little Page, 'as
clear as crystal!' and the King doubled his salary a second time. 'What
an honour!' cried all the courtiers.

After the banquet there was to be a Ball. The bride and bridegroom

I

were to dance the Rose-dance together, and the King had promised to play the flute. He played very badly, but no one had ever dared to tell him so, because he was the King. Indeed, he knew only two airs, and was never quite certain which one he was playing; but it made no matter, for, whatever he did, everybody cried out, 'Charming! charming!'

The last item on the programme was a grand display of fireworks, to be let off exactly at midnight. The little Princess had never seen a firework in her life, so the King had given orders that the Royal Pyrotechnist should be in attendance on the day of her marriage.

'What are fireworks like?' she had asked the Prince, one morning, as she was walking on the terrace.

'They are like the Aurora Borealis,' said the King, who always answered questions that were addressed to other people, 'only much more natural. I prefer them to stars myself, as you always know when they are going to appear, and they are as delightful as my own flute-playing. You must certainly see them.'

So at the end of the King's garden a great stand had been set up, and as soon as the Royal Pyrotechnist had put everything in its proper place, the fireworks began to talk to each other.

'The world is certainly very beautiful,' cried a little Squib. 'Just look at those yellow tulips. Why! if they were real crackers they could not be lovelier. I am very glad I have travelled. Travel improves the mind wonderfully, and does away with all one's prejudices.'

'The King's garden is not the world, you foolish Squib,' said a big Roman Candle; 'the world is an enormous place, and it would take you three days to see it thoroughly.'

'Any place you love is the world to you,' exclaimed a pensive Catharine Wheel, who had been attached to an old deal box in early life, and prided herself on her broken heart; 'but love is not fashionable any more, the poets have killed it. They wrote so much about it that nobody believed them, and I am not surprised. True love suffers, and is silent. I remember myself once – But it is no matter now. Romance is a thing of the past.'

'Nonsense!' said the Roman Candle, 'Romance never dies. It is like the moon, and lives for ever. The bride and bridegroom, for instance, love each other very dearly. I heard all about them this morning from a brown-paper cartridge, who happened to be staying in the same drawer as myself, and knew the latest Court news.'

But the Catharine Wheel shook her head. 'Romance is dead, Romance is dead, Romance is dead,' she murmured. She was one of those people who think that, if you say the same thing over and over a great many times, it becomes true in the end.

Suddenly, a sharp, dry cough was heard, and they all looked round. It came from a tall, supercilious-looking Rocket, who was tied to the end of a long stick. He always coughed before he made any observations, so as to attract attention.

'Ahem, ahem!' he said, and everybody listened except the poor Catharine Wheel, who was still shaking her head, and murmuring, 'Romance is dead.'

'Order! order!' cried out a Cracker. He was someting of a politician, and had always taken a prominent part in the local elections, so he knew the proper Parliamentary expressions to use.

'Quite dead,' whispered the Catharine Wheel, and she went off to sleep.

As soon as there was perfect silence, the Rocket coughed a third time and began. He spoke with a very slow, distinct voice, as if he was dictating his memoirs, and always looked over the shoulder of the person to whom he was talking. In fact, he had a most distinguished manner.

'How fortunate it is for the King's son,' he remarked, 'that he is to be married on the very day on which I am to be let off. Really, if it had not been arranged before hand, it could not have turned out better for him; but Princes are always lucky.'

'Dear me!' said the little Squib, 'I thought it was quite the other way, and that we were to be let off in the Prince's honour.'

'It may be so with you,' he answered; 'indeed, I have no doubt that it is, but with me it is different. I am a very remarkable Rocket, and come of remarkable parents. My mother was the most celebrated Catharine Wheel of her day, and was renowned for her graceful dancing. When she made her great public appearance she spun round nineteen times before she went out, and each time that she did so she threw into the air seven pink stars. She was three feet and a half in diameter, and made of the very best gunpowder. My father was a Rocket like myself, and of French extraction. He flew so high that the people were afraid that he would never come down again. He did, though, for he was of a kindly disposition, and he made a most brilliant descent in a shower of golden rain. The newspapers wrote about his performance in very flattering terms. Indeed, the Court Gazette called him a triumph of Pylotechnic art.'

'Pyrotechnic, Pyrotechnic, you mean,' said a Bengal Light; 'I know it is Pyrotechnic, for I saw it written on my own canister.'

'Well, I said Pylotechnic,' answered the Rocket, in a severe tone of voice, and the Bengal Light felt so crushed that he began at once to bully the little squibs, in order to show that he was still a person of some importance.

'I was saying,' continued the Rocket, 'I was saying – What was I saying?'

'You were talking about yourself,' replied the Roman Candle.

3

'Of course; I knew I was discussing some interesting subject when I was so rudely interrupted. I hate rudeness and bad manners of every kind, for I am extremely sensitive. No one in the whole world is so sensitive as I am, I am quite sure of that.'

'What is a sensitive person?' said the Cracker to the Roman Candle.

'A person who, because he has corns himself, always treads on other people's toes,' answered the Roman Candle in a low whisper; and the Cracker nearly exploded with laughter.

'Pray, what are you laughing at?' inquired the Rocket; 'I am not laughing.'

'I am laughing because I am happy,' replied the Cracker.

'That is a very selfish reason,' said the Rocket angrily. 'What right have you to be happy? You should be thinking about others. In fact, you should be thinking about me. I am always thinking about myself, and I expect everybody else to do the same. That is what is called sympathy. It is a beautiful virtue, and I possess it in a high degree. Suppose, for instance, anything happened to me to-night, what a misfortune that would be for every one! The Prince and Princess would never be happy again, their whole married life would be spoiled; and as for the King, I know he would not get over it. Really, when I begin to reflect on the importance of my position, I am almost moved to tears.'

'If you want to give pleasure to others,' cried the Roman Candle, 'you had better keep yourself dry.'

'Certainly,' exclaimed the Bengal Light, who was now in better spirits; 'that is only common sense.'

'Common sense, indeed!' said the Rocket indignantly; 'you forget that I am very uncommon, and very remarkable. Why, anybody can have common sense, provided that they have no imagination. But I have imagination, for I never think of things as they really are; I always think of them as being quite different. As for keeping myself dry, there is evidently no one here who can at all appreciate an emotional nature. Fortunately for myself, I don't care. The only thing that sustains one through life is the consciousness of the immense inferiority of everybody else, and this is a feeling that I have always cultivated. But none of you have any hearts. Here you are laughing and making merry just as if the Prince and Princess had not just been married.'

'Well, really,' exclaimed a small Fire-balloon, 'why not? It is a most joyful occasion, and when I soar up into the air I intended to tell the stars all about it. You will see them twinkle when I talk to them about the pretty bride.'

'Ah! what a trivial view of life!' said the Rocket; 'but it is only what I expected. There is nothing in you; you are hollow and empty. Why, perhaps the Prince and Princess may go to live in a country where there is a deep river, and perhaps they may have one only son, a little fair-haired boy with violet eyes like the Prince himself; and perhaps some day he may go out to walk with his nurse; and perhaps the nurse may go to sleep under a great elder-tree; and perhaps the little boy may fall into the deep river and be drowned. What a terrible misfortune! Poor people, to lose their only son! It is really too dreadful! I shall never get over it.'

'But they have not lost their only son,' said the Roman Candle; 'no misfortune has happened to them at all.'

'I never said that they had,' replied the Rocket; 'I said that they might. If they had lost their only son there would be no use in saying more about the matter. I hate people who cry over spilt milk. But when I think that they might lose their only son, I certainly am very much affected.'

'You certainly are!' cried the Bengal Light. 'In fact, you are the most affected person I ever met.'

'You are the rudest person I ever met,' said the Rocket, 'and you cannot understand my friendship for the Prince.'

'Why, you don't even know him,' growled the Roman Candle.

'I never said I knew him,' answered the Rocket. 'I dare say that if I knew him I should not be his friend at all. It is a very dangerous thing to know one's friends.'

'You had really better keep yourself dry,' said the Fire-balloon. 'That is the important thing.'

'Very important for you, I have no doubt,' answered the Rocket, 'but I shall weep if I choose'; and he actually burst into real tears, which flowed down his stick like rain-drops, and nearly drowned two little beetles, who were just thinking of setting up house together, and were looking for a nice dry spot to live in.

'He must have a truly romantic nature,' said the Catharine Wheel, 'for he weeps when there is nothing at all to weep about'; and she heaved a deep sigh and thought about the deal box.

But the Roman Candle and the Bengal Light were quite indignant, and kept saying, 'Humbug! humbug!' at the top of their voices. They were extremely practical, and whenever they objected to anything they called it humbug.

Then the moon rose like a wonderful silver shield; and the stars began to shine, and a sound of music came from the palace.

The Prince and Princess were leading the dance. They danced so beautifully that the tall white lilies peeped in at the window and watched them, and the great red poppies nodded their heads and beat time.

Then ten o'clock struck, and then eleven, and then twelve, and at the last stroke of midnight every one came out on the terrace, and the

King sent for the Royal Pyrotechnist.

'Let the fireworks begin,' said the King; and the Royal Pyrotechnist made a low bow, and marched down to the end of the garden. He had six attendants with him, each of whom carried a lighted torch at the end of a long pole.

It was certainly a magnificent display.

Whizz! Whizz! went the Catharine Wheel, as she spun round and round. Boom! Boom! went the Roman Candle. Then the Squibs danced all over the place, and the Bengal Lights made everything look scarlet. 'Good-bye,' cried the Fire-balloon, as he soared away, dropping tiny blue sparks. Bang! Bang! answered the Crackers, who were enjoying themselves immensely. Every one was a great success except the Remarkable Rocket. He was so damp with crying that he could not go off at all. The best thing in him was the gunpowder, and that was so wet with tears that it was of no use. All his poor relations, to whom he would never speak, except with a sneer, shot up into the sky like wonderful golden flowers with blossoms of fire. Huzza! Huzza! cried the Court; and the little Princess laughed with pleasure.

'I suppose they are reserving me for some grand occasion,' said the Rocket; 'no doubt that is what it means,' and he looked more supercilious than ever.

The next day, the workmen came to put everything tidy. 'This is evidently a deputation,' said the Rocket; 'I will receive them with becoming dignity'; so he put his nose in the air, and began to frown severely, as if he were thinking about some very important subject. But they took no notice of him at all till they were just going away. Then one of them caught sight of him. 'Hallo!' he cried, 'what a bad rocket!' and he threw him over the wall into the ditch.

'BAD Rocket? BAD Rocket?' he said, as he whirled through the air; 'impossible! GRAND Rocket, that is what the man said. BAD and GRAND sound very much the same, indeed they often are the same'; and he fell into the mud.

'It is not comfortable here,' he remarked, 'but no doubt it is some fashionable watering-place, and they have sent me away to recruit my health. My nerves are certainly very much shattered, and I require rest.'

Then a little Frog, with bright jewelled eyes, and a green mottled coat, swam up to him.

'A new arrival, I see!' said the Frog. 'Well, after all there is nothing like mud. Give me rainy weather and a ditch, and I am quite happy. Do you think it wil be a wet afternoon? I am sure I hope so, but the sky is quite blue and cloudless. What a pity!'

'Ahem! ahem!' said the Rocket, and he began to cough.

'What a delightful voice you have!' cried the Frog. 'Really it is quite

6

like a croak, and croaking is, of course, the most musical sound in the world. You will hear our glee-club this evening. We sit in the old duck-pond close by the farmer's house, and as soon as the moon rises we begin. It is so entrancing that everybody lies awake to listen to us. In fact, it was only yesterday that I heard the farmer's wife say to her mother that she could not get a wink of sleep at night on account of us. It is most gratifying to find oneself so popular.'

'Ahem! ahem!' said the Rocket angrily. He was very much annoyed that he could not get a word in.

'A delightful voice, certainly,' continued the Frog; 'I hope you will come over to the duck-pond. I am off to look for my daughters. I have six beautiful daughters, and I am so afraid the Pike may meet them. He is a perfect monster, and would have no hesitation in breakfasting off them. Well, good-bye; I have enjoyed our conversation very much, I assure you.'

'Conversation, indeed!' said the Rocket. 'You have talked the whole time yourself. That is not conversation.'

'Somebody must listen,' answered the Frog, 'and I like to do all the talking myself. It saves time, and prevents arguments.'

'But I like arguments,' said the Rocket.

'I hope not,' said the Frog complacently. 'Arguments are extremely vulgar, for everybody in good society holds exactly the same opinions. Good-bye a second time; I see my daughters in the distance'; and the little Frog swam away.

'You are a very irritating person,' said the Rocket, 'and very ill-bred. I hate people who talk to themselves, as you do, when one wants to talk about oneself, as I do. It is what I call selfishness, and selfishness is a most detestable thing, especially to any one of my temperament, for I am well known for my sympathetic nature. In fact, you should take example by me, you could not possibly have a better model. Now that you have the chance you had better avail yourself of it, for I am going back to Court almost immediately. I am a great favourite at Court; in fact, the Prince and Princess were married yesterday in my honour. Of course you know nothing of these matters, for you are a provincial.'

'There is no good talking to him,' said a Dragonfly, who was sitting on the top of a large brown bulrush; 'no good at all, for he has gone away.'

'Well, that is his loss, not mine,' answered the Rocket. 'I am not going to stop talking to him merely because he pays no attention. I like hearing myself talk. It is one of my greatest pleasures. I often have long conversations all by myself, and I am so clever that sometimes I don't understand a single work of what I am saying.'

'Then you should certainly lecture on Philosophy,' said the

Dragonfly, and he spread a pair of lovely gauze wings and soared away into the sky.

'How very silly of him not to stay here!' said the Rocket. 'I am sure that he has not often got such a chance of improving his mind. However, I don't care a bit. Genius like mine is sure to be appreciated some day'; and he sank down a little bit deeper in to the mud.

After some time a large White Duck swam up to him. She had yellow legs, and webbed feet, and was considered a great beauty on account of her waddle.

'Quack, quack, quack,' she said. 'What a curious shape you are! May I ask were you born like that, or is it the result of an accident?'

'It is quite evident that you have always lived in the country,' answered the Rocket, 'otherwise you would know who I am. However, I excuse your ignorance. It would be unfair to expect other people to be as remarkable as oneself. You will no doubt be surprised to hear that I can fly up into the sky, and come down in a shower of golden rain.'

'I don't think much of that,' said the Duck, 'as I cannot see what use it is to any one. Now, if you could plough the fields like the ox, or draw a cart like the horse, or look after the sheep like the collie-dog, that would be something.'

'My good creature,' cried the Rocket in a very haughty tone of voice, 'I see that you belong to the lower orders. A person of my position is never useful. We have certain accomplishments, and that is more than sufficient. I have no sympathy myself with industry of any kind, least of all with such industries as you seem to recommend. Indeed, I have always been of the opinion that hard work is simply the refuge of people who have nothing whatever to do.'

'Well, well,' said the Duck, who was of a very peaceful disposition, and never quarrelled with any one, 'everybody has different tastes. I hope, at any rate, that you are going to take up your residence here.'

'Oh! dear no,' cried the Rocket. 'I am merely a visitor, a distinguished visitor. The fact is that I find this place rather tedious. There is neither society here, nor solitude. In fact, it is essentially suburban. I shall probably go back to Court, for I know that I am destined to make a sensation in the world.'

'I had thought of entering public life once myself,' remarked the Duck; 'there are so many things that need reforming. Indeed, I took the chair at a meeting some time ago, and we passed resolutions condemning everything that we did not like. However, they did not seem to have much effect. Now I go in for domesticity, and look after my family.'

'I am made for public life,' said the Rocket, 'and so are all my relations, even the humblest of them. Whenever we appear we excite great attention. I have not actually appeared myself, but when I do so it will be a magnificent sight. As for domesticity, it ages one rapidly, and distracts one's mind from higher things.'

'Ah! the higher things of life, how fine they are!' said the Duck; 'and that reminds me how hungry I feel'; and she swam away down the stream, saying, 'Quack, quack, quack.'

'Come back! come back!' screamed the Rocket, 'I have a great deal to say to you'; but the Duck paid no attention to him. 'I am glad that she has gone,' he said to himself, 'she has a decidedly middle-class mind'; and he sank a little deeper still into the mud, and began to think about the loneliness of genius, when suddenly two little boys in white smocks came running down the bank with a kettle and some faggots.

'This must be the deputation,' said the Rocket, and he tried to look very dignified.

'Hallo!' cried one of the boys, 'look at this old stick; I wonder how it came here'; and he picked the rocket out of the ditch.

'OLD stick!' said the Rocket, 'impossible! GOLD stick, that is what he said. Gold Stick is very complimentary. In fact, he mistakes me for one of the Court dignitaries!'

'Let us put it into the fire!' said the other boy, 'it will help to boil the kettle.'

So they piled the faggots together, and put the Rocket on top, and lit the fire.

'This is magnificent,' cried the Rocket, 'they are going to let me off in broad daylight, so that every one can see me.'

'We will go to sleep now,' they said, 'and when we wake up the kettle will be boiled': and they lay down on the grass, and shut their eyes.

The Rocket was very damp, so he took a long time to burn. At last, however, the fire caught him.

'Now I am going off!' he cried, and he made himself very stiff and straight. 'I know I shall go much higher than the stars, much higher than the moon, much higher than the sun. In fact, I shall go so high that –'

Fizz! Fizz! Fizz! and he went straight up into the air.

'Delightful!' he cried, 'I shall go on like this for ever. What a success I am!'

But nobody saw him.

Then he began to feel a curious tingling sensation all over him.

'Now I am going to explode,' he cried. 'I shall set the whole world on fire, and make such a noise, that nobody will talk about anything else for a whole year.' And he certainly did explode. Bang! Bang! Bang! went the gunpowder. There was no doubt about it.

But nobody heard him, not even the two little boys, for they were sound asleep.

Then all that was left of him was the stick, and this fell down on the back of a Goose who was taking a walk, by the side of the ditch.

'Good heavens!' cried the Goose. 'It is going to rain sticks'; and she rushed into the water.

'I knew I should create a great sensation,' gasped the Rocket, and he went out.

OSCAR WILDE

Introduction

Fireworks proclaim their art in brilliant and instructive deception. The beholder watches their first epiphany and registers images which seem to take a certain form and colour; then form and colour change, the dimensions alter, the meaning and message are transformed, perhaps obviously, perhaps subtly. They are not what we had thought they were, and as we contemplate them they break up our first conclusions and demand that we find other ones, to be questioned in their turn. So 'The Remarkable Rocket', the last of Wilde's fairy stories in *The Happy Prince and Other Tales*, published in May 1888, may seem a delicate satire personifying what should be inanimate creations, and written in the tradition of Hans Andersen; a closer reading might prompt the reflection of the satire towards Wilde's increasingly hostile former friend and patronising mentor James Abbott McNeill Whistler; and closer reasoning still, as has been applied by Dr Emmanuel Vernadakis in his Sorbonne doctoral thesis *La Prétexte de Salomé* (which illustrates work after work of Wilde's with its own inspirational flashes), offers Wilde himself as another target of his own gentle malice. The fireworks make ludicrous many objects against which they are discharged; and among them is a flickering light of self-mockery. After his fall Wilde, especially in the great letter from prison later known as *De Profundis*, became his own remorseless self-accuser. The fireworks, symbolic of his Odyssey to success before the terrible ordeal which destroyed him as a public man, were conceived in a competitive world whose training had taught him never to show faint-heartedness in pyrotechnics, so that early forms of self-mockery were not easily discernible, but they were necessary to him, and they were there. But ostensibly the rocket suggested Whistler, above all his controversial painting of 1875, *Nocturne in Black and Gold – The Falling Rocket*.

Whistler's *Rocket* had been inspired by the fireworks at Cremorne, as also were other paintings of his, such as *Nocturne in Blue and Silver – The Fiery Wheel*. Whistler's devoted biographers, Joseph and Elizabeth Robins Pennell, record in their *Life* of him that

> In October, he sent to the Winter Exhibition at the Dudley Gallery a *Nocturne in Blue and Gold, no. III*, which it is impossible to identify, and *Nocturne in Black and Gold – The Falling Rocket*, which Ruskin presently

identified beyond possibility of doubt . . .

That was two years later, when in his *Fors Clavigera* John Ruskin produced his reaction to its further exhibition at the Grosvenor Gallery:

> For Mr Whistler's own sake, no less than for the protection of the purchaser, Sir Coutts Lindsay ought not to have admitted works into the gallery in which the ill-educated conceit of the artist so nearly approached the aspect of wilful imposture. I have seen and heard much of Cockney impudence before now but never expected to hear a coxcomb ask two hundred guineas for flinging a pot of paint in the public's face.

On 25 November 1878 *Whistler v Ruskin* was heard in the Court of Exchequer Division before Baron Huddlestone and a jury. Whistler was the first witness, during which *The Falling Rocket* was brought in upside down. But if Ruskin's leading counsel, Attorney-General Sir John Holker, believed the same would be true of any other pyrotechnics Whistler produced in court, he was mistaken. William Gaunt's *The Aesthetic Adventure* captures the mood of the cross-examination:

> A 'stiffish price', suggested the Attorney-General, 'two hundred guineas' and, with a sneer, 'How soon did you *knock it off?*' (Laughter.) . . .
>
> Attorney-General: 'I am afraid I am using a term that applies rather to my own work.'
>
> Whistler, self-possessed, disdainful, condescended. 'Oh, no! permit me, I am too greatly flattered to think that you apply to a work of mine any term that you are in the habit of using with reference to your own.'
>
> 'Let us say, then, how long did I take to' – he went through the pantomime of recalling and forcing himself to utter the curious and distasteful jargon of the lawyer and paused – 'how long did I take to "knock off" (I think that is it) – to knock off', he repeated, 'that Nocturne? Well. . .' It was a moment for a deliberate trailing of the coat. Perhaps he had already prepared in his quick mind the trap in which the lawyer might be caught by his own astuteness. 'As well as I remember, about a day . . . I may still have put a few more touches to it the next day if the painting were not dry. I had better say, then, that I was two days at work on it.'
>
> It almost seemed as if Whistler were giving his case away in thus complacently emphasizing and elaborating upon the short space of time which the picture had occupied.
>
> The lawyer rushed upon the point, triumphant. 'The labour of two days then is that for which you ask two hundred guineas?'
>
> Then came the lunge. Whistler had got Sir John just where he wanted him. He produced the brilliant riposte: 'No; I ask it for the knowledge of a lifetime.'

And a little later:

> 'You don't approve of criticism.' . . .

'I should not disapprove of technical criticism by a man whose life is passed in the practice of the science which he criticizes; but for the opinion of a man whose life is not so passed, I would have as little regard as you would if he expressed an opinion upon the law.'

The fireworks in art, then, were challenge; the fireworks in speech were response, defence, guard, creed. They offered an effective form of concealed warfare. They suggested display, flamboyant and short-lived, and a vulnerable self-regard. Too late for their opponent, they showed their descent from a gunpowder plot threatening the pillars of society and the agreed conventions of civilization. That they also had the power to maim and perhaps destroy their manipulator and more innocent bystanders was a less obvious lesson. Whistler won his case, received damages of a farthing, had to pay his costs, and was as a result adjudged bankrupt. His beautiful house in Chelsea was sold, his possessions were dispersed for ludicrous sums under the hammer of an auctioneer wielded for the receiver. He wrote above his front door as he departed, 'Except the Lord build the house, they labour in vain that build it. E. W. Godwin, FSA, built this one', but he was later forced to witness the occupancy of his house by his prime target Philistine whom he ceremonially shaved of his initial aspirate, 'Arry Quilter.

Wilde could have been present in the Court. He certainly watched in the wings, no farther away than Oxford where on 22 November he satisfied the examiners in the Rudiments of Religion (making play in subsequent anecdote with his own supposed ignorance of the Bible, on which his boyhood visits to an uncle in holy orders had probably given him groundwork). On 28 November he graduated as Bachelor of Arts of Oxford University. He had attended Ruskin's lectures there in Autumn 1874 and helped him as a volunteer worker in an abortive road-making project. In 1879 Ruskin took Wilde to see Henry Irving playing Shylock at the Lyceum Theatre in London. Wilde seems to have met Whistler in 1877 when, as an undergraduate, he reviewed the Grosvenor Gallery Exhibition for an Irish periodical associated with his first university, the *Dublin University Magazine*. He admired Whistler's work, but at this time with conventional preferences such as the portrait of Thomas Carlyle. On *The Falling Rocket* he 'banters', wrote Richard Ellmann, 'like a simple-minded realist: it "is worth looking at for about as long as one looks at a real rocket, that is, for somewhat less than a quarter of a minute".' The trial of *Whistler v Ruskin* would have told him things he had not known about fireworks, and while Ruskin had the bigger artistic artillery to fire in evidence on his side, witnesses such as Edward Burne-Jones, Whistler did have Albert Moore, a painter Wilde admired, and W. G. Wills, a playwright with whom he claimed kinship. Wilde's sonnet to Ellen Terry would later be based on her appearance in Wills's *Charles I*.

As Ellmann says, 'Wilde contrived to remain on good terms with Ruskin and Burne-Jones on the one hand, and with Whistler on the other, in the circumstances an acrobatic feat'. But in the aftermath of the trial it was with Whistler that his friendship flourished; Ellmann is surely right in suspecting he had outgrown Ruskin. Yet Ruskin had his fireworks too, more sonorous than Whistler's, evident even in the paragraph which was brought to trial, as though he had been inspired by the pyrotechnic he despised. Wilde would learn the art of firework-manipulation in the kill-or-be-killed mode of conversation which constituted friendship as well as enmity with Whistler, but from Ruskin he may have drawn some of the fuller resonance which distinguishes his sparkle from Whistler's. Whistler's effects were like lightning when they struck; perhaps to Macaulay (whose *History* had drawn on the topographical expertise of Wilde's father), Ruskin – and perhaps directly, if surreptitiously, Wilde himself – owed something of the sound of thunder.

Wilde travelled happily in Whistler's wake when he came to London from Oxford, but the painter, twenty years his senior, viewed him with increasingly scornful and jealous eyes, and the fireworks grew more deadly as he sent them hissing in Wilde's direction. Wilde had been interested as well as repelled by the fireworks of Whistler's painting in 1877 and in his judicious replies to a Whistler attack ('The Ten O'Clock Lecture') had spoken of the fireworks in Whistler's art, writing and speech. 'The Remarkable Rocket' could be taken, as Ellmann has taken it, to be his verdict on the self-destruction of Whistler's vanity; but Wilde again and again returned to the idea of the loss of conviction at the moment of victory, for instance in his *The Portrait of Mr W. H.* (which turns on the theory that Shakespeare wrote his sonnets to the actor who created his major female roles) or in his unfinished play *La Sainte Courtesane*. So, as Dr Vernadakis says, 'The Remarkable Rocket' is self-diagnosis as well as Whistler-diagnosis; the murdered painter Basil Hallward in *The Picture of Dorian Gray*, as Ellmann so brilliantly showed, was originally Whistler but it also contains some self-portraiture as Wilde himself acknowledged; Wilde's ill-fated libel action against Lord Queensberry in 1895 featured a display of fireworks in the witness-box surely prompted by Whistler's, and it was followed by bankruptcy amid his overwhelming ruin. Wilde long resisted full-scale war against Whistler in the mid-1880s, and when the break came its form showed he had become more Whistlerian in manner as he outgrew him in thought. 'Admirable as are Mr Whistler's fireworks on canvas, his fireworks in prose are abrupt, violent and exaggerated', he wrote on 26 January 1889 in the *Pall Mall Gazette*, but this is less a repudiation of fireworks than a demand for improvement in their realization. Whistler, conscious of Wilde's indebtedness to him for ideas on art, published in *Truth* on 2 January 1890

> He went forth . . . as my St John – but, forgetting that humility should be his chief characteristic, . . . he not only trifled with my shoe, but bolted with the latchet!
>
> . . . in . . . 'The Decay of Lying', Mr Wilde has deliberately and incautiously incorporated, 'without a word of comment', a portion of the well-remembered letter in which, after admitting his rare appreciation and amazing memory, I acknowledge that 'Oscar has the courage of the opinions – of others!'

It was a suitably and sourly ironic overture to the '90s, a decade which would be dominated by Wilde's triumph and disaster, and which Wilde began by settling his accounts with Whistler:

> The definition of a disciple as one who has the courage of the opinions of his master is really too old even for Mr Whistler to be allowed to claim it, and as for borrowing Mr Whistler's ideas about art, the only thoroughly original ideas I have ever heard him express have had reference to his own superiority over painters greater than himself.

As between Whistler and Ruskin Wilde's position had been too ambiguous, and perhaps his humane desire to leave in all possible peace the now increasingly mind-sick Ruskin too great, for him now to add the truthful corollary that Ruskin had established Wilde's foundations of artistic appreciation long before Whistler cast Wilde for apprentice and plagiarist. But he went to some trouble to ensure that Ruskin had received a copy of his *The Happy Prince and Other Tales*, no doubt to please him by the aesthetic Socialism of the title-story but probably also with the thought that Ruskin might see himself avenged in 'The Remarkable Rocket'. However much he might deplore Whistler's prose pyrotechnics, they constituted his chief debt to Whistler, save that Wilde greatly improved on them. He brought into life and literature the fireworks which Whistler at his most constructive, creative and challenging had made to enrich, and in some ways to symbolize, his own painting. As he had maliciously indicated, both Whistler and himself had many antecedents in firework-display, but the experience of personal tutelage so quickly becoming personal duelling sharpened his wit as well as his wits. The conclusion in 1890 was already implicit in the telegram exchange of early November 1883 when *Punch* with its usual laboriousness had attempted a version of their conversation, supposedly about actresses. Wilde wrote:

> *Punch* too ridiculous. When you and I are together we never talk about anything except ourselves.

And Whistler answered:

> No, no, Oscar, you forget. When you and I are together, we never talk about anything except me.

As Wilde would put such a relationship in 1893 at the close of his first Act of *A Woman of No Importance*:

> LORD ILLINGWORTH . . . if you wish, let us stay here. Yes, let us stay here. The Book of Life begins with a man and a woman in a garden.
> MRS ALLONBY It ends with Revelations.
> LORD ILLINGWORTH You fence divinely. But the button has come off your foil.
> MRS ALLONBY I still have the mask.

Thus far in the exchange she might be Whistler, but Wilde would hardly have replied, like Illingworth: 'It makes your eyes lovelier.' Nor would Whistler have thanked him for saying it. Yet Ellmann is characteristically incisive in seeing a sense of betrayal on Wilde's part in his relationship with Whistler. The younger man did not, in this instance, seek to be loved, but he did seek affection, sympathy and in some sense protection, and all he received was an insistence on proprietorship, even in the telegram handed to him on his wedding-day: 'Fear I may not be able to reach you in time for the ceremony. Don't wait.'

As Ellmann says, betrayal constituted a theme in *The Happy Prince and Other Tales*. Even in Mrs Allonby's Whistlerian deflation of Illingworth's sentiments we are in the presence of betrayal, though not by her. Her mask of ambiguity, like Whistler's in 1883, remains in place. It is Mrs Arbuthnot, whose letter Illingworth sees the next moment, who provides the tragic proof of Mrs Allonby's indiscriminate pyrotechnics. Mrs Allonby will indeed betray Illingworth by exploiting his vanity to make him betray himself and bring his schemes to disaster. But Illingworth, it proves, has far more physically betrayed Mrs Arbuthnot, as he recalls in a line inviting the audience to recall Mrs Allonby's little squib now not with a smile but with a shudder: 'I was twenty-one, I believe, when the whole thing began in your father's garden.' The use of fireworks for Wilde, then, for all of his insistence on their existence for their own sake, was a function producing its best when they leave impressions of their passage in what may prove a later, deeper darkness. It is this which makes an anthology such as the present a particularly suspect business. His fireworks give a magnificent show; yet we miss much of their profundity and brilliance by wrenching them from larger contexts in their settings in his writings and life. There is an awesome relevance in Jonson's lines on Shakespeare's portrait. The fireworks tell us what it was like to be in Wilde's company, and in that sense show us his picture, but Jonson seems to glower a warning to look not at his fireworks, but at his books.

But would we really refuse to pass a couple of hours in the company of Wilde because we had not read him sufficiently? It would probably inspire us to read more of him, and that is certainly a moral of this book, a quality Wilde would in other circumstances term a grave fault in any book whether or not he meant it.

It is not always firework-time with Wilde. Caryl Brahms and S. J. Simon offer the classic illustration of when it might not be, in their *Don't, Mr Disraeli*, a novel constructed of anachronisms such as Mr Greville, who died in the year of Max Beerbohm's birth, as witness:

> A rainy day. The cobbles of the Haymarket look like toffee but taste like mud. Max Beerbohm, overshoed, umbrella'd and meditating an epigram, is hurrying towards Piccadilly. Oscar Wilde, meditating an epigram, overshoed and umbrella'd, is hurrying towards Trafalgar Square. Mr Greville, overshoed and umbrella'd and in no hurry whatever, pops behind the pillars of the Haymarket Theatre. What materials for his diary! He pulls out his notebook and stands damply, pencil in hand, ready to record the masterly ripostes of the two wittiest men in town.
> 'Good morning, Max', said Oscar Wilde.
> 'Good morning, Oscar', said Max Beerbohm.
> They looked at each other. They thought furiously. They hurried on.
> Under his perch at the Haymarket Theatre Mr Greville looked at his material. He shook his head.

After all, rain dampens fireworks. And at least the episode would be pleasing to Wilde as offering, in contrast to the pessimistic thesis in his famous essay, a proof that Lying is not perpetually in Decay. He might reply by saying Mr Greville's anachronistic presence simply proved the truth of his saying that the Gods had given Max the gift of eternal old age, as Max in any case went on to prove. Curiously enough, the pillars of the Haymarket Theatre were the audience for a comparable encounter, all the more appropriate as it was not recorded in print until Wilde's son Vyvyan published it in his *Son of Oscar Wilde* fourteen years after the appearance of *Don't, Mr Disraeli*. Max Beerbohm's half-brother Herbert Beerbohm Tree, then lessee of the Haymarket, was in 1893 in rehearsal of *A Woman of No Importance* which he was directing and in which he was playing Illingworth. Wilde, like Shaw afterwards, insisted on attending rehearsals, and doubtless anticipated Shaw's fury at Tree's inability to retain his lines accurately and his insistence on bringing in business at variance with the intent of the playwright. Tree, on his side, subsequently insisted that he directed 'with the interference of Wilde'. Both men met under the pillars, and as Tree drew off a magnificent new top-hat, Wilde complimented him extravagantly on its rich red lining. 'Do you like it?' asked Tree. 'Like it?', said Wilde, doubtless delighted to find a firm point of agreement before the inevitable commencement of hostilities, 'I think it's wonderful'. 'Then it's yours', replied Tree, ripping out the lining, handing it to Wilde, and vanishing into the theatre, correctly convinced (he said afterwards – though his stories were no more reliable than his lines) that Wilde would never follow him inside after having been the loser in an exchange. Fireworks encumber their master's business.

The brothers Beerbohm were pyrotechnicians in their own right, and with Wilde it was not necessary for disciples (as Max was, and Herbert wasn't, at least voluntarily) to allow the Master to shine as he so often had allowed Whistler. (Max wickedly acknowledged as much when he transposed the ages of Wilde and Whistler, and retold the old – and possibly apocryphal – story of Wilde saying 'I wish I had said that' of a Whistler witticism to be answered by 'You will, Oscar, you will', only to have the venerable Wilde, in the Max version, retort 'No, I won't'.) Apart from a button-foiled Wilde in their years of friendship, so many of Whistler's adversaries – Tom Taylor, Sir John Holker, 'Arry Quilter – were hopelessly outmatched by their tormentor. Wilde gave of his best in equal competition, or at least in competition with some chance of being equal. When Wilde was dying, Reggie Turner, devoted friend of both Max and himself, was told with horror of a dreadful dream in which Wilde had found himself dining with the dead, and to Wilde's delight answered 'And I am sure you were the Life and Soul of the party'.

He looked for equality of debate; he did not seek for Boswells, witness his not entirely unprophetic remark, 'Every great man has his disciples, and it is usually Judas who writes the biography'. The Judas touch can take many forms: it is not necessarily a kiss, and it was not, in the case of Frank Harris, who noisily asserted his own heterosexuality to the four corners of the world in the just hope of shocking them. Harris's *Oscar Wilde: His Life and Confessions* has been long recognised as a judicious mixture of plagiarism and invention. 'I may be a liar; most men are', replied Harris to the complaint of Carlyle's indignant relatives that the Sage of Chelsea would hardly have chosen him as audience for a tearful confession of sexual impotence. Not even Harris could completely steal and lie his way through an account of the life of Wilde, whom as an editor he had printed, to whom as a companion he had occasionally listened, and towards whom as a benefactor in the years of ruin he had shown an intermittent generosity. No statement made by him merits acceptance without corroboration, although in the absence of any it is occasionally necessary to consider a few with the accompaniment of ferocious health warnings on veracity. But Robert Ross summed up the case against Harris's work as reporter of Wilde with feline succinctness, saying that it was remarkable how like Harris the Wilde of his revelations talked. And in efforts to trick out their memoirs, other memorialists invite similar suspicion for seeking to recreate Wilde in their own images. Sir Charles Holmes may cruelly tantalise in reminding us how quickly the memory of fireworks passes, but his honesty in *Self and Partners* has a bleak glory:

> The last appearance of Wilde at The Vale which I remember was also the most brilliant. Walter Sickert was there, boyish, clean-shaven, aureoled with a mass of blond hair, playing with a crinolined doll and flashing out now and then with some lively repartee; Steer sat by me in monumental silence; while Ricketts, perched on the edge of the table, engaged in a long verbal combat. So swiftly came parry and *riposte*, that my slow brain could only follow the tongue-play several sentences behind, and cannot remember a word of what passed, except 'Oh! nonsense, Oscar!' from Ricketts, although it lives in memory as the most dazzling dialogue I was ever privileged to hear.

It is not enough to tell ourselves Holmeses are not meant to be Watsons. Much of what has been allowed to pass unchallenged as authentic Wilde may derive from memories no better stocked than Holmes's with consciences much less lively.

Robert Ross on one occasion tried his hand as amanuensis for the pyrotechnician, only to have his efforts commandeered by Wilde for use in a play. And this turns us back to the works. It is an appropriately Wildean paradox: we cannot fully appreciate the fireworks without their setting in the composition, yet at some points the setting was certainly contrived to accommodate previously-composed fireworks, and our existing texts also bear largely invisible marks of fireworks inserted and later withdrawn before display. For instance, when *A Woman of No Importance* was in rehearsal, Wilde was being blackmailed by a male prostitute named Wood, who had stolen a highly demonstrative letter from Wilde to Lord Alfred Douglas, sent a copy to the actor-manager Herbert Beerbohm Tree, and lay in wait for Wilde at the Haymarket stage door. Tree advised Wilde of the situation, and warned him against indiscreet letters and importuning suitors (possibly learning or deducing that Wilde had enjoyed Wood as a sexual partner, possibly not). Wilde refused to pay blackmail, but good-naturedly gave Wood's agents money when they voluntarily returned the incriminating correspondence. So as an expression of thanks to Tree, the play received an additional firework intended primarily for his entertainment:

> LADY HUNSTANTON Well, dear, I hope you like the park. It is said to be well timbered.
> MRS ALLONBY The trees are wonderful, Lady Hunstanton. But I think that is rather the drawback of the country. In the country there are so many trees one can't see the temptations.
> LADY HUNSTANTON My dear!

It was a characteristic Wilde firework: the explosion of a *cliché*, this time the old one about not seeing the wood for the trees, but its precise point of explosion must necessarily have been lost on anyone but Tree, and perhaps one or two young men, possibly including Ross and Douglas. Tree was probably amused by it, but may have enjoined its suppression. Anyhow, Wilde took it out again, leaving to Mrs Allonby only the assurance that 'The trees are wonderful'. That could bring no objection from the actress cast to play Mrs Allonby: Mrs Tree. It probably raised laughter, if the lady chose to give it emphasis or was so directed by her husband and manager. Lady Stutfield was given a supportive line to prolong the impudent pit-catcher: 'Quite, quite wonderful'. She was to be an intense character, and it established her intensity on a matter whose crowd captivation was outrageous enough to make her intervention memorable. Her subsequent use of 'quite, quite' would now invite reminiscent as well as immediate amusement. She had to be established somehow, for an early reference to her had also been deleted by Wilde, this time because too many characters as yet unseen were being discussed for the audience to remember them before their first entrances. After dissecting Mrs Allonby for the first time, Lady Caroline Pontefract, now ruthlessly ruling her fourth husband, was initially intended to say:

> As for Lady Stutfield, she is quite irreproachable, of course, but she is just a little too romantic for a woman who has been married. Whenever I find a married woman romantic, I always feel there must have been something seriously wrong. However she was very devoted to poor Lord Stutfield, very devoted indeed. I have heard that when he died her hair turned quite gold from grief. But it may have been for another reason.

Having deleted this here, Wilde put it to some use nearly two years later, in *The Importance of Being Earnest*, and in the process showed he had learned how to burn his fireworks on a longer fuse.

> LADY BRACKNELL I'm sorry if we are a little late, Algernon, but I was obliged to call on dear Lady Harbury. I haven't been there since her poor husband's death. I never saw a woman so altered; she looks quite twenty years younger. . . .

There is then dialogue in which Algernon's consumption of cucumber sandwiches before his aunt's arrival is concealed by Lane's supportive mendacious assurance that there were no cucumbers in the market.

> LADY BRACKNELL It really make no matter, Algernon, I had some crumpets with Lady Harbury, who seems to me to be living entirely for pleasure now.
> ALGERNON I hear her hair has turned quite gold from grief.
> LADY BRACKNELL It certainly has changed its colour. From what

cause I, of course, cannot say.

It is not that his greater experience in the theatre was leading him to recognise that the best firework manipulation was achieved by entrusting it to at least two characters rather than one. He was also more deliberately directing his fireworks into illumination of the characters chosen to ignite them. Lady Caroline had been sufficiently established, and was of no great importance to the plot; Lady Stutfield, also of little consequence, was better left to establish herself. He had retained enough of the atmosphere of women priding themselves on playing games of love to point the ugly contrast when he showed in Mrs Arbuthnot the woman who had taken love seriously and been ruined by it. In *The Importance of Being Earnest* the distribution of the improved version of Lady Caroline's suppressed firework became an overture for Lady Bracknell's blend of formal rebuke to, and covert conspiracy with, the younger characters which, when not derailed by handbags, continued throughout the play. The fireworker was giving more thought to his audience than his artistic preceptor had cared to do.

But the intended audience, as the incident of Wood and the Trees reveals, could be a dual one: there was the private view to be considered as well as the public one, and their joint existence in the same theatre space was not always a barrier to Wilde thinking sometimes most particularly of the favoured inner circle which knew so much more about him than did the general theatre-going public. Of this Shaw proved himself well aware when reviewing *An Ideal Husband*: 'The six worst epigrams are mere alms handed with a kind smile to the average suburban playgoers: the three best remain secrets between Mr Wilde and a few choice spirits.' The classic instance is surely the title *The Importance of Being Earnest*. Here the joke at the end of the play seems the feeblest pun ever laboured to bring down a curtain. Jack by the Wildest coincidence proves to have met his beloved's insistence that she will only marry a man called Ernest. He is permitted to embrace her.

LADY BRACKNELL . . . you seem to be displaying signs of triviality.
JACK On the contrary, Aunt Augusta, I've now realised for the first time in my life the vital Importance of Being Earnest.

Lady Bracknell's complaint seems in the circumstances her most unreasonable in the entire play. But it was needed for much more serious intent than anyone save Wilde's inner coterie could know. It was to induce a proclamation. For 'earnest' was their secret code-name for what is now generally termed 'gay'. Jack, having found his identity machinations concluded by certain marriage, tells the homosexuals in the audience how vital a homosexual identity is to an irrevocably prospective husband. To the world at large, it must have seemed the most anti-climactic of all the succession of fireworks, in themselves the most brilliant and most scientifically deployed of all Wilde's pyrotechnical displays on the theatre stage. It succeeds only because an anticlimax seems the last paradox of a symphony in paradox. But to the homosexual audience it would be the finest and Wildest firework of all, the grand finale most alluring in its invisibility to all other viewers. The firework is cruel only when we do what in firework displays we must not do: look at the fireworker himself; it is a statement justifying a way of life for Wilde which was impoverishing his family and increasingly risking their happiness, and was indeed on the verge of plunging his innocent wife and two sons into horrifying tragedy which would mortally wound the lives of all three. But in the play it is simple equalisation of intent. The women are simply more open as to the choices that remain to them in marriage. When Jack, still unaware that he is really Ernest, asks Gwendolen if she is obdurate on the name:

GWENDOLEN I never change, except in my affections.
CECILY What a noble nature you have, Gwendolen!

The play's last and hidden firework answers that.

Wilde's career as playwright of pyrotechnics is normally taken as beginning with *Lady Windermere's Fan*, produced by George Alexander in 1892 and written in the summer of 1891. It is now clear that the long-credited story of its having been commissioned by Alexander is not true: Wilde had written it in the summer of 1891 and initially sought a production by Augustin Daly before finding an enthusiastic recipient in Alexander. Like Whistler's experimentalism, Wilde's was pursued initially at his own instance, not as the result of patronage. *The Picture of Dorian Gray*, originally published in its magazine form on 20 June 1890, held many passages of epigrammatic dialogue which suggest a playwright struggling to find his medium. 'The Critic as Artist', appearing in the *Nineteenth Century* during July and September of the same year, and 'The Decay of Lying', in the same journal in January 1889, used dialogue for the better delivery of ideas and, like dialogue in fiction, satisfactorily distanced the author from what he was saying. Wilde's doctrine of limited conviction, or conviction destroyed by conversion of an antagonist, was linked to his sense of art as independent of any message – again in itself a point he saw vulnerable to expression as a credo. In the witness-box in *Regina (Wilde) v Queensberry* his own fireworks had a far more profound and far-reaching pedagogic intent than Whistler's had in *Whistler v Ruskin*, important though the principle at stake in that trial was. He might mock us by the thought that giving evidence on oath naturally limited expression of truth far more than free discourse, but his fireworks are useful as well as artistic. His former fellow-student at Trinity College Dublin, Edward Carson, was

22

cross-examining:

> Listen, sir. Here is one of the 'Phrases and Philosophies for the Use of the Young' which you contributed: 'Wickedness is a myth invented by good people to account for the curious attractiveness of others'. You think that is true? – I rarely think that anything I write is true.
>
> Did you say 'rarely'? – I said 'rarely'. I might have said 'never' – not true in the actual sense of the world.

The firework is created, is made visible, and thus works to its effect independent of its creator. Because Wilde's sense of fireworks was so dominated by Whistler's creation of them in painting, it is the more important to listen to them, or read them, for their own sake and appreciate or be stimulated by them as we choose. They become their own intentions; and, sure enough, Wilde called his collected volume of essays including 'The Decay of Lying' and 'The Critic as Artist' *Intentions*. His case against Whistler in part rested on Whistler's having impaired his artistic status by talking about it: hence his own verbal fireworks must succeed by being realised in art-forms where Whistler's, linked to himself, his vanity and his feuds, had failed. When both were still on outwardly friendly terms, Wilde, in his criticism of the 'Ten O'Clock Lecture', made a derisive reference to Benjamin West and Paul Delaroche, to which Whistler responded even more derisively. Wilde answered, on or around 23 February 1885:

> By the aid of a biographical dictionary I discovered that there were once two painters, called Benjamin West and Paul Delaroche, who recklessly took to lecturing on Art.
>
> As of their works nothing at all remains, I concluded that they explained themselves away. Be warned in time, James; and remain, as I do, incomprehensible; to be great is to be misunderstood.

That the last seven words were a quotation from Emerson's 'Self-Reliance' may have had its charms in the circumstances, Whistler, the American rebel, being answered from Emerson, now a sternly orthodox monument of American culture. But Emerson had been a great rebel in his own day, and Wilde was happy to assume the mask he had prepared, all the more since few readers (quite probably including Whistler) would have identified the original firework-maker.

In the irony of Wilde's relationship to his own work, as transformed by his fall, the great repository of the most perfected pyrotechnics, *The Importance of Being Earnest*, became an object of distaste to him, and hence it flourishes all the more independent of its creator. He would add some fireworks in character-description in revising *An Ideal Husband* for publication after his imprisonment (Wilde had no time before his trials to see either it or *Earnest* through the press as he had with all his other completed plays save his verse-drama *The Duchess of Padua*).

The first description of Lord Goring in *An Ideal Husband*, possibly the closest of all his creations to himself, concludes: '*He is fond of being mis-understood. It gives him a post of vantage.*' The words were written in 1899 and, together with the other notes to *An Ideal Husband*, are Wilde's very last writing for publication. But he had made no such emendations to *The Importance of Being Earnest* a few months before, even though it had been abridged from the four-act version he had intended. The best he would say for it (writing to Reggie Turner in March 1899) was

> I like the play's irresponsibility and its *obiter dicta*, but it is essentially an acting play: it should have been a classic for the English Theatre, but alas! the author was struck by madness from the moon.

Wilde's fireworks may seem impossible to separate from his life and, for all of his intentions, are thereby even more severely imprisoned than Whistler's, but he wanted them to travel by themselves, and if their students cannot release them from their creator's past, they should at least be given some remission from his future. Art and Life diverged, however much Life became Art – the Art of Tragedy – in itself. Even the fireworks to Carson have their own life beyond the trial.

But for how long had Wilde been moving towards the theatre as the true vehicle for his pyrotechnics? The theatre has cared little about it, but his first pyrotechnical work for the stage had ushered in not his own decade, the 1890s, but its predecessor, when Wilde was making his way on a path of elegance and awkwardness. *Vera*, his drama of love and Russian Nihilism, was first composed in 1880. Hesketh Pearson's remarkable biography, which held pride of place for forty years until it was displaced by Richard Ellmann's great work, drew attention to the character of its villain, Prince Paul Maraloffski, Prime Minister, Svengali of tyranny, *ancien régime* cynic, Machiavellian epitome, and insatiable epigrammatist. He appears for the first time on the opening of Act Two:

> PRINCE PETROVITCH So our young scatter-brained Czarevitch has been forgiven at last, and is to take his seat here again.
> PRINCE PAUL Yes; if that is not meant as an extra punishment. For my part, at least, I find these Cabinet Councils extremely tiring.
> PRINCE PETROVITCH Naturally; you are always speaking.
> PRINCE PAUL No; I think it must be that I have to listen sometimes. It is so exhausting not to talk.

As Professor Katharine Worth has argued in her *Oscar Wilde*, the play is much better than Ross, for instance, deemed it, but Wilde ran risks in juxtaposing Vera's 'rhetorical organ notes and the Prince's light mocking tones' in the third Act when Prince Paul, disgraced by the new (and Nihilist) Czar who has succeeded his father (assassinated at the close of Act Two), joins the Nihilists:

> VERA Welcome! What welcome should we give you but the dagger or the noose?
>
> PRINCE PAUL I had no idea, really, that the Nihilists were so exclusive. Let me assure you that if I had not always had an entrée to the very best society, and the very worst conspiracies, I could never have been Prime Minister of Russia.

'Wilde takes an obvious risk here – Vera's rhetoric could easily be pushed over the edge of the absurd by the Prince's cool reasoning,' continues Professor Worth. 'Yet it does not quite happen, perhaps because her style is after all more in tune with the violence of the play's events.' As published it does not quite happen, and publication in its initial form antedated the only theatrical production by three years, but there exists in the William Andrews Clark Library an early draft in which it is clear that Wilde knew all about his obvious risk, and in his initial efforts failed to avoid it. In the draft, Prince Paul's fireworks reduce the Nihilists to total and ludicrous logical disaster. In answering Vera's bitter denunciation of his having been responsible for the death of her father (contrived by other agents in the final text), the Prince explains that he was merely anticipating her own Nihilistic dogmas as to the abolition of the family. As early as 1880, then, Wilde saw the stage as the proper medium for his fireworks: what he had to learn was the business of craftmanship which would give them the harmony in which to do their work.

Whistler could have been an inspiration: even as early as 1880 Wilde may have known Whistler well enough to see instinctive treachery to associates and disciples who might prove later rivals, and Prince Paul is as contemptuous of his Cabinet collaborators as he is treacherous to his subsequent Nihilist fellow-conspirators. But there are other antecedents. Ellmann points out that Young Ireland nationalism provided some of the rhetoric in which denunciation of Czarist oppression of Russia is couched. In the draft of *Vera* there is even more support for this origin. There Vera is not Russian but Polish, and Prince Paul has extensive Polish estates on which as the child of a serf she was born. The Irish nationalist comparison of Ireland to Poland was particularly vigorous in Young Ireland circles. One can go further than Ellmann and recognise that the Fenian conspiracy of the 1860s and 1870s offered a live model for Wilde's Nihilists, as did agrarian secret societies, passwords and all, on his own doorstep, when the doorstep was that on his father's estate in Co. Galway where the Wildes went for some holidays. A Czarevitch telling his father's cabinet of his membership in a Nihilist conspiracy has echoes of an Archdeacon's granddaughter intervening in a treason-felony trial, as Wilde's mother did in 1848, to accuse herself and acquit the prisoner of authorship of a much-denounced editorial. An absurd Nihilist polemicist, Professor Marfa (a character given more detail in the draft) has a name suspiciously close to Wilde's ferociously Unionist tutor at Trinity, Professor John Pentland Mahaffy. For Mahaffy as for Whistler, Wilde believed the polemical preoccupations had the effect of injuring the intellectual achievement:

> PROFESSOR MARFA My forte is more in writing pamphlets than in taking shots. Still a regicide has always a place in history.
> MICHAEL If your pistol is as harmless as your pen, this young tyrant will have a long life.
> PRINCE PAUL You ought to remember, too, Professor, that if you were seized, as you probably would be, and hung, as you certainly would be, there would be nobody left to read your own articles.

But Mahaffy is probably also present in Prince Paul: the name 'Maraloffski' has also some points in common with 'Mahaffy', and the reactionary wit a great deal more. Wilde first heard fireworks in Ireland. Ellmann cites the story of Mahaffy's being asked to sign a petition protesting against Russian peasants being knouted by order of the Czar, and characteristically refusing, 'Why, my dear fellow, if he doesn't knout them, they'll knout themselves'. Wilde's review of Mahaffy's *Greek Life and Thought* in 1887 dissected in some detail the author's constant interpolation of denunciations of modern democracy and Irish Home Rule, with retroactive effect:

> Mr Mahaffy . . . begins his history by frankly expressing his regret that Demosthenes was not summarily put to death for his attempt to keep the spirit of patriotism alive among the citizens of Athens! Indeed, he has no patience with what he calls 'the foolish and senseless opposition to Macedonia'; regards the revolt of the Spartans against 'Alexander's Lord Lieutenant for Greece' as an example of 'parochial politics'; indulges in Primrose League platitudes against a low franchise and the iniquity of allowing 'every pauper' to have a vote; and tells us that the 'demagogues' and 'pretended patriots' were so lost to shame that they actually preached to the parasitic mob of Athens the doctrine of Autonomy – 'not now extinct', Mr Mahaffy adds regretfully – and propounded, as a principle of political economy, the curious idea that people should be allowed to manage their own affairs!

Wilde in 1887 was an enthusiastic supporter of Parnell; Mahaffy, like many another Irish Unionist, had been roused to paranoid fury by the success of the Parnellite Home Rule cause, all the more because its leader came from his own Irish Protestant Ascendancy caste (as did Wilde). Home Rule had been temporarily defeated in 1886, but Parnell's alliance with Gladstone meant that a Second Home Rule Bill was only a matter of time. But when Wilde was Mahaffy's pupil at Trinity College Dublin in 1871-74, and when he travelled with him in Italy in 1875 and in Greece in 1877, Home Rule politics had already entered on their first phase. Prince Paul's entry among the Nihilists and subversion of their cause in his own interest might well have derived from a sardonic reflection on Mahaffy's capacity for survival were he suddenly thrust into a gathering of really virulent Irish nationalist conspirators, and behind Prince Paul's cold wit lie ominous lessons as to the vulnerability of enthusiastic revolutionary ideologues confronted by a seasoned political operator. For all of his ignorance of Russia – and there is little sign of such ignorance in his remarks on Russian literature – Wilde proved a true prophet in seeing the perpetuation of oppression regardless of any triumph of revolution. It is just possible that Prince Paul might not have survived his night among the Nihilists. His last line, and the reply it sustains, leaves the matter appropriately ambiguous:

> PRINCE PAUL (*aside*) This is the ninth conspiracy I have been in in Russia. They always end in a *voyage en Sibérie* for my friends and a new decoration for myself.
>
> MICHAEL It is your last conspiracy, Prince.

Michael has just assassinated the Czar, and arranged for the assassination of his successor: on the other hand he establishes closer accord with Prince Paul in this Act than does any other Nihilist.

Some years after *Vera* Wilde referred to 'Marfa' as the name of the widow of Ivan the Terrible, thus placing in *Vera* two poles of political interpretation of Mahaffy – subtle political survivor and old-woman professor, both with symbols of dependence on despotism.

But whatever political arguments Wilde may have had with Mahaffy or heard from him, Mahaffy left no doubt (until he ceased to speak of Wilde when the scandal broke in 1895) that he had taught his pupil the art of conversation. As Ellmann noted, Wilde had already shown his prowess as a talker at school in Portora, and he would have had the consistent stimulus of Dublin conversational pyrotechnicians in the home of his highly literary parents, but it is probable that Mahaffy talked more about talking than anyone else he ever met in Dublin. Mahaffy's *The Art of Conversation* appeared in 1887, but it must have had many years of germination in self-admiring discourses to students. Wilde was critical of the book's style, but despite the anonymity of his *Pall Mall Gazette* reviews made it clear that the reviewer was well acquainted with Mahaffy as talker, with the inference that the subjects had included the art of conversation. For this reason our selection of amusing and instructive quotations from Wilde's reviews, usually limited to one or two passages, departs from the norm at this point. The review and the book it notices brings us closer to Wilde's formal tutelage as a pyrotechnician than does any other document. We get some flavour of what Mahaffy taught Wilde, and more uncertain indications of Wilde's reactions to the teaching, at the time and subsequently. There are but a few of Wilde's direct contradictions to Mahaffy's assertions, possibly the same proportion of dissents he ventured to utter during his time as a pupil. The real significance is that it shows what Wilde had to think about in being put to the study of conversation. That Wilde did not file more dissents in reporting Mahaffy's maxims does not mean agreement with them: he is exceptionally intangible in his general verdict ('These are the broad principles contained in Mr Mahaffy's clever little book, and many of them will, no doubt, commend themselves to our readers.'). Ellmann noted the nearness in time to the earlier harsh review of *Greek Life and Thought* which may account for Wilde's present gentleness in being 'almost ready to stomach Mahaffy's absurd manual'. One covert sign of revolt was evident in the mockery of Mahaffy's Aristotelianism: Wilde proclaimed himself a Platonist, and nowhere more so than in conversational instruction, as he was shortly to show in 'The Decay of Lying' and 'The Critic as Artist', where he offered his duologues in place of Mahaffy's monologue. He would also have enjoyed the irony of supposedly reactionary Platonism being espoused by the radical pupil, and allegedly progressive Aristotelianism being linked to the conservative teacher: and Aristotle had been Plato's greatest pupil as well as his greatest critic. The review itself was pyrotechnic even more than its contents. Moreover Wilde, for once apparently silent in his own judgements, presents Mahaffy's theses almost as lecture-notes, the form in which Aristotle was said to have survived, with only an occasional official gloss of his own and a firm hint that his version presented Mahaffy better than did Mahaffy's book.

There is certainly an ironic subtext, although it may have had no wider charmed circle of 'choice spirits' than Wilde's mother, who would have agreed with her son about Mahaffy's politics. The rendition of Mahaffy's declaration of the pre-eminence of tact in conversation is so utterly at variance with what is known of Mahaffy that it must have made delicious reading for Lady Wilde, who had entertained Mahaffy at her Dublin *salon* and was consequently all too familiar with his tact in political discourse. The bitterness of the earlier review suggests that Wilde's citation of Mahaffy's 'principle' on the cruelty of great wits and the vulgarity of great humourists recalled some victimisation of the pupil by the teacher. Mahaffy was a bully, and had an unpleasant line in contemptuous dismissals: his congratulation on Wilde's scholarship to Magdalen College Oxford in 1874 carried its barb 'You're not quite clever enough for us here, Oscar. Better run up to Oxford'. In the fashion of Dublin wit, no friendship was proof against the chance of a treacherous epigram, and for all of his pride of family, personal attainments and ambitious courage, Wilde was still the pupil and obliged to keep his foil buttoned when the master could lunge painfully and precisely whenever he chose. So with Mahaffy as with Whistler, Wilde retained a sense of affection betrayed.

If Wilde learned pyrotechnics from Mahaffy as well as from Whistler, did he also absorb some of their conversational and controversial cruelty? It is difficult to indict him for betraying anyone, until his fall involuntarily betrayed everyone. Scholars who devoted years to studying him, from Hesketh Pearson to Sir Rupert Hart-Davis, united in singling out his kindness and kindliness. Yet Conor Cruise O'Brien finished reading Ellmann's biography with the sense that Wilde was cruel, ready to humiliate persons weaker than himself. One may question the accuracy of specific stories on which such a view is based, but some uneasiness may still remain. To take up Wilde's own thesis that the victorious antagonist is converted from his own principles, it would be easy to postulate a victim of pyrotechnical cruelties falling into imitation of brutality which had hurt him. Irish immigrants to many countries were victimised and later turned the same victimisation on later immigrants from other cultures, and quite apart from Wilde's having studied his fireworks in hard schools, he is a case-study of Irish immigration into Britain for all of the official Union of the two islands. In early life in England his assertiveness and apparent assurance suggests uncertainty and defensiveness; and the speed with which he won success as a playwright in 1892 increased the appearance of arrogance. After his fall he, who had been so badly hurt, hit out time and again with the pain of mortal wounds, and before 1895 he sometimes showed an insensitivity akin to Mahaffy's or Whistler's. But in his case it seems far less intentional, save in a few specific, and hotly disputed, incidents; verifiable cases where it was intentional show strong provocation. As he would remind us, Hamlet had not envenomed the rapier with which he stabbed Laertes; and yet Hamlet admitted he shot his arrow o'er the house and hurt his brother.

But in another sense Wilde had the coldness of most great creative artists where human material is concerned, whether in observation or in dissection. Science – or, as he would say, art – led him to actions he would probably have shunned for private gratification. The main effect of Mahaffy's analysis of conversation for his pupil was neither acceptance nor rejection: it was utilisation. Mahaffy laid down the law about bad conversationalists: Wilde turned them into stage conversationalists. In *A Woman of No Importance* he takes one of Mahaffy's targets, 'the raw country-bred girl who always says what she means', translates her from Mahaffy's undoubted point of reference, rural Ireland, to America, makes her the football of English Society sophisticates, and makes her triumph over their hero, Lord Illingworth, at the end. Then, in *The Importance of Being Earnest*, he transforms her, as Cecily, into a creature of absolute charm (which as Hester Worsley in *A Woman of No Importance* she emphatically is not), and with some inspiration from Hannah More gives her individual triumphs over every London sophisticate in the play. This was not a matter of proving Mahaffy wrong: Wilde contented himself, as to that, with gentle revelations of Mahaffy's snobbery about commercial travellers, or mild repudiations of the desirability of professional anecdotage about Victor Emmanuel, or sardonic deduction that Mahaffy's 'principles' implied an egalitarianism their author abominated. But as a playwright he simply adopted Mahaffy's argument that conversation was being perpetually impaired by solecisms and showed how their presentation, rather than their prevention, was what the theatre needed. In conversation Wilde became a great performer; but his finest pyrotechnics derived from his knowledge of how others performed. His genius lay in preserving their weaknesses while enabling them to be themselves, but themselves with sparkle. Even the apparently irredeemably dull would be made to catch fire from the blazes alongside them.

The mass of Wilde reviews in the 1880s, from which many exceprts are included here, show the fireworks in preparation, and some are present not in explosion but in manufacture or in the laying of a fuse or powder-train. His delighted discovery of the imaginary life and correspondence of Hannah More, the great Evangelical, coupled with her social success, gives us a glimpse of his assimilation of material to be detonated by Cecily in *The Importance of Being Earnest*. These years also show instances of his evangelism-apostasy, or the thesis prompting antithesis. On some questions he learns, matures, becomes master. On others he questions earlier enthusiasms, only to call them back later still in mingling of nostalgia and reappraisal. On others still he was conscious of counter-attractions and counter-repulses. He was at once the metropolitan sophisticate and the loyal son of the Celtic periphery. He was disgusted by stage-Irishry and stage-Scottishness, and formally repudiated dialect, yet his consciousness of metropolitan cultural near-bankruptcy made him all the more ready to seek wisdom from Irish integrity, could it be discovered. What he found in the young Yeats does honour to his heart, but also tells us something of what his head was inquiring. He was more hostile to Scottish self-assertiveness, and in a sense could be clearer. What we would now call the Kailyard obviously annoyed him, and received its squibs and rockets: but he diagnosed a search for some form of cultural innovation based on Scottish and Irish self-respect. He may seem in conflict with the forms of Irish and Scottish Renaissance of the next century as expressed by John Millington Synge and Hugh MacDiarmid, yet much of what he had to say makes him a satisfactorily ambiguous John the Baptist for Yeats and MacDiarmid. The political undertones are also significant: he missed few opportunities for cool and deadly thrusts against Parnell's enemies, whether in mocking the polemics of the arch-Unionist James Anthony Froude (whose novel he called a 'Blue Book' (i.e. a Report to Parliament)) or the imprisonment of the pro-Parnell Wilfrid Blunt by his cousin, Chief Secretary A. J. Balfour, but when Parnell's fall dashed Wilde's hopes he reacted with the white heat of so many other literary Parnellites. Domiciled in England, he denounced the hypocrisy of English journalism where the youthful Joyce in Ireland mourned Parnell's martyrdom at the hands of the pusillanimous Irish. The Parnell movement itself symbolised Wilde's larger conflict of past against future: he hailed its modernism, above all in the American character it had now assumed (and he rightly described Charles Stewart Parnell as Irish-American), yet it was part of what Yeats and Lady Wilde exhibited in their rediscovery of Celtic mythology. Parnell himself was a master-pyrotechnician in conduct rather than in speech or writing (although he had a fine dry wit mingled with a sense of emotive public slogan), and the Irish political success in unexpected tactical challenge was an inspirational music in the background of Wilde's own cultural embattlement. Shaw, Yeats, Wilde, even Joyce, all became their own Parnells, most conspicuously in Wilde's case with his own triumph and disaster in the years immediately after Parnell's fall. Our texts from Wilde, then, show fireworks in print: we must remember that some of them were written in journals recording Parnellite fireworks in House of Commons confrontation.

The reviews possessed also the necessity for pyrotechnics by occupation. Hesketh Pearson felt Wilde was too kind to be a satisfactorily severe critic, but Richard Ellmann, less impressed by the logical alternative critic, Shaw, than was Pearson, put Wilde in a more professional context (one which might at least have appealed to Shaw as the author of *Cashel Byron's Profession*): 'So Wilde wheeled about in the literature of his time, lending an ear here and boxing one there.' Wilde and Shaw were in fact on the same side in many respects – an Irish Protestant nationalism becoming Socialism, an immigrant hostility to London cultural atrophy, a highly evangelical inheritance which led them noisily to preach the gospels of less extrovert prophets like Walter Pater and Sidney Webb, a determined readiness to compel attention and for the moment lose respect by public play-acting ('he was Oscar the comic, I was G.B.S. the clown'), a conviction that their novels – and then, as matters developed for both of them, their plays – would bring London to the European standards behind which it lagged so far and so ignorantly. Wilde might appear less naturally censorious than Shaw, but he was sometimes the more deadly pyrotechnician. His air of lazy benevolence made his demolition-work more devastating than that of the obviously embattled and energetic combat-seeker Shaw. Nor was his critical brief necessarily marked for forensic combat: in the columns of the *Pall Mall Gazette* it had such an option, but as editor of the *Woman's World* he had to report on women's literary and cultural achievements, encourage them, and lead them as tactfully as he could in diplomatic feminism. Sometimes his two briefs could be interpreted by himself to do the same work, as in fighting the cause of Yeats. Sometimes they could not: the *Woman's World* was no place for the indiscriminate igniting of Catharine wheels. The women nonetheless saw some of his fireworks, and might be led to set off others which he had assembled and put in place.

Wilde declares firmly in *The Portrait of Mr W. H.* how momentary and thin sincerity may be, and his life among fireworks had shown him how sincere affection might confidently buttress itself with pyrotechnic banter which ultimately burned the affection away. But it did not of necessity do so, and his own fireworks were a means of conveying affection. Familiarity might ultimately breed condescension with the living: 'I hope you heard me?' asked Pater after one of his near-inaudible lectures; 'we overheard you', smiled Wilde; 'really, Mr Wilde, you have a phrase for everything' – Pater had much experience in dampening a firework, having frequently dampened his own. As Macaulay (to whose prose, transmitted by its influence on Ruskin, Wilde owed far more than he would wish to realise) had said, the great literary dead are the true friends, and Wilde remained unshakeable in his discipleship to idols among the dead such as Flaubert, who could not lose their lustre in personal acquaintance. It did not prevent him from affectionately mocking his own enthusiasm. The deliberate anticlimax of Flaubert's *Hérodias* with its description of the disciples of John the Baptist or Iokanaan carrying away his head in turns, for it was very heavy, was glossed by his biographical explanation: 'Flaubert's father was a doctor'. So, of course, was Wilde's, which may have increased his ease of entry into Flaubert's mind, of which he gave such proofs in *Salomé*. He paid his highest compliment to the literary and (then) Parnellite M.P. Justin Huntly McCarthy in May 1889 'Your book is charming, and your prose worthy of the sinless master whom mortals call Flaubert', but both he and his fellow-Irish recipient knew well he was ironically borrowing from Poe's 'rare and radiant maiden whom the angels name Lenore' in 'The Raven', with the obvious intention of investing worship with a smile. 'Lord Arthur Savile's Crime' is, among other things, a delicious satire on the sense of destiny and doom in Flaubert's 'Legend of St Julian Hospitator' while 'The Canterville Ghost' mercilessly lampoons supernatural literature and then, with the audience weak by laughing, makes a formidable addition to the *genre* – the fireworks induce first entertainment, then awe, and the object of ridicule becomes one of profound sympathy while farce is transformed into fear. Poe and Le Fanu are targets and inspirations there rather than Flaubert, but Flaubert himself had used rationalism – without much obvious humour – in *Hérodias* so effectively that Wilde could take it as having cleared the ground and left himself free to build new mystical conflicts of religious and sexual intensity in *Salomé*. Flaubert helped Wilde in turning confidently to the past in order to assert new forms of literary expression for the future, so that Wilde under his influence continued to mock and pray simultaneously. He took both activities much farther than Flaubert would have wished, but doctors also have to improve on the work of admired precursors. Fireworks can hardly be recommended as an act of homage, save to Handel, and Wilde knew relatively little about music. Part of Wilde's Flaubert joke lay in treating Flaubert as a saint; Flaubert himself had played most ambiguously with religious devotion on the part of his own characters. Wilde was not Flaubert's parrot, except insofar as he became his agent of canonisation.

The critic in search of ammunition in confronting the present volume may desire to explode its declaration of firework-content by declaring its idea of fireworks merely an avoidance of long-tried terms such as 'aphorisms' or 'epigrams', already utilised for anthologies of quotations from Wilde by G. N. Sutton (1914) and Alvin Redman (1952) respectively. Whatever the merits of this dismissal, it runs into difficulties with *Salomé*. The play is ruthlessly innocent of epigram – indeed ruthless innocence is one of its most memorable qualities. It is now clear that Wilde wrote it in French directly, and internal evidence in any case would support such a conclusion, for it seems to defy any attempt at satisfactory translation into English. It demands recognition for pyrotechnical as for other qualities, yet sentences extracted on their own do not convey them. Something of its intricate and rich tapestry may be seen in specific speeches. The great Irish actor, Micheál Mac Liammóir, whose magnificent one-person show *The Importance of Being Oscar*, first presented in 1960, has been a profound influence on the present work, chose to include in it a memorable rendition of Herod's speech in which he seeks to buy off Salomé's demand for the head of Iokanaan by offers of exotic jewels. The marvellous cadences of Mac Liammóir's sensual, gutteral French echo still in my ears, and he would, I think, sympathise with the wish of a grateful admirer to applaud with inevitable inadequacy and try something else. I have

chosen to include all of Salomé's own lines, which taken together on
their own give a terrible directness to her frustration, her demand, and
her destruction. This is firework, but firework of a wholly different
kind to Wilde's epigrammatic English. *Salomé* is perpetually associated
with her dance of the seven veils. Formally, Wilde does nothing with it
save give curt direction for it to happen. Flaubert conveyed it in immortal language: Wilde's is essentially a voyage around Flaubert,
deliberately crossing his path as little as possible. Beardsley's drawings bring us much closer to it, and indeed illustrate Flaubert's *Hérodias* more directly at several points than they do Wilde's *Salomé*. (His
'Enter Herodias', for instance, is much more in keeping with the Herodias of Flaubert than the Herodias of Wilde, for all of his intrusion of a
caricature of Wilde into this and other of his illustrations. Wilde is said
to have complained that Beardsley's drawings were 'cruel and evil and
so like dear Aubrey, who has a face like a silver hatchet with grass-
green hair': it seemed appropriate for our front cover, based on a
Beardsley caricature of Wilde writing *Salomé*, to reply in kind.) Pro-
ductions of *Salomé*, and its adaptation as in Richard Strauss's opera,
depend heavily on the dance. Yet it seems to me that Wilde's whole
presentation of *Salomé* herself throughout the play with its remorseless
self-stripping of illusions is a metaphor for the ultimate dance, and,
considered on their own, her lines symbolise it both before and after
the dance itself. The necessity of including Salomé's words (and
Herod's final line) in French should not deter readers. As Beardsley's
illustration maliciously reminds us, Wilde wrote in good, easy French,
for all that he made it do his work as he wished. Perhaps its introduction here may stimulate the use of the play in schools.

There is nothing in this book dating from later than Wilde's conviction for homosexual practices. Thereafter any fireworks were for
private conversation and correspondence, and the domination of
either art by his tragedy retires the idea of fireworks from effective con-
sideration. We can certainly trace lines of thought and style from the
years before his fall to those that followed it, but his presentation of
words becomes a different activity from the moment of his conviction.
Apart from his editions of his last two plays, survivals from his years of
splendour, his *Ballad of Reading Gaol* and his two profound and moving
letters to the *Daily Chronicle* on prison conditions, he made no public
display of his work, and I decline to search his writings in the shadow
of imprisonment and disgrace for something that might be fireworks in
another context. He would not have wanted me to, and I owe him a
great deal. Such an activity would have produced, not an illuminating
distortion but a destructive one. His last firework, then, is his protest
at the silence into which he was thrust, and the burden it bears destroys the *genre* for what lies beyond it in time. The display of pyrotech-

nics is over, and the pyrotechnician is exploded far more remorselessly than the Bunbury imagined by Algernon in *The Importance of Being Earnest* (Bunbury, explosion and all, proved too large a continuous display for inclusion here unless we were to include the entire play, which in one sense a full treatment of the fireworks might seem to demand). The fireworks have been restricted at all times to those for public audience: letters have been used only when they were intended for public prints, or for reading at public gatherings, such as the Thirteen Club which prided itself on defying superstitions and which therefore received a mock castigation from Wilde. The private fireworks may be studied in Sir Rupert Hart-Davis's admirable and invaluable editions of Wilde's letters to which (and to whose great editor) I am profoundly indebted. His *Selected Letters of Oscar Wilde* and *More Letters of Oscar Wilde* are still happily in print.

What is present here is nonetheless a public intellectual biography, written by its subject. We can see the growth of his genius (for all of his denial of any maturing process) and the varying forms of artistic expression and declarations of ideological interest. If the removal of his fireworks from their setting, or from the train of argument which led to each of them, makes for distortion, it may also help to highlight the argument in them where it can be lost in sheer accumulation of prose. In this form he invites us to consider his thought in staccato form, forcing us to confront his high points directly instead of being drawn too rapidly onwards in the excitement of his continuous narrative. I have been bound by what he presented to the world. I have not, for instance, included extracts from the text of the four-act version of *The Importance of Being Earnest*, cut down to three acts when George Alexander insisted on it to allow for a 'curtain-raiser'. The publication of the four-act version was welcome, and it has been presented with some success on the stage. But it is obviously unfinished: he had much work to do in cutting and polishing his gems, as may be seen by comparison with the finished versions in the final three-act text. Lady Bracknell's superb remark on the possible public response to her missing any more trains is in the four-act version a repetitive and much less funny series of allusions to train-missing. One can guess at the form the four-act version's epigrams would have taken from the evidence of the three-act text: I revised the four-act text myself along such lines for a BBC radio production by Ian Cotterell ten years ago. But it does not offer a set of fireworks as finally presented by Wilde himself. I have included a few discarded epigrams from the text of 'Mrs Arbuthnot', the draft of *A Woman of No Importance* evidently used in rehearsal. But these clearly were in a form in which they could have been employed, and therefore made for a few amusing exceptions to the iron law as to public performance of fireworks. I felt so strongly about the public principle that a failure to violate it would have been inartistic. To throw a little more doubt on my consistency it should be said that 'Mrs Arbuthnot' also includes usages not present in the final text: Gerald is 'Aleck' (was this a private joke about Wilde's previous producer, George Alexander, known as 'Aleck', in that Gerald/Aleck receives much tutelage from the Wildean Lord Illingworth?); and Illingworth's family name is 'Harbord', which being an existing aristocratic name was dropped in favour of 'Harford'. As Lord Illingworth advises, it was necessary for Wilde to study the *Peerage*.

The dates of composition of the fireworks are in many cases problematical and I have adopted the very rough and ready method of taking first publication or first production (whichever came first) of a given work as the means of establishing a chronological order. In some cases final texts came many years after first appearances. In one such case, 'Shakespeare and Stage Costume', later published in book form as *The Truth of Masks*, I have indicated the later date of composition of one entirely new firework but left it in the company of the earlier material to which it refers and on which it depends. *Vera* was first published in 1880 and revised for its 1882 edition where a prologue (not used by me) is added. *The Portrait of Mr W. H.* appeared in its shorter form in July 1889. Its larger, revised version, never published in Wilde's lifetime but clearly completed by him for publication, may not have been finalised until 1893, to judge from the important study by Dr Horst Schroeder, to which and to whom I am much obliged. *The Picture of Dorian Gray* was substantially revised and enlarged between its magazine publication in June 1890 and its appearance in book form in April 1891. My concession to the later date has been to print the work's 'preface', written in response to adverse criticism, after both the selections from the novel itself and the letters to three hostile newspapers: Wilde's only other answers to adverse commentators. The dates of composition may in some cases have been considerably earlier than first publication. Wilde complained to George Macmillan (*More Letters*, p. 80) that 'London Models' was initially written and despatched to its editor, Joseph Comyns Carr, in March 1886, and that it only appeared in the *English Illustrated Magazine* in January 1889. But it may have had further revisals, and an exception would only have opened up problems about doubtful cases impossible of resolution. In any case its appearance probably involved reflections by its author which worked their way to fruition in *Dorian Gray*, from which I would not have wished to distance it unduly.

Apart from the enjoyment I have had in working with Wilde on this book, it had the incidental charm of enabling me to make one new discovery. Reference in a review of a minor novel by Dostoevsky, *Injury and Insult*, a review I did not use, made it clear that Wilde had previously reviewed *Crime and Punishment*, and that his review later eluded the vigilance of his literary executor, Robert Ross, and his bibliographer, Stuart Mason (i.e. Christopher Sclater Millard), or, if known to either of them, was deliberately or accidentally overlooked by them. Accordingly, I have reprinted my discovery in an appendix. When I mentioned it to the critic Philip French, he promptly inquired what was the relation of its date of appearance to that of *Lord Arthur Savile's Crime*, and in fact it is clear from the chronology that the story was one immediate effect of Wilde's encounter with the great Russian novel. (Another, I suspect, is the role of Dorian Gray's consistently altering portrait as his Inquisitor. A third is probably certain passages, quoted here, in 'The Soul of Man Under Socialism.') I also observed that while Mason in his *Bibliography* lists a translation – the first into English – of Turgenev's 'A Fire at Sea' (originally, and exceptionally, written in French) – as executed anonymously by Wilde for *Macmillan's Magazine*, May 1886, this has never been included in any collection of his writing and the authorship of the translation is apparently unknown to students of Turgenev. Mason cited a portion of the manuscript in support of the ascription, which seems conclusive. I am content to defend the appearance of both works in the appendix on the ground that *Crime and Punishment* supplied the unknown basis for important fireworks, and that the definition of a firework must surely include work on 'A Fire at Sea'. If any student of Wilde has, unknown to me, reprinted either item I can only offer them my apologies, coupled with my knowledge of the pleasure their discovery must have given them.

And now to the names of those but for whom this work would never have transpired, whose encouragement in Wilde studies has sustained me down the years though most are innocent of any complicity with this venture, and some, alas, will never know of it.

Sir Rupert Hart-Davis; June, Lady Hart-Davis; the late Ruth, Lady Hart-Davis; the late Richard Ellmann; Nicholas Barker; Alf Mac Lochlainn; Edna C. Davis, late of the William Andrews Clark Library of Los Angeles; Dr Patrick Henchy; Professor Thomas P. O'Neill; Dr Isobel Murray; the late Jocelyn Baines; John Bell; Richard Garnett; the late Michael O'Neill Walshe; S. E. Allen Figgis; Terence de Vere White; the late Micheál Mac Liammóir; Allen Wright; Professor W. W. Robson; Professor Dan H. Laurence; Dr Emmanuel Vernadakis; Dr Horst Schroeder; Allan Massie; Ronald Mason; Michael Worton; Ian Cotterell; Denis Rafter; the Very Rev. Anthony Ross, O.P.; Professor George Shepperson; my father, the late R. Dudley Edwards; my mother, the late Síle Ní Shúilleabháin.

Euan Cameron of Barrie & Jenkins has inspired and guided this work from inception to appearance, and he and his family have become much-loved friends in the course of it. Clara Grant, student of English Literature at Edinburgh University, gave me excellent advice on the choices; Elspeth Morrison, student in History and English literature, also at Edinburgh University, was invaluable on Wilde's Russian interests; Dr Adam Naylor and Dr Colin Affleck, my former students, were as always sage counsel in cumber; Tadeusz Deręgowski gave good advice on painters; Roger Savage, my invaluable colleague in English Literature, most kindly read and strengthened this work in proof, and together with Randall Stevenson and Sarah Carpenter enabled me to test some of its ideas in drama seminars; T. Michael Williams crowned many years of thought-provoking comment by his work reflected here.

My wife, Bonnie Lee Dudley Edwards, my children Leila, Sara and Michael, my mother-in-law Elizabeth Balbirnie Lee, our friend Mark Kennedy, all made individual and irreplaceable contributions to the book's development.

The Librarian and staff of the Library of Congress, the staff of the William Andrews Clark Library, the Director and staff of the British Library; the Director and staff of the National Library of Ireland – are all deserving of my deepest thanks over many years. To the Librarian and staff of Edinburgh University Library my great gratitude is due for their unfailing good nature and support in most trying times. The Edinburgh Public Library at George IV Bridge was exceptionally helpful, most particularly in its admirable Reference Room. To the Director of the National Library of Scotland, to Dr James Donaldson and all my helpers and friends in the Reading Rooms, no thanks could be adequate for their assistance and resourcefulness on every occasion.

Mr Merlin Holland has most generously consented to my request for permission to include unpublished matter, and his enthusiasm for the book is particularly heart-warming, bringing as it does the same kindness for which his grandfather, Oscar Wilde, was distinguished.

I dedicate this book to my aunt, Mrs Elizabeth Wall. My primary motive is to give some expression, however inadequately, for her life-time's love and goodness to me. But I do so also because of her conversation, from which I first learned how much language can be made simultaneously the instrument of love, laughter and learning, and it is because of that I fell in love with the fireworks of Oscar Wilde.

OWEN DUDLEY EDWARDS
University of Edinburgh
21 May 1989

The Fireworks of
OSCAR WILDE

The use of three black stars (★ ★ ★) in the pages that follow indicates a change of attribution. A single hollow star (☆) shows that the attributions are continuous. The source of attribution is repeated at the top of every left hand page.

The Fireworks of
OSCAR WILDE
1880

PRINCE PAUL When you are as old as I am, Prince, you will understand
   that there are few things easier than to live badly and die well.
CZAREVITCH Easy to die well! A lesson experience cannot have taught
   you, much as you know of a bad life.
PRINCE PAUL Experience, the name men give to their mistakes. I never
   commit any.

Vera, Act II

☆

PRINCE PAUL To make a good salad is to be a brilliant diplomatist – the
   problem is entirely the same in both cases. To know exactly how
   . much oil one must put with one's vinegar.

☆

PRINCE PAUL Culture depends on cookery. For myself, the only immortality I desire is to invent a new sauce.

☆

COUNT ROUVALOFF There seems to be nothing in life about which you
   would not jest.
PRINCE PAUL Ah! my dear Count, life is much too important a thing
   ever to talk seriously about it.
CZAREVITCH I don't think Prince Paul's nature is such a mystery. He
   would stab his best friend for the sake of writing an epigram on
   his tombstone.
PRINCE PAUL *Parbleu!* I sould sooner lose my best friend than my worst
   enemy. To have friends, you know, one need only be good-
   natured; but when a man has no enemy left there must be something mean about him.

☆

PRINCE PAUL (*bitterly*) I love to drive through the streets and see how
   the rabble scowl at me from every corner. It makes me feel I am a
   power in Russia; one man against millions! Besides, I have no
   ambition to be a popular hero, to be crowned with laurels one
   year and pelted with stones the next; I prefer dying peaceably in

41

my own bed.

CZAREVITCH And after death?

PRINCE PAUL (*shrugging his shoulders*) Heaven is a despotism. I shall be at home there.

Vera, Act II

☆

CZAR Who is that man over there? I don't know him. What is he doing? Is he a conspirator? Have you searched him? Give him till to-morrow to confess, then hang him! – hang him!

PRINCE PAUL Sire, you are anticipating history. This is Count Petou-chof, your new Ambassador to Berlin.

☆

CZAREVITCH Who are we who dare lay this ban of terror on a people? Have we less vices than they have, that we bring them to the bar of judgment before us?

PRINCE PAUL What a Communist the Prince is! He would have an equal distribution of sin as well as of property.

☆

CZAREVITCH The star of freedom is risen already, and far off I hear the mighty wave Democracy break on these cursed shores.

PRINCE PAUL (*to* PRINCE PETROVITCH) In that case you and I must learn how to swim.

☆

PRINCE PAUL You have so many spies that I should think you want in-formation. Well, you will find me the best-informed man in Russia on the abuses of our Government. I made them nearly all myself.

Vera, Act III

☆

PRESIDENT The Nihilists never forget their friends, or forgive their enemies.

PRINCE PAUL Really? I did not think you were so civilised.

☆

PRINCE PAUL (*reading*) 'The rights of humanity'! In the old times men carved out their rights for themselves as they lived, but nowadays every baby seems born with a social manifesto in its mouth much bigger than itself. 'Nature is not a temple, but a workshop: we demand the right to labour.' Ah, I shall surrender my own rights in that respect. ... 'The family as subversive of true socialistic

42

and communal unity is to be annihilated.' Yes, President, I agree completely with Article 5. A family is a terrible incumbrance, especially if one is not married.

☆

PRESIDENT This must be a new atmosphere for you, Prince Paul. We speak the truth to one another here.
PRINCE PAUL How misleading you must find it!

☆

PRINCE PAUL Good kings are the only dangerous enemies that modern democracy has...

1882

As regards Hester Grazebrook's dresses . . . the masterpiece was undoubtedly the last, a symphony in silver-grey and pink, a pure melody of colour which I feel sure Whistler would call a *Scherzo*, and take as its visible motive the moonlight wandering in silver mist through a rose-garden; unless indeed he saw this dress, in which case he would paint it and nothing else, for it is a dress such as Velasquez only could paint, and Whistler very wisely always paints those things which are within reach of Velasquez only.

Notice of Lily Langtry as Hester Grazebrook in Tom Taylor, *An Unequal Match*, Wallack's Theatre, New York, *New York World*, 7 November 1882

☆

The scenery was, of course, prepared in a hurry. . . . The last scene was exceedingly clever and true to nature as well, being that combination of lovely scenery and execrable architecture which is so specially characteristic of a German spa.

☆

As for the drawing-room scene, I cannot regard it as in any way a success. The heavy ebony doors are entirely out of keeping with the satin panels; the silk hangings and festoons of black and yellow are quite meaningless in their position and consequently quite ugly; the carpet is out of all colour relation with the rest of the room, and the table-cover is mauve. Still, to have decorated even so bad a room in six days must, I suppose, be a subject of respectful wonder, though I should have fancied that Mr Wallack had many very much better sets in his own stock.

☆

. . . the beauty of Hester Grazebrook . . . may also influence the art of America as it has influenced the art of England, for of the rare Greek type it is the most absolutely perfect example. The Philistine may, of course, object that to be absolutely perfect is impossible. Well, that is so: but then it is only the impossible things that are worth doing nowadays!

44

1883

... everybody seems in a hurry to catch a train. This is a state of things which is not favourable to poetry or romance. Had Romeo or Juliet been in a constant state of anxiety about trains, or had their minds been agitated by the question of return-tickets, Shakespeare could not have given us those lovely balcony scenes which are so full of poetry and pathos.

Lecture, 'Personal Impressions of America', 10 July 1883

☆

In England an inventor is regarded almost as a crazy man, and in too many instances invention ends in disappointment and poverty. In America an inventor is honoured, help is forthcoming, and the exercise of ingenuity, the application of science to the work of man, is there the shortest road to wealth. There is no country in the world where machinery is so lovely as in America. ... It was not until I had seen the water-works at Chicago that I realised the wonders of machinery; the rise and fall of the steel rods, the symmetrical motion of the great wheels is the most beautiful rhythmic thing I have ever seen.

☆

One is impressed in America, but not favourably impressed, by the inordinate size of everything. The country seems to try to bully one into a belief in its power by its impressive bigness.

☆

I was disappointed in Niagara – most people must be disappointed in Niagara. Every American bride is taken there, and the sight of the stupendous waterfall must be one of the earliest, if not the keenest, disappointments in American married life.

☆

To appreciate it really one has to see it from underneath the fall, and to do that it is necessary to be dressed in a yellow oil-skin, which is as ugly as a mackintosh – and I hope none of you ever wears one. It is a consolation to know, however, that such an artist as Madame Bern-

hardt has not only worn that yellow, ugly dress, but has been photo-
graphed in it.

Lecture, 'Personal Impressions of America', 10 July 1883

☆

Perhaps the most beautiful part of America is the West, to reach
which, however, involves a journey by rail of six days, racing along
tied to an ugly tin-kettle of a steam engine. I found but poor consolation for this journey in the fact that the boys who infest the cars
and sell everything that one can eat – or should not eat – were selling
editions of my poems vilely printed on a kind of grey blotting paper,
for the low price of ten cents. Calling these boys on one side I told
them that though poets like to be popular they desire to be paid, and
selling editions of my poems without giving me a profit is dealing a
blow at literature which must have a disastrous effect on poetical aspi-
rants. The invariable reply that they made was that they themselves
made a profit out of the transaction and that was all they cared about.

☆

It is a popular superstition that in America a visitor is invariably
addressed as 'Stranger'. I was never once addressed as 'Stranger'.
When I went to Texas I was called 'Captain'; when I got to the centre
of the country I was addressed as 'Colonel', and, on arriving at the
borders of Mexico, as 'General'.

☆

It is perhaps worth while to note that what many people call
Americanisms are really old English expressions which have lingered
in our colonies while they have been lost in our own country. Many
people imagine that the term 'I guess', which is so common in
America, is purely an American expression, but it was used by John
Locke in his work on 'The Understanding', just as we now use 'I
think'.

☆

It is in the colonies, and not in the mother country, that the old life of
the country really exists. If one wants to realise what English Puritanism is – not at its worst (when it is very bad), but at its best, and
then it is not very good – I do not think one can find much of it in
England, but much can be found about Boston and Massachusetts.
We have got rid of it. America still preserves it, to be, I hope, a short-
lived curiosity.

☆

San Francisco is a really beautiful city. China Town, peopled by

Chinese labourers, is the most artistic town I have ever come across. The people – strange, melancholy Orientals, whom many people would call common, and they are certainly very poor – have determined that they will have nothing about them that is not beautiful. In the Chinese restaurant, where these navvies meet to have supper in the evening, I found them drinking tea out of china cups as delicate as the petals of a rose-leaf, whereas at the gaudy hotels I was supplied with a *delf* cup an inch and a half thick. When the Chinese bill was presented it was made out on rice paper, the account being done in Indian ink as fantastically as if an artist had been etching little birds on a fan.

☆

Salt Lake City contains only two buildings of note, the chief being the Tabernacle, which is in the shape of a soup-kettle. It is decorated by the only native artist, and he has treated religious subjects in the naive spirit of the early Florentine painters, representing people of our own day in the dress of the period side by side with people of Biblical history who are clothed in some romantic costume.

☆

The building next in importance is called the Amelia Palace, in honour of one of Brigham Young's wives. When he died the present president of the Mormons stood up in the Tabernacle and said that it had been revealed to him that he was to have the Amelia Palace, and that on this subject there were to be no more revelations of any kind!

☆

From Salt Lake City one travels over the great plains of Colorado and up the Rocky Mountains, on the top of which is Leadville, the richest city in the world. It has also got the reputation of being the roughest, and every man carries a revolver. I was told that if I went there they would be sure to shoot me or my travelling manager. I wrote and told them that nothing that they could do to my travelling manager would intimidate me.

☆

They are miners – men working in metals, so I lectured to them on the Ethics of Art. I read them passages from the autobiography of Benvenuto Cellini and they seemed much delighted. I was reproved by my hearers for not having brought him with me. I explained that he had been dead for some little time which elicited the enquiry 'Who shot him?'

☆

They afterwards took me to a dancing saloon where I saw the only

47

rational method of art criticism I have ever come across. Over the piano was printed a notice:

> PLEASE DO NOT SHOOT THE PIANIST.
> HE IS DOING HIS BEST.

The mortality among pianists in that place is marvellous.

Lecture, 'Personal Impressions of America', 10 July 1883

☆

Then they asked me to supper, and having accepted, I had to descend a mine in a rickety bucket in which it was impossible to be graceful. Having got into the heart of the mountain I had supper, the first course being whisky, the second whisky, and the third whisky.

☆

I went to the Theatre to lecture and I was informed that just before I went there two men had been seized for committing a murder, and in that theatre they had been brought on to the stage at eight o'clock in the evening, and then and there tried and executed before a crowded audience. But I found these miners very charming and not at all rough.

☆

Among the more elderly inhabitants of the South I found a melancholy tendency to date every event of importance by the late war. 'How beautiful the moon is to-night' I once remarked to a gentleman who was standing next to me. 'Yes', was his reply, 'but you should have seen it before the war.'

☆

So infinitesimal did I find the knowledge of Art, west of the Rocky Mountains, that an art patron – one who in his day had been a miner – actually sued the railroad company for damages because the plaster cast of Venus of Milo, which he had imported from Paris, had been delivered minus the arms. And, what is more surprising still, he gained his case and the damages.

☆

Pennsylvania, with its rocky gorges and woodland scenery, reminded me of Switzerland. The prairie reminded me of a piece of blotting-paper.

☆

The Spanish and French have left behind them memorials in the beauty of their names. All the cities that have beautiful names derive them from the Spanish or the French. The English people give intensely ugly names to places. One place had such an ugly name that I refused to lecture there. It was called Grigsville. Supposing I had founded a school of Art there – fancy 'Early Grigsville'. Imagine a School of Art teaching 'Grigsville Renaissance'.

☆

American youths are pale and precocious, or sallow and supercilious, but American girls are pretty and charming – little oases of pretty unreasonableness in a vast desert of practical common-sense.

☆

Every American girl is entitled to have twelve young men devoted to her. They remain her slaves and she rules them with charming nonchalance.

☆

The men are entirely given to business; they have, as they say, their brains in front of their heads. They are also exceedingly acceptive of new ideas. Their education is practical. We base the education of children entirely on books, but we must give a child a mind before we can instruct the mind. Children have a natural antipathy to books – handicraft should be the basis of education. Boys and girls should be taught to use their hands to make something, and they would be less apt to destroy and be mischievous.

☆

In going to America one learns that poverty is not a necessary accompaniment to civilisation.

☆

There at any rate is a country that has no trappings, no pageants and no gorgeous ceremonies. I saw only two processions – one was the Fire Brigade preceded by the Police, the other was the Police preceded by the Fire Brigade.

☆

Every man when he gets to the age of twenty-one is allowed a vote, and thereby immediately acquires his political education. The Americans are the best politically educated people in the world. It is well worth one's while to go to a country which can teach us the beauty of the word FREEDOM and the value of the thing LIBERTY.

1884

. . . as regards high heels, I quite admit that some additional height in the shoe or boot is necessary if long gowns are to be worn in the street; but what I object to is that the height should be given to the heel only, and not to the sole of the foot also. The modern high-heeled boot is, in fact, merely the clog of the time of Henry VI, with the front prop left out, and its inevitable effect is to throw the body forward, to shorten the steps, and consequently to produce that want of grace which always follows want of freedom.

To the Editor, *Pall Mall Gazette*, printed 14 October 1884

☆

I am not proposing any antiquarian revival of an ancient costume, but trying merely to point out the right laws of dress, laws which are dictated by art and not by archaeology, by science and not by fashion; and just as the best work of art in our days is that which combines classic grace with absolute reality, so from a combination of the Greek principles of beauty with the German principles of health will come, I feel certain, the costume of the future.

☆

. . . now to the question of men's dress . . . The broad-brimmed hat of 1640 kept the rain of winter and the glare of summer from the face. . .; a wide turned-down collar is a healthier thing than a strangling stock, and a short cloak much more comfortable than a sleeved overcoat . . . a cloak is easier to put on and off, lies lightly on the shoulder in summer, and, wrapped round one in winter, keeps one perfectly warm. A doublet, again, is simpler than a coat and waistcoat; instead of two garments we have one; by not being open, also, it protects the chest better.

Short loose trousers are in every way to be preferred to the tight knee-breeches which often impede the proper circulation of the blood . . . soft leather boots, which could be worn above or below the knee, are more supple, and give consequently more freedom. . .

☆

I say nothing about the question of grace and picturesqueness, for I

suppose that no one . . . would prefer a macaroni to a cavalier, a Law-
rence to a Vandyke, or the third George to the first Charles; but for
ease, warmth and comfort this seventeenth-century dress is infinitely
superior to anything that came after it, and I do not think it is excelled
by any preceding form of costume. I sincerely trust that we may soon
see in England some national revival of it.

★　　★　　★

I am not denying the force, or even the popularity, of the '' 'Eave arf a
brick' school of criticism, but I acknowledge it does not interest me.
The *gamin* in the gutter may be a necessity, but the *gamin* in discussion
is a nuisance.

'More Radical Ideas Upon Dress Reform', *Pall Mall Gazette*,
11 November 1884

☆

. . . tails have no place in costume, except on some Darwinian theory of
heredity. . .

☆

Mr Wentworth Huyshe solemnly announces that 'he and those who
think with him' cannot permit this question of beauty to be imported
into the question of dress; that he and those who think with him take
'practical views on the subject', and so on.

　　Well, I will not enter here into a discussion as to how far any one
who does not take beauty and the value of beauty into account can
claim to be practical at all. The word practical is nearly always the last
refuge of the uncivilised.

☆

. . . beauty is essentially organic; that is, it comes, not from without,
but from within – not from any added prettinesses, but from the perfection of its own being; and that consequently, as the body is beautiful, so all apparel that rightly clothes it must be beautiful also in its
construction and in its lines.

☆

Fashion in her high-heeled boots has screamed, and the dreadful word
'anachronism' has been used. Now, whatever is useful cannot be an
anachronism. Such a word is applicable only to the revival of some
folly. . .

☆

. . . all charges of a want of womanly character in these forms of dress
are really meaningless; every right article of apparel belongs equally to

both sexes, and there is absolutely no such thing as a definitely femi-
nine garment.

1885

The present style of burying and sorrowing for the dead seems to me to make grief grotesque and to turn mourning to a mockery. . . . The ceremony by which we part from those whom we have loved should not merely be noble in its meaning but simple in its sincerity. The funeral of Ophelia does not seem to me 'a maimed rite' when one thinks of the flowers strewn on her grave. . . . the coffin should be privately conveyed at night-time to the churchyard chapel, and . . . there the mourners should next day meet. By these means the public procession through the streets would be avoided; and the publicity of funerals is surely the real cause of their expense.

Public letter to the Rev. J. Page Hopps, read at Funeral and
Mourning Reform meeting at Leicester, 15 January 1885

☆

If we are to have funeral memorials at all, far better models are to be found in the beautiful crosses of Ireland, such as the cross at Monasterboice, or in the delicate bas-reliefs on Greek tombs. Above all, such art, if we are to have it, should concern itself more with the living than the dead – should be rather a noble symbol for the guiding of life than an idle panegyric on those who are gone. If a man needs an elaborate tombstone in order to remain in the memory of his country, it is clear that his living at all was an act of absolute superfluity. Keats's grave is a hillock of green grass with a plain headstone, and is to me the holiest place in Rome. There is in Westminster Abbey a periwigged admiral in a nightgown hurried off to heaven by two howling cherubs, which is one of the best examples I know of ostentatious obscurity.

★   ★   ★

Last night, at Prince's Hall, Mr Whistler made his first public appearance as a lecturer on art, and spoke for more than an hour with really marvellous eloquence on the absolute uselessness of all lectures of the kind. . . . this fashionable assemblage seemed somewhat aghast, and not a little amused, at being told that the slightest appearance among a civilised people of any joy in beautiful things is a grave impertinence to all painters; but Mr Whistler was relentless, and with charming ease, and much grace of manner, explained to the public that the only

53

thing they should cultivate was ugliness, and that on their permanent stupidity rested all the hopes of art in the future.

'Mr Whistler's Ten O'Clock', *Pall Mall Gazette*, 21 February 1885

☆

. . . he stood there, a miniature Mephistopheles, mocking the majority! He was like a brilliant surgeon lecturing to a class composed of subjects destined ultimately for dissection, and solemnly assuring them how valuable to science their maladies were, and how absolutely uninteresting the slightest symptoms of health on their part would be.

☆

. . . there were some arrows, barbed and brilliant, shot off, with all the speed and splendour of fireworks, at the archaeologists, who spend their lives in verifying the birthplaces of nobodies, and estimate the value of a work of art by its date or its decay, at the art critics who always treat a picture as if it were a novel, and try and find out the plot; at dilettanti in general, and amateurs in particular; and (*O mea culpa!*) at dress reformers most of all. 'Did not Velasquez paint crinolines? What more do you want?'

☆

Having thus made a holocaust of humanity, Mr Whistler turned to Nature, and in a few moments convicted her of the Crystal Palace, Bank holidays, and a general overcrowding of detail, both in omnibuses and in landscapes; and then, in a passage of singular beauty, not unlike one that occurs in Corot's letters, spoke of the artistic value of dim dawns and dusks, when the mean facts of life are lost in exquisite and evanescent effects, when common things are touched with mystery and transfigured with beauty; when the warehouses become as palaces, and the tall chimneys of the factory seem like campaniles in the silver air.

☆

Finally, after making a strong protest against anybody but a painter judging of painting, and a pathetic appeal to the audience not to be lured by the aesthetic movement into having beautiful things about them, Mr Whistler concluded his lecture with a pretty passage about Fusiyama on a fan . . . I strongly deny that charming people should be condemned to live with magenta ottomans and Albert-blue curtains in their rooms in order that some painter may observe the side-lights on the one and the values of the other. Nor do I accept the dictum that only a painter is a judge of painting. I say that only an artist is a judge of art; there is a wide difference.

☆

... there are not many arts, but one art merely and poem, picture Parthenon, sonnet and statue – all are in their essence the same, and he who knows one knows all. But the poet is the supreme artist, for he is the master of colour and of form, and the real musician besides, and is lord over all life and all arts; and so to the poet beyond all others are these mysteries known; to Edgar Allan Poe and to Baudelaire, not to Benjamin West and Paul Delaroche. However, I would not enjoy anybody else's lectures unless in a few points I disagreed with them, and Mr Whistler's lecture last night was, like everything that he does, a masterpiece.

★   ★   ★

Were we able to carry our *chiaroscuro* about with us, as we do our umbrellas, all would be well; but this being impossible, I hardly think that pretty and delightful people will continue to wear a style of dress as ugly as it is useless, and as meaningless as it is monstrous, even on the chance of such a master as Mr Whistler spiritualising them into a symphony, or refining them into a mist. For the arts are made for life, and not life for the arts.

'The Relation of Dress to Art: A Note in Black and White on Mr
Whistler's Lecture', *Pall Mall Gazette*, 28 February 1885

☆

... all costumes are caricatures. The basis of Art is not the Fancy Ball.

☆

... Art is not to be taught in Academies. It is what one looks at, not what one listens to, that makes the artist. The real schools should be the streets.

☆

A nation arrayed in stove-pipe hats, and dress improvers, might have built the Pantechnichon, possibly, but the Parthenon, never.

☆

Speaking ... from his own passionless pedestal, Mr Whistler in pointing out that the power of the painter is to be found in his power of vision, not in his cleverness of hand, has expressed a truth which needed expression, and which, coming from the lord of form and colour, cannot fail to have its influence. His lecture, the Apocrypha though it be for the people, yet remains from this time as the Bible for the painter, the masterpiece of masterpieces, the song of songs. It is true he has pronounced the panegyric of the Philistine, but I can fancy Ariel praising Caliban for a jest: and, in that he has read the Commination Service over the critics, let all men thank him, the critics themselves indeed most of all, for he has now relieved them from the necessity of a tedious existence.

'The Relation of Dress to Art: A Note in Black and White on Mr Whistler's Lecture', *Pall Mall Gazette*, 28 February 1885

☆

. . . among all our public speakers, I know but few who can combine, so felicitously as he does, the mirth and malice of Puck, with the style of the minor prophets.

★   ★   ★

. . . the British cook is a foolish woman, who should be turned, for her iniquities, into a pillar of that salt which she never knows how to use.

Review: *Dinners and Dishes, Pall Mall Gazette,* 7 March 1885

★   ★   ★

. . . we can strongly recommend to the School-Board the *Lines on the Old Town Pump* as eminently suitable for recitation by children. Such a verse, for instance, as –

> I hear the little children say
> (For the tale will never die)
> How the old pump flowed both night and day
> When the brooks and the wells ran dry,

has all the ring of Macaulay in it, and is a form of poetry which cannot possibly harm anybody, even if translated into French. Any inaccurate ideas of the laws of nature, which the children might get from the passage in question, could easily be corrected afterwards by a lecture on Hydrostatics.

Review: Atherton Furlong, *Echoes of Memory, Pall Mall Gazette,* 27 March 1885

★   ★   ★

On the roots of verbs Philology may be allowed to speak, but on the roots of flowers she must keep silence. We cannot allow her to dig up Parnassus.

To the Editor, *Pall Mall Gazette*, printed 1 April 1885

★   ★   ★

> We caught the tread of dancing feet,
> We loitered down the moonlit street,
> And stopped beneath the harlot's house.
>
> Inside, above the din and fray,
> We heard the loud musicians play
> The 'Treues Liebes Herz' of Strauss.

Like strange mechanical grotesques,
Making fantastic arabesques,
The shadows raced across the blind.

We watched the ghostly dancers spin
To sound of horn and violin,
Like black leaves wheeling in the wind.

Like wire-pulled automatons,
Slim silhouetted skeletons
Went sidling through the slow quadrille.

They took each other by the hand,
And danced a stately saraband;
Their laughter echoed thin and shrill.

Sometimes a clockwork puppet pressed
A phantom lover to her breast,
Sometimes they seemed to try to sing.

Sometimes a horrible marionette
Came out, and smoked its cigarette
Upon the steps like a live thing.

Then, turning to my love, I said,
'The dead are dancing with the dead,
The dust is whirling with the dust.'

But she – she heard the violin,
And left my side, and entered in:
Love passed into the house of lust.

Then suddenly the tune went false,
The dancers wearied of the waltz,
The shadows ceased to wheel and whirl.

And down the long and silent street,
The dawn, with silver-sandalled feet,
Crept like a frightened girl.

'The Harlot's House', *Dramatic Review*, 11 April 1885

★   ★   ★

. . . I have rarely witnessed such enthusiasm . . . I would like, in fact, to use the word ovation, but a pedantic professor has recently informed us, with the Batavian buoyancy of misapplied learning, that this expression is not to be employed except when a sheep has been sacrificed. At the Lyceum last week I need hardly say nothing so dreadful occurred. The only inartistic incident of the evening was the hurling of a bouquet from a box at Mr Irving while he was engaged in portraying

the agony of Hamlet's death, and the pathos of his parting with Hora-
tio. The Dramatic College might take up the education of spectators as
well as that of players, and teach people that there is a proper moment
for the throwing of flowers as well as a proper method.

Dramatic Review, 9 May 1885

★   ★   ★

Of Shakespeare it may be said he was the first to see the dramatic
value of doublets, and that a climax may depend on a crinoline.

'The Truth of Masks', initially 'Shakespeare and Stage Costume',
Nineteenth Century, May 1885

☆

... in the inventory, still in existence, of the costume-wardrobe of a
London theatre in Shakespeare's time, there are mentioned particular
costumes ... which evidence a good deal of archaeological research on
the part of the manager of the theatre. It is true that there is a mention
of a bodice for Eve, but probably the *donnée* of the play was after the
Fall.

☆

Indeed, anybody who cares to examine the age of Shakespeare will see
that archaeology was one of its special characteristics... The curious
objects that were being constantly brought to light by excavations
were not left to moulder in a museum, for the contemplation of a callous curator, and the *ennui* of a policeman bored by the absence of
crime.

☆

... the stage is not merely the meeting place of all the arts, but is also
the return of art to life.

☆

I can understand archaeology being attacked on the ground of its excessive realism, but to attack it as pedantic seems to be very much
beside the mark. However, to attack it for any reasons, is foolish; one
might just as well speak disrespectfully of the equator. For archaeology, being a science, is neither good nor bad, but a fact simply. Its
value depends entirely on how it is used, and only an artist can use it.

☆

It has been said that the anachronisms in the plays themselves show us
that Shakespeare was indifferent to historical accuracy, and a great
deal of capital has been made out of Hector's indiscreet quotation from
Aristotle. Upon the other hand, the anachronisms are really few in

58

number, and not very important, and, had Shakespeare's attention been drawn to them by a brother artist, he would probably have corrected them. For, though they can hardly be called blemishes, they are certainly not the great beauties of his work . . .

☆

. . . up to the time of the unfortunate triumph of the Philistines in 1645, the chapels and cathedrals of England were the great national museums of archaeology, and in them were kept the armour and attire of the heroes of English history.

☆

And this is the important thing. Better to take pleasure in a rose than to put its root under a microscope. Archaeological accuracy is merely a condition of illusionist stage effect; it is not its quality.

☆

The Puritan dislike of colour, adornment, and grace in apparel was part of the great revolt of the middle classes against Beauty in the seventeenth century. A historian who disregarded it would give us a most inaccurate picture of the time, and a dramatist who did not avail himself of it would miss a most vital element in producing an illusionist effect.

☆

But it is not enough that a dress should be accurate; it must be also appropriate to the stature and appearance of the actor, and to his supposed condition, as well as to his necessary action in the play. In Mr Hare's production of *As You Like It* at the St James's Theatre, for instance, the whole point of Orlando's complaint that he is brought up like a peasant, and not like a gentlemen, was spoiled by the gorgeousness of his dress, and the splendid apparel worn by the banished Duke and his friends was quite out of place. Mr Lewis Wingfield's explanation that the sumptuary laws of the period necessitated their doing so, is, I am afraid, hardly sufficient. Outlaws, lurking in a forest and living by the chase, are not very likely to care much about ordinances of dress.

☆

The facts of art are diverse, but the essence of artistic effect is unity. Monarchy, Anarchy, and Republicanism may contend for the government of nations; but a theatre should be in the power of a cultured despot. There may be division of labour, but there must be no division of mind. . . In fact, in art there is no specialism, and a really artistic production should bear the impress of one master, and one master only, who not merely should design and arrange everything, but should have complete control over the way in which each dress is to be worn.

'The Truth of Masks', initially 'Shakespeare and Stage Costume',
Nineteenth Century, May 1885

☆

More dress rehearsals would also be of value in explaining to the actors that there is a form of gesture and movement that is not merely appropriate to each style of dress, but really conditioned by it. The extravagant use of the arms in the eighteenth century, for instance, was the necessary result of the large hoop, and the solemn dignity of Burleigh owed as much to his ruff as to his reason. Besides until an actor is at home in his dress, he is not at home in his part.

☆

Not that I agree with everything that I have said in this essay. There is much with which I entirely disagree. The essay simply represents an artistic standpoint, and in aesthetic criticism attitude is everything. For in art there is no such thing as a universal truth. A Truth in art is that whose contradictory is also true. And just as it is only in art-criticism, and through it, that we can apprehend the Platonic theory of ideas, so it is only in art-criticism, and through it, that we can realise Hegel's system of contraries. The truths of metaphysics are the truths of masks.

These lines were added silently by Wilde when he included the essay
now entitled 'The Truth of Masks' to his *Intentions* for its publication
in May 1891

★   ★   ★

... in spite of the roaring of the young lions at the Union, and the screaming of the rabbits in the home of the vivisector, in spite of Keble College, and the tramways, and the sporting prints, Oxford still remains the most beautiful thing in England, and nowhere else are life and art so exquisitely blended, so perfectly made one.

Dramatic Review, 23 May 1885

☆

... while we look to the dramatist to give romance to realism, we ask of the actor to give realism to romance.

★   ★   ★

Odysseus, not Achilles, is the type of the modern Greek. Merchandise has taken precedence of the Muses and politics are preferred to Parnassus.

Review: *Greek Lays, Idylls, Legends, etc.* trans. E. M. Edmonds, *Pall Mall Gazette*, 27 May 1885

★   ★   ★

. . . life remains eternally unchanged; it is art which, by presenting it to us under various forms, enables us to realise its many-sided mysteries, and to catch the quality of its most fiery-coloured moments. The originality, . . . which we ask from the artist, is originality of treatment, not of subject. It is only the unimaginative who ever invents. The true artist is known by the use he makes of what he annexes, and he annexes everything.

Dramatic Review, 30 May 1885

☆

Perfect heroes are the monsters of melodramas, and have no place in dramatic art. Life possibly contains them, but Parnassus often rejects what Peckham may welcome. I look forward to a reaction in favour of the cultured criminal.

1886

The nineteenth century may be a prosaic age, but we fear that, if we are to judge by the general run of novels, it is not an age of prose.

Pall Mall Gazette, 1 February 1886

★ ★ ★

. . . absolute catholicity of taste is not without its dangers. It is only an auctioneer who should admire all schools of art.

Pall Mall Gazette, 8 February 1886

★ ★ ★

. . . while one should always study the method of a great artist, one should never imitate his manner. The manner of an artist is essentially individual, the method of an artist is absolutely universal. The first is personality, which no one should copy; the second is perfection, which all should aim at.

Dramatic Review, 20 February 1886

★ ★ ★

. . . our ordinary English novelists . . . fail . . . in concentration of style. Their characters are far too eloquent and talk themselves to tatters. What we want is a little more reality and a little less rhetoric. . . we wish that they would talk less and think more. They lead us through a barren desert of verbiage to a mirage that they call life: we wander aimlessly through a very wilderness of words in search of one touch of nature. However, one should not be too severe on English novels; they are the only relaxation of the intellectually unemployed.

Pall Mall Gazette, 4 August 1886

★ ★ ★

We cannot tell, and Shakespeare himself does not tell us, why Iago is evil, why Regan and Goneril have hard hearts, or why Sir Andrew Aguecheek is a fool. It is sufficient that they are what they are, and that nature gives warrant for their existence. If a character in a play is life-like, if we recognise it as true to nature, we have no right to insist on the author explaining its genesis to us. We must accept it as it is: and in the hands of a good dramatist mere presentation can take the place of analysis, and indeed is often a more dramatic method, because a more direct.

Pall Mall Gazette, 20 September 1886

★ ★ ★

... the tramp ... if any one should possess that freedom of mood which is so essential to the artist, for he has no taxes to pay and no relations to worry him. The man who possesses a permanent address, and whose name is to be found in the Directory, is necessarily limited and localised. Only the tramp has absolute liberty of living. Was not Homer himself a vagrant, and did not Thespis go about in a caravan?

Pall Mall Gazette, 27 September 1886

★ ★ ★

A poet can survive everything but a misprint.

Pall Mall Gazette, 14 October 1886

★ ★ ★

Astray: A Tale of a Country Town, is a very serious volume. It has taken four people to write it, and even to read it requires assistance. Its dulness is premeditated and deliberate and comes from a laudable desire to rescue fiction from flippancy. It is in fact tedious from the noblest motives and wearisome through its good intentions ... Still, in this tale of a country town there are certain solid qualities, and it is a book that one can with perfect safety recommend to other people.

Miss Rhoda Broughton belongs to a very different school. No one can ever say of her that she has tried to separate flippancy from fiction, and, whatever harsh criticisms may be passed on the construction of her sentences, she at least possesses that one touch of vulgarity that makes the whole world kin.

Reviews: *Astray: A Tale of a Country Town* by Charlotte M. Yonge,
Mary Bramston, Christabel Coleridge and Esmé Stuart; and *Betty's
Visions* by Rhoda Broughton. *Pall Mall Gazette*, 28 October 1886

★ ★ ★

Although it is against etiquette to quote Greek in Parliament, Homer has always been a great favourite with our statesmen and indeed may be said to be almost a factor in our political life. For as the cross-benches form a refuge for those who have no minds to make up, so those who cannot make up their minds always takes to Homeric studies. Many of our leaders have sulked in their tents with Achilles after some violent political, crisis and enraged at the fickleness of fortune, more than one has given up to poetry what was obviously meant for party.

Pall Mall Gazette, 3 November 1886

★ ★ ©

There is a healthy bank-holiday atmosphere about this book which is extremely pleasant. Mr Quilter is entirely free from affectation of any kind. He rollicks through art with the recklessness of the tourist and describes its beauties with the enthusiasm of the auctioneer. To many, no doubt, he will seem to be somewhat blatant and bumptious, but we prefer to regard him as being simply British.

Review: Harry Quilter, *Sententiae Artis: First Principles of Art for Painters and Picture Lovers. Pall Mall Gazette,* 18 November 1886

1887

... a poet without hysterics is rare.
Pall Mall Gazette, 8 March 1887

★   ★   ★

Indeed, in many respects, she was quite English, and was an excellent example of the fact that we have really everything in common with America nowadays, except, of course, language.
'The Canterville Ghost', *Court and Society Review*, 23 February and
2 March 1887

☆

'What a monstrous climate!' said the American Minister calmly, as he lit a long cheroot. 'I guess the old country is so overpopulated that they have not enough decent weather for everybody. I have always been of opinion that emigration is the only thing for England.'

☆

He thought of the Dowager Duchess, whom he had frightened into a fit as she stood before the glass in her lace and diamonds; of the four housemaids, who had gone off into hysterics when he merely grinned at them through the curtains of one of the spare bedrooms; of the rector of the parish, whose candle he had blown out as he was coming late one night from the library, and who had been under the care of Sir William Gull ever since, a perfect martyr to nervous disorders; and of old Madame de Tremouillac, who, having wakened up one morning early and seen a skeleton seated in an arm-chair by the fire reading her diary, had been confined to her bed for six weeks with an attack of brain fever, and, on her recovery, had become reconciled to the Church, and had broken off her connection with that notorious sceptic Monsieur de Voltaire.

☆

He remembered the terrible night when the wicked Lord Canterville was found choking in his dressing-room, with the knave of diamonds half-way down his throat, and confessed, just before he died, that he had cheated Charles James Fox out of £50,000 at Crockford's by

means of that very card, and swore that the ghost had made him
swallow it.

'The Canterville Ghost', *Court and Society Review*, 23 February and
2 March 1887

☆

All his great achievements came back to him again, from the butler
who had shot himself in the pantry because he had seen a green hand
tapping at the window pane, to the beautiful Lady Stutfield, who was
always obliged to wear a black velvet band round her throat to hide
the mark of five fingers burnt upon her white skin, and who drowned
herself at last in the carp-pond at the end of the King's Walk.

☆

With the enthusiastic egotism of the true artist he went over his most
celebrated performances, and smiled bitterly to himself as he recalled
to mind his last appearance as 'Red Reuben, or the Strangled Babe',
his *début* as 'Gaunt Gibeon, the Blood-sucker of Bexley Moor', and the
furore he had excited one lovely June evening by merely playing ninepins with his own bones upon the lawn-tennis ground. And after all
this, some wretched modern Americans were to come and offer him
the Rising Sun Lubricator, and throw pillows at his head!

☆

... Lord Francis Stilton had once bet a hundred guineas with Colonel
Carbury that he would play dice with the Canterville ghost, and was
found the next morning lying on the floor of the card-room in such a
helpless paralytic state, that though he lived on to a great age, he was
never able to say anything again but 'Double Sixes'. The story was
well known at the time, though, of course, out of respect to the feelings
of the two noble families, every attempt was made to hush it up; and a
full account of all the circumstances connected with it will be found in
the third volume of Lord Tattle's *Recollections of the Prince Regent and his
Friends*.

☆

... he made arrangements for appearing ... in his celebrated im-
personation of 'The Vampire Monk, or, the Bloodless Benedictine', a
performance so horrible that when old Lady Startup saw it, which she
did on one fatal New Year's Eve, in the year 1764, she went off into the
most piercing shriek, which culminated in violent apoplexy, and died
in three days, after disinheriting the Cantervilles, who were her near-
est relations, and leaving all her money to her London apothecary.

☆

'... you know you have been very wicked. Mrs Umney told us, the first day we arrived here, that you had killed your wife.'

'Well, I quite admit it', said the Ghost petulantly, 'but it was a purely family matter, and concerned no one else.'

'It is very wrong to kill any one', said Virginia, who at times had a sweet Puritan gravity, caught from some old New England ancestor.

'Oh, I hate the cheap severity of abstract ethics! My wife was very plain, never had my ruffs properly starched, and knew nothing about cookery. . .'

☆

'. . . Once in New York, you are sure to be a great success. I know lots of people there would give a hundred thousand dollars to have a grandfather, and much more than that to have a family Ghost.'

☆

'. . you must weep with me for my sins, because I have no tears, and pray with me for my soul, because I have no faith, and then, if you have always been sweet, and good, and gentle, the Angel of Death will have mercy on me. You will see fearful shapes in darkness, and wicked voices will whisper in your ear, but they will not harm you, for against the purity of a little child the powers of Hell cannot prevail.'

☆

'. . . For my own part, I confess I am a good deal surprised to find any child of mine expressing sympathy with mediaevalism in any form, and can only account for it by the fact that Virginia was born in one of your London suburbs shortly after Mrs Otis had returned from a trip to Athens.'

★   ★   ★

A terrible danger is hanging over the Americans in London. Their future and their reputation this season depend entirely on the success of Buffalo Bill and Mrs Brown-Potter. The former is certain to draw; for English people are far more interested in American barbarism than they are in American civilisation.

'The American Invasion', *Court and Society Review*, 23 March 1887

☆

. . . the American invasion has done English society a great deal of good. American women are bright, clever, and wonderfully cosmopolitan. . . They take their dresses from Paris and their manners from Piccadilly, and wear both charmingly. They have a quaint pertness, a delightful conceit, a native self-assertion. They insist on being paid compliments and have almost succeeded in making Englishmen eloquent.

☆

It is true that they lack repose and that their voices are somewhat harsh and strident when they land first at Liverpool; but after a time one gets to love these pretty whirlwinds in petticoats that sweep so recklessly through society and are so agitating to all duchesses who have daughters.

'The American Invasion', *Court and Society Review*, 23 March 1887

☆

Nothing is more amusing than to watch two American girls greeting each other in a drawing-room or in the Row. They are like children with their shrill staccato cries of wonder, their odd little exclamations. Their conversation sounds like a series of exploding crackers; they are exquisitely incoherent and use a sort of primitive, emotional language. After five minutes they are left beautifully breathless and look at each other half in amusement and half in affection.

☆

On the whole, American girls have a wonderful charm and, perhaps, the chief secret of their charm is that they never talk seriously except about amusements.

☆

From its earliest years every American child spends most of its time in correcting the faults of its father and mother; and no one who has had the opportunity of watching an American family on the deck of an Atlantic steamer, or in the refined seclusion of a New York boarding-house, can fail to have been struck by this characteristic of their civilisation. In America the young are always ready to give to those who are older than themselves the full benefits of their inexperience. A boy of only eleven or twelve years of age will firmly but kindly point out to his father his defects of manner or temper; will never weary of warning him against extravagance, idleness, late hours, unpunctuality, and the other temptations to which the aged are so particularly exposed . . . it may be truly said that no American child is ever blind to the deficiencies of its parents, no matter how much it may love them.

☆

The American father . . . is never seen in London. He passes his life entirely in Wall Street and communicates with his family once a month by means of a telegram in cipher.

☆

. . . the American girl is always welcome. . . In the race for coronets she often carries off the prize; but, once she has gained the victory, she is

68

generous and forgives her English rivals everything, even their beauty.

☆

Warned by the example of her mother that American women do not grow old gracefully, she tries not to grow old at all and often succeeds. She has exquisite feet and hands, is always *bien chausée et bien gantée* and can talk brilliantly upon any subject, provided that she knows nothing about it. Her sense of humour keeps her from the tragedy of a *grande passion*, and, as there is neither romance nor humility in her love, she makes an excellent wife.

★   ★   ★

K. E. V.'s little volume is a series of poems on the Saints. Each poem is preceded by a brief biography of the Saint it celebrates – which is a very necessary precaution, as few of them ever existed. It does not display much poetic power, and such lines as these on St Stephen –

> Did ever man before so fall asleep?
> A cruel shower of stones his only bed,
> For lullaby the curses loud and deep,
> His covering with blood red,

may be said to add another terror to martyrdom. Still it is a thoroughly well-intentioned book, and eminently suitable for invalids.
Review: The Circle of Saints. By K.E.V. Pall Mall Gazette, 8 March
1882.

★   ★   ★

Remembering that of all forms of error prophecy is the most gratuitous, we will not take upon ourselves to decide the question of Dickens's immortality. If our descendants do not read him they will miss a great source of amusement, and if they do, we hope they will not model their style upon his. Of this however there is but little danger, for no age ever borrows the slang of its predecessor.
Review: Frank T. Marzials, Life of Charles Dickens. Pall Mall Gazette,
31 March 1887

★   ★   ★

It is a pity that the finest line Ben Jonson ever wrote about Shakespeare should be misquoted at the very beginning of the book . . . but it is quite useless to dwell on these things, as nobody nowadays seems to have any time either to correct proofs, or to consult authorities.
Review: Annals of the Life of Shakespeare. Pall Mall Gazette, 12 April 1887

★   ★   ★

On the whole the book is well worth reading, so well worth reading indeed, that we hope the foolish remarks on the Greek Drama will be amended in a second edition, or, which would be better still, struck out altogether. They show a want of knowledge that must be the result of years of study.

> Review: *Studies in Italian Literature.* By Catherine Mary Phillimore.
> *Ibid.*

★ ★ ★

Formerly we used to canonise our great men; now-a-days we vulgarise them. . . the best we can say of it is that it is just the sort of biography Guildenstern might have written of Hamlet.

> Review: Joseph Knight, *Life of Dante Gabriel Rossetti. Pall Mall Gazette*,
> 18 April 1887

☆

Better, after all, that we only knew a painter through his vision and a poet through his song, than that the image of a great man should be marred and made mean for us by the clumsy geniality of good intentions.

☆

We are sorry too to find an English dramatic critic misquoting Shakespeare, as we had always been of opinion that this was a privilege reserved specially for our English actors.

☆

A pillar of fire to the few who knew him, and of cloud to the many who knew him not, Dante Gabriel Rossetti lived apart from the gossip and tittle-tattle of a shallow age. He never trafficked with the merchants for his soul, nor brought his wares into the market-place for the idle to gape at.

★ ★ ★

. . . the poor American man remains permanently in the background, and never rises beyond the level of the tourist. . . The telephone is his test of civilisation, and his wildest dreams of Utopia do not rise beyond elevated railways and electric bells. His chief pleasure is to get hold of some unsuspecting stranger, or some sympathetic countryman, and then to indulge in the national game of 'matching'. With a *naïveté* and a nonchalance that are absolutely charming, he will gravely compare St James' Palace to the grand central depot at Chicago, or Westminster Abbey to the Falls of Niagara. Bulk is his canon of beauty, and size his standard of excellence. To him the greatness of a country consists in the number of square miles that it contains; and he is never tired of telling the waiters at his hotel that the state of Texas is larger than France and Germany put together.

> 'The American Man', *Court and Society Review*, 13 April 1887

☆

For him Art has no marvel, and Beauty no meaning, and the Past no message. He thinks that civilisation began with the introduction of steam . . .

☆

The ruin and decay of Time has no pathos in his eyes. He turns away from Ravenna, because the grass grows in her streets, and can see no loveliness in Verona, because there is rust on her balconies. His one desire is to get the whole of Europe into thorough repair.

☆

In a word, he is the Don Quixote of common sense, for he is so utilitarian that he is absolutely unpractical.

☆

. . . the strange thing about American civilisation is, that the women are most charming when they are away from their own country, the men most charming when they are at home.

☆

They seem to get a hold on life much earlier than we do. . . They know men much better than they know books, and life interests them more than literature.

☆

There is no such thing as a stupid American. Many Americans are horrid, vulgar, intrusive, and impertinent, just as many English people are also; but stupidity is not one of the national vices. Indeed, in America there is no opening for a fool. They expect brains even from a boot-black, and get them.

☆

As for marriage, it is one of their most popular institutions. The American man marries early, and the American woman marries often; and they get on extremely well together.

☆

On the whole, the great success of marriage in the States is due partly to the fact that no American man is ever idle, and partly to the fact that no American wife is considered responsible for the quality of her husband's dinners.

☆

Even the American freedom of divorce, questionable though it undoubtedly is on many grounds, has at least the merit of bringing into
marriage a new element of romantic uncertainty. When people are tied
together for life they too often regard manners as a mere superfluity,
and courtesy a thing of no moment; but where the bond can be easily
broken, its very fragility makes its strength, and reminds the husband
that he should always try to please, and the wife that she should never
cease to be charming.

'The American Man', *Court and Society Review*, 13 April 1887

☆

American humour is a mere travellers' tale. It has no real existence.
Indeed, so far from being humourous, the male American is the most
abnormally serious creature who ever existed. He talks of Europe as
being old; but it is he himself who has never been young.

☆

He has always been prudent, always practical, and pays a heavy
penalty for having committed no mistakes.

☆

It is evident that where it takes one twenty-four hours to go across a
single parish, and seven days' steady railway travelling to keep a
dinner engagement in another State, the ordinary resources of human
speech are quite inadequate to the strain put on them, and new linguistic forms have to be invented, new methods of description resorted
to. But this is nothing more than the fatal influence of geography upon
adjectives . . .

☆

. . . what seemed a paradox when we listened to it in London, becomes
a platitude when we hear it in Milwaukee.

☆

America has never quite forgiven Europe for having been discovered
somewhat earlier in history than itself.

☆

. . . though the American man may not be humorous, he is certainly
humane. He is keenly conscious of the fact that there is a great deal of
human nature in man, and tries to be pleasant to every stranger who
lands on his shores.

☆

If the English girl ever met him, she would marry him; and if she married him, she would be happy. For, though he may be rough in manner, and deficient in the picturesque insincerity of romance, yet he is invariably kind and thoughtful, and has succeeded in making his own country the Paradise of Women.

This, however, is perhaps the reason why, like Eve, the women are always so anxious to get out of it.

★   ★   ★

Every great man nowadays has his disciples, and it is usually Judas who writes the biography. Mr Whistler, however, is more fortunate than most of his *confrères*, as he has found in Mr Walter Dowdeswell the most ardent of admirers, indeed, we might almost say the most sympathetic of secretaries.

'The Butterfly's Boswell', *Court and Society Review*, 20 April 1887

☆

. . . an extremely graphic picture of this remarkable artist, from his tall hat and wand . . . down to the sly smile that we have all heard echoing through the Suffolk Street Gallery on the occasion of a private view, and that used, in old days, to deafen the Royal Academicians at their annual *soirée*.

☆

. . . his family tree seems to go back perilously near to those old mediaeval days that he himself has often so charmingly satirized, and always so cleverly misunderstood. The particular branch, however, from which the President of the British Artists is immediately descended is partly Irish and American, a fact that explains a great deal of the peculiar quality of his wonderful wit, just as to his early residence in Russia, where his father was a distinguished engineer, we may attribute the origin of that winning and fascinating manner that makes the disciples murmur to each other after each exhibition '*Grattez le maître, et vous trouverez le Tartare!*'

☆

. . . Mr Dowdeswell displays a really remarkable power, not merely of writing, but of writing from dictation, especially in his very generous and appreciative estimate of Mr Whistler's genius.

☆

. . . he has pointed out possibilities of beauty hitherto undreamt of, and . . . by his keen critical faculty, no less than by the dominance of his assertive personality, he has given to Art itself a new creative impulse. Indeed, when the true history of Art comes to be written, a task that Mr Whistler is eminently capable of doing himself, at least in the form

73

of an autobiography, there can be no doubt but that his name will stand high amongst the highest on its record, for he has opened the eyes of the blind, and given great encouragement to the short-sighted.

'The Butterfly's Boswell', *Court and Society Review*, 20 April 1887

☆

He has done etchings with the brilliancy of epigrams, and pastels with the charm of paradoxes, and many of his portraits are pure works of fiction.

☆

... as Mr Whistler once himself remarked, no man alive is life-size; and it would be ungracious to criticize with too much severity an article that shows such memory on the part of the writer, and such journalistic ability on the part of the subject.

★   ★   ★

Though the Oracles are dumb, and the Prophets have taken to the turf, and the Sibyls are reduced to telling fortunes at bazaars, the ancient power of divination has not yet left the world. Mr Mark Twain's fascinating article, in the current number of the *Century Magazine*, on 'English as She is Taught' in his native country, throws an entirely new light on that *enfant terrible* of a commercial civilisation, the American child, and reminds us that we may all learn wisdom from the mouths of babes and sucklings. For the mistakes made by the interesting pupils of the American Board-Schools are not mistakes springing from ignorance of life or dulness of perception; they are, on the contrary, full of the richest suggestion, and pregnant with the very highest philosophy. No wonder that the American child educates its father and mother, when it can give us such luminous definitions as the following:–

> *Republican* a sinner mentioned in the Bible
> *Demagogue* a vessel containing beer and other liquids
> *The Constitution of the United States* that part of the book at the end that nobody reads
> *Plagiarist* a writer of plays
> *Equestrian* one who asks questions
> *Tenacious* ten acres of land
> *Quaternions* a bird, with a flat beak and no bill, dwelling in New Zealand
> *Franchise* anything belonging to the French

The last definition points very clearly to the fact that the fallacy of an extended Franchise is based on the French theory of equality, to which the child-philosopher seems also to allude when he says that:

Things which are equal to each other are equal to anything else,

while the description of the Plagiarist is the most brilliant thing that has been said on modern literature for some time.

'The Child-Philosopher', *Court and Society Review*, 20 April 1887

☆

If mendacious only means 'what can be mended', mercenary 'one who feels for another', and parasite 'a kind of umbrella', it is evident that latent, in the very lowest citizen of our community, lies capacities for platform oratory hitherto unsuspected. Even women, most complex of all modern problems, are analysed with a knowledge that in Europe is confined to poets and dandies. 'They make fun of boys', says the child-philosopher, 'and then turn round and love them.'

☆

Mr Mark Twain deserves our warmest thanks for bringing to light the true American genius. American patriots are tedious, American millionaires go bankrupt, and American beauties don't last, but the schoolboy seems to be eternally delightful; and when the world has grown weary of Boston novelists, and tired of the civilisation of the telephone, the utterances of the child-philosopher will be treasured by the scientific historian as the best criticism upon modern education, the best epigram upon modern life.

★   ★   ★

The annual attacks upon the Royal Academy, with which we are all so familiar, and of which most of us are so tired, have, as a rule, been both futile and depressing. The dull have cried out upon dulness, and the mediocre have denounced mediocrity, and each side has taken itself very seriously indeed. It is always a sorry spectacle when the Philistines of Gath go out against the Philistines of Gaza . . .

'The Rout of the R.A.', *Court and Society Review*, 27 April 1887

☆

. . . dulness has become the basis of respectability, and seriousness the only refuge of the shallow.

★   ★   ★

The establishment of a Talking Club in our midst may seem to some the beginning of a new reign of terror, in which the wisdom of silence will be forgotten, and the dignity of culture have to give place to the shrill voice of chatter, the noise of empty words; others may protest against a scheme that proposes to war against misrepresentation, which is the secret of criticism, and misunderstanding, which is the basis of love . . .

'Should Geniuses Meet?', *Court and Society Review*, 4 May 1887

☆

... it would be a very good thing if people were taught how to speak. Language is the noblest instrument we have, either for the revealing or the concealing of thought; talk itself is a sort of spirtualised action; and conversation is one of the loveliest of the arts.

'Should Geniuses Meet?', *Court and Society Review*, 4 May 1887

☆

... take the case of Mr Whistler and Mr Ruskin. Mr Whistler had to submit to the decision of an incompetent tribunal, to plead before a judge who knew nothing of nocturnes, and a jury to whom Symphonies were a rock of offence. His 'Harmonies in Blue and Gold' were treated as *pièces de conviction*, his 'Notes in Violet and Silver' as obvious proof of guilt. How much better it would have been had the two combatants appeared face to face, without the intervention of the criminal bar, and settled their dispute in a civilized manner. But though Mr Whistler would undoubtedly have been present, armed to the teeth with brilliant epigram, and barbed with clever caustic jest, we hardly think that Mr Ruskin would have stirred from the water-side of the Coniston Lake, or troubled himself to play the prize-fighter to a gallery of Impressionists.

☆

Nothing ... is permanent. Day by day the old order of things changes, and new modes of thought pass over our world, and it may be that, before many years, talking will have taken place of literature, and the personal screech silenced the music of impersonal utterance.

★   ★   ★

Gorgeous peeresses chatted affably to violent Radicals, popular preachers brushed coat-tails with eminent sceptics, a perfect bevy of bishops kept following a stout prima-donna from room to room, on the staircase stood several Royal Academicians, disguised as artists, and it was said that at one time the supper-room was absolutely crammed with geniuses.

'Lord Arthur Savile's Crime', *Court and Society Review*, 11, 18, 25 May 1887

☆

Early in life she had discovered the important truth that nothing looks so like innocence as an indiscretion; and by a series of reckless escapades, half of them quite harmless, she had acquired all the privileges of a personality. She had more than once changed her husband;

76

indeed, Debrett credits her with three marriages; but as she had never changed her lover, the world had long ago ceased to talk scandal about her.

☆

'. . . Next year . . . I am in great danger, both by land and sea, so I am going to live in a balloon, and draw up my dinner in a basket every evening. It is all written down on my little finger, or on the palm of my hand, I forget which.'

'But surely that is tempting Providence, Gladys.'

'My dear Duchess, surely Providence can resist temptation by this time . . .'

☆

. . . many people seemed afraid to face the odd little man with his stereotyped smile, his gold spectacles, and his bright, beady eyes; and when he told poor Lady Fermor right out before every one, that she did not care a bit for music, but was extremely fond of musicians, it was generally felt that cheiromancy was a most dangerous science . . .

☆

'. . . if Mr Podgers finds out that you have a bad temper, or a tendency to gout, or a wife living in Bayswater, I shall certainly let her know all about it.'

Lord Arthur smiled and shook his head. 'I am not afraid', he answered. 'Sybil knows me as well as I know her.'

'Ah! I am a little sorry to hear you say that. The proper basis for marriage is a mutual misunderstanding. No, I am not at all cynical. I have merely got experience, which, however, is very much the same thing . . .'

☆

Most men and women are forced to perform parts for which they have no qualifications. Our Guildensterns play Hamlet for us, and our Hamlets have to jest like Prince Hal. The world is a stage, but the play is badly cast.

☆

. . . it was not the mystery, but the comedy of suffering that struck him; its absolute uselessness, its grotesque want of meaning. How incoherent everything seemed! How lacking in all harmony! He was amazed at the discord between the shallow optimism of the day, and real facts of existence. He was still very young.

☆

77

Perhaps, some day, his own name might be placarded on the walls of London. Some day, perhaps, a price would be set on his head also.

'Lord Arthur Savile's Crime', *Court and Society Review*, 11, 18, 25 May
1887

☆

He wondered how he could have been so foolish as to rant and rave about the inevitable. The only question that seemed to trouble him was, whom to make away with; for he was not blind to the fact that murder, like the religions of the Pagan world, requires a victim as well as a priest. Not being a genius, he had no enemies, and indeed he felt that this was not the time for the gratification of any personal pique or dislike . . .

☆

He had every reason, then, to decide in favour of poison. It was safe, sure, and quiet, and did away with any necessity for painful scenes, to which, like most Englishmen, he had a rooted objection.

☆

Where to produce an explosive machine was, of course, quite another matter. The London Directory gave him no information on the point, and he felt that there was very little use in going to Scotland Yard about it, as they never seemed to know anything about the movements of the dynamite faction till after an explosion had taken place, and not much even then.

☆

'. . . Papa says Liberty was invented at the time of the French Revolution. How awful it seems! . . .'

☆

'I have no time to be happy, Sybil. I always like the last person who is introduced to me; but, as a rule, as soon as I know people I get tired of them.'

☆

'. . . lions are only good for one season. As soon as their manes are cut, they are the dullest creatures going . . .

☆

'. . . He has really made me hate cheiromancy. I go in for telepathy now. It is much more amusing.'

★   ★   ★

His father had bequeathed him his cavalry sword, and a *History of the*

Peninsular War in fifteen volumes.

'The Model Millionaire'. *World*, 22 June 1887

☆

He had gone on the Stock Exchange for six months; but what was a butterfly to do among bulls and bears?

☆

'The only people a painter should know', he used to say, 'are people who are *bête* and beautiful, people who are an artistic pleasure to look at and an intellectual repose to talk to. Men who are dandies and women who are darlings rule the world, at least they should do so.'

☆

'How much does a model get for sitting?'. . .
'A shilling an hour.'
'And how much do you get for your picture, Alan?'
'Oh, for this I get two thousand!'
'Pounds?'
'Guineas. Painters, poets, and physicians always get guineas.'
'Well, I think the model should have a percentage', cried Hughie, laughing; 'they work quite as hard as you do.'
'Nonsense, nonsense! Why, look at the trouble of laying on the paint alone, and standing all day long at one's easel! It's all very well, Hughie, for you to talk, but I assure you that there are moments when Art almost attains to the dignity of manual labour . . .'

☆

'. . . He could buy all London to-morrow without overdrawing his account. He has a house in every capital, dines off gold plate, and can prevent Russia going to war when he chooses.'

★   ★   ★

The only form of fiction in which real characters do not seem out of place is history.

Saturday Review, 7 May 1887

★   ★   ★

It is quite right that blank verse should be spoken naturally, but there is no necessity to turn it into bad prose.

Review of *The Winter's Tale* at the Lyceum, *Court and Society Review*,
14 September 1887

☆

The mere mechanical *technique* of acting can be taught, but the spirit that is to give life to lifeless forms must be born in a man. No dramatic college can teach its pupils to think or to feel. It is Nature who makes our artists for us, though it may be Art who taught them their right mode of expression.

* * *

The stage management is of that quick steeplechase kind which is so popular in plays of this description. Every room has five or six doors, and the characters rush in and out, and chase each other, and misunderstand each other, and fall exhausted on sofas, and make scenes and tableaux, and distribute a gentle air of lunacy over life. In fact, *The Barrister* is a pure nineteenth-century comedy. What our descendants will think of such a work of art is an open question. However, posterity has as yet done nothing for us!

Review of *The Barrister* at the Comedy Theatre, *ibid.*

* * *

Everybody pays a penalty for peeping through keyholes, and the keyhole and the backstairs are essential parts of the method of the modern biographers. . . Mr Rossetti commits the great mistake of separating the man from the artist. The facts of Keats's life are interesting only when they are shown in relation to his creative activity. The moment they are isolated they are either uninteresting or painful. Mr Rossetti complains that the early part if Keats's life is uneventful and the latter part depressing, but the fault lies with the biographer, not with the subject.

Review: *Life of John Keats*, by William Michael Rossetti. *Pall Mall Gazette*, 27 September 1887

* * *

The Apostolic dictum, that women should not be suffered to teach, is no longer applicable to a society such as ours, with its solidarity of interests, its recognition of natural rights, and its universal education, however suitable it may have been to the Greek cities under Roman rule. Nothing in the United States struck me more than the fact that the remarkable intellectual progress of that country is very largely due to the efforts of American women, who edit many of the most powerful magazines and newspapers, take part in the discussion of every question of public interest, and exercise an important influence upon the growth and tendencies of literature and art. Indeed, the women of America are the one class in the community that enjoys that leisure which is so necessary for culture.

'Literary and Other Notes', *Woman's World*, November 1887

*

. . . it is really only the idle classes who dress badly. Wherever physical

labour of any kind is required, the costume used is, as a rule, absolutely right, for labour necessitates freedom, and without freedom
there is no such thing as beauty in dress at all. In fact, the beauty of
dress depends on the beauty of the human figure, and whatever limits,
constrains, and mutilates is essentially ugly, though the eyes of many
are so blinded by custom that they do not notice the ugliness till it has
become unfashionable.

★   ★   ★

There is always something peculiarly impotent about the violence of a
literary man. It seems to bear no reference to facts, for it is never kept
in check by action. It is simply a question of adjectives and rhetoric, of
exaggeration and over-emphasis.

> Review: *Greek Life and Thought: from the Age of Alexander to the Roman
> Conquest*, by J. P. Mahaffy. *Pall Mall Gazette*, 9 November 1887

☆

The aim of social comedy, in Menander no less than in Sheridan, is to
mirror the manners, not to reform the morals of its day, and the cen-
sure of the Puritan, whether real or affected, is always out of place in
literary criticism, and shows a want of recognition of the essential distinction between art and life. After all, it is only the Philistine who
thinks of blaming Jack Absolute for his deception, Bob Acres for his
cowardice, and Charles Surface for his extravagance, and there is very
little use in airing one's moral sense at the expense of one's artistic
appreciation.

★   ★   ★

It is quite true that language is apt to degenerate into a system of
almost algebraic symbols, and the modern city-man who takes a ticket
for Blackfriars Bridge, naturally never thinks of the Dominican monks
who once had their monastery by Thames-side, and after whom the
spot is named. But in earlier times it was not so. Men were then keenly
conscious of the real meaning of words, and early poetry, especially, is
full of this feeling, and, indeed, may be said to owe to it no small portion of its poetic power and charm.

> Review: *The Odyssey of Homer*. Done into English Verse by William
> Morris. Volume II. *Pall Mall Gazette*, 24 November 1887

☆

These last twelve books of the *Odyssey* have not the same marvel of
romance, adventure and colour that we find in the earlier part of the
epic. There is nothing in them that we can compare to the exquisite
idyll of Nausicäa, or to the Titanic humour of the episode in the
Cyclops' cave. Penelope has not the glamour of Circe, and the song of

the Sirens may sound sweeter than the whizz of the arrows of Odysseus as he stands on the threshold of his hall. Yet for sheer intensity of passionate power, for concentration of intellectual interest, and for masterly dramatic construction, these latter books are quite unequalled. Indeed they show very clearly how it was that, as Greek art developed, the epos passed into the drama. The whole scheme of the argument, the return of the hero in disguise, his disclosure of himself to his son, his terrible vengeance on his enemies and his final recognition by his wife, reminds us of the plot of more than one Greek play, and shows us what the great Athenian poet meant when he said that his own dramas were merely scraps from Homer's table.

★   ★   ★

The *Aeneid* bears almost the same relation to the *Iliad* that the *Idylls of the King* do to the old Celtic romances of Arthur. Like them it is full of felicitous modernisms, of exquisite literary echoes, and of delicate and delightful pictures; as Lord Tennyson loves England so did Virgil love Rome; the pageants of history and the purple of empire are equally dear to both poets; but neither of them has the grand simplicity, or the large humanity, of the early singers, and as a hero, Aeneas is no less a failure than Arthur.

Pall Mall Gazette, 30 November 1887

★   ★   ★

... it is no doubt quite right that the saints should take themselves very seriously.

'Literary and Other Notes', *Woman's World,* December 1887

☆

The poor are not to be fed upon facts. Even Shakespeare and the Pyramids are not sufficient; nor is there much use in giving them the results of culture, unless we also give them those conditions under which culture can be realised. In these cold, crowded cities of the North, the proper basis for morals, using the word in its wide Hellenic signification, is to be found in architecture, not in books.

☆

Modern realistic art has not yet produced a Hamlet, but at least it may claim to have studied Guildenstern and Rosencrantz very closely ...

☆

This note of realism in dealing with national types of character has always been a distinguishing characteristic of Irish fiction, from the days of Miss Edgeworth down to our own days ... I fear, however, that few people read Miss Edgeworth nowadays, though both Scott

82

and Tourgénieff acknowledged their indebtedness to her novels, and her style is always admirable in its clearness and precision.

☆

From the sixteenth century to our own day there is hardly any form of torture that has not been inflicted on girls, and endured by women, in obedience to the dictates of an unreasonable and monstrous Fashion ... instances of absolute mutilation and misery are so common in the past that it is unnecessary to multiply them; but it is really sad to think that in our own day a civilised woman can hang on to a cross-bar while her maid laces her waist into a fifteen-inch circle... Fashion's motto is, *Il faut souffrir pour être belle*; but the motto of art and of common-sense is, *Il faut être bête pour souffrir*.

☆

... I see more vulgarity than vice in the tendencies of the modern stage; nor do I think it possible to elevate dramatic art by limiting its subject-matter *On tue une littérature quand on lui interdit la vérité humaine.* As far as the serious presentation of life is concerned, what we require is more imaginative treatment, greater freedom from theatric language and theatric convention. It may be questioned, also, whether the consistent reward of virtue and punishment of wickedness be really the healthiest ideal for an art that claims to mirror nature.

☆

The best way to make children good is to make them happy ...

★　　　★　　　★

In society, says Mr Mahaffy, every civilised man and woman ought to feel it their duty to say something, even when there is hardly anything to be said, and in order to encourage this delightful art of brilliant chatter he has published a social guide without which no *débutante* or dandy should ever dream of going out to dine.

Review: *The Principles of the Art of Conversation: a Social Essay.* By J. P. Mahaffy. *Pall Mall Gazette*, 16 December 1887

☆

In discussing this important question of conversation, he has not merely followed the scientific method of Aristotle which is perhaps excusable, but he has adopted the literary style of Aristotle, for which no excuse is possible.

☆

'Even a consummate liar', says Mr Mahaffy, is a better ingredient in a company than 'the scrupulously truthful man, who weighs every statement, questions every fact, and corrects every inaccuracy.' The liar at any rate recognises that recreation, not instruction, is the aim of conversation, and is a far more civilised being than the blockhead who loudly expresses his disbelief in a story which is told simply for the amusement of the company.

Review: The Principles of the Art of Conversation: a Social Essay. By J. P. Mahaffy. Pall Mall Gazette, 16 December 1887

☆

Mr Mahaffy . . . makes an exception in favour of the eminent specialist and tells us that intelligent questions addressed to an astronomer, or a pure mathematician, will elicit many curious facts which will pleasantly beguile the time. Here, in the interest of society, we feel bound to enter a formal protest. Nobody, even in the provinces, should ever be allowed to ask an intelligent question about pure mathematics across a dinner table. A question of this kind is quite as bad as inquiring suddenly about the state of a man's soul, a sort of *coup* which, as Mr Mahaffy remarks elsewhere, 'many pious people have actually thought a decent introduction to a conversation'.

☆

Modesty . . . may easily become a social vice, and to be continually apologising for one's own ignorance or stupidity is a grave injury to conversation, for, 'what we want to learn from each member is his free opinion on the subject in hand, not his own estimate of the value of that opinion'. Simplicity, too, is not without its dangers. The *enfant terrible*, with his shameless love of truth, the raw country-bred girl, who always says what she means, and the plain, blunt man who makes a point of speaking his mind on every possible occasion without ever considering whether he has a mind at all, are the fatal examples of what simplicity leads to.

☆

Tact, which is an exquisite sense of the symmetry of things, is, according to Mr Mahaffy, the highest and best of all the moral conditions for conversation. The man of tact, he most wisely remarks, 'will instinctively avoid jokes about Bluebeard' in the company of a woman who is a man's third wife; he will never be guilty of talking like a book, but will rather avoid too careful an attention to grammar and the rounding of periods; he will cultivate the art of graceful interruption, so as to prevent a subject being worn threadbare by the aged or the inexperienced; and should he be desirous of telling a story, he will look round, and consider each member of the party, and if there be a single stranger present will forego the pleasure of anecdotage rather than make the social mistake of hurting even one of the guests . . . Great

84

wits, too, are often very cruel, and great humourists often very vulgar, so it will be better to try and 'make good conversation without any help from these brilliant but dangerous gifts'.

☆

In a *tête-à-tête* one should talk about persons, and in general society about things. The state of the weather is always an excusable exordium, but it is convenient to have a paradox or heresy on the subject always ready, so as to direct the conversation into other channels.

☆

Really domestic people are almost invariably bad talkers, as their very virtues in home life have dulled their interests in outer things. The very best mothers will insist on chattering of their babies, and prattling about infant education. In fact most women do not take sufficient interest in politics, just as most men are deficient in general reading. Still, anybody can be made to talk, except the very obstinate, and even a commercial traveller may be drawn out, and become quite interesting.

☆

In the case of meeting a genius and a Duke at dinner, the good talker will try to raise himself to the level of the former, and to bring the latter down to his own level. To succeed among one's social superiors one must have no hesitation in contradicting them. Indeed, one should make bold criticisms and introduce a bright and free tone into a Society whose grandeur and extreme respectability make it, Mr Mahaffy remarks as pathetically as inaccurately, 'perhaps somewhat dull'.

☆

The best conversationalists are those whose ancestors have been bilingual, like the French and Irish, but the art of conversation is really within the reach of almost every one, except those who are morbidly truthful, or whose high moral worth requires to be sustained by a permanent gravity of demeanour, and a general dulness of mind.

☆

The maxim, 'If you find the company dull, blame yourself', seems to us somewhat optimistic, and we have no sympathy at all with the professional story-teller, who is really a great bore at a dinner-table; but Mr Mahaffy is quite right in insisting that no bright social intercourse is possible without equality, and it is no objection to his book to say that it will not teach people how to talk cleverly.

★   ★   ★

. . . now that the Celtic spirit has become the leaven of our politics, there is no reason why it should not contribute something to our decorative art. This result, however, will not be obtained by a patriotic misuse of old designs, and even the most enthusiastic Home Ruler must not be allowed to decorate his dining-room with a dado of Oghams.

Review: *Early Christian Art in Ireland*, by Margaret Stokes. *Pall Mall Gazette*, 17 December 1887

1888

. . . the personality of the player passes away, and with it that pleasure-giving power by virtue of which the arts exist. Yet the artistic method of a great actor survives. It lives on in tradition, and becomes part of the science of a school. It has all the intellectual life of a principle. In England, at the present moment, the influence of Garrick on our actors is far stronger than that of Reynolds on our painters of portraits, and if we turn to France it is easy to discern the tradition of Talma, but where is the tradition of David?

'Literary and Other Notes', *Woman's World*, January 1888

☆

. . . the mere artistic process of acting, the translation of literature back again into life, and the presentation of thought under the conditions of action, is in itself a critical method of a very high order; . . . It may be true that actors pass too quickly away from the form, in order to get at the feeling that gives the form beauty and colour, and that, where the literary critic studies the language, the actor looks simply for the life; and yet, how well the great actors have appreciated that marvellous music of words which in Shakespeare at any rate is so vital an element of poetic power . . .

☆

As for Mr Birrell's statement that actors have the words of literature for ever on their lips, but none of its truths engraved on their hearts, all that one can say is that, if it be true, it is a defect which actors share with the majority of literary critics.

☆

. . . true originality is to be found rather in the use made of a model than in the rejection of all models and masters. *Dans l'art comme dans la nature on est toujours fils de quelqu'un,* and we should not quarrel with the reed if it whispers to us the music of the lyre. A little child once asked me if it was the nightingale who taught the linnets how to sing.

☆

In France they have had one great genius, Balzac, who invented the modern method of looking at life; and one great artist, Flaubert, who is the impeccable master of style; and to the influence of these two men we may trace almost all contemporary French fiction. But in England we have had no schools worth speaking of. The fiery torch lit by the Brontës has not been passed on to other hands; Dickens has influenced only journalism; Thackeray's delightful superficial philosophy, superb narrative power, and clever social satire have found no echoes; nor has Trollope left any direct successors behind him – a fact which is not much to be regretted, however, as admirable though Trollope undoubtedly is for rainy afternoons and tedious railway journeys, from the point of view of literature he is merely the perpetual curate of Pudlington Parva.

'Literary and Other Notes', *Woman's World*, January 1888

☆

Mr Ruskin in prose, and Mr Browning in poetry, were the first who drew for us the workings of the artist soul, the first who led us from the painting or statue to the hand that fashioned it, and the brain that gave it life. They seem to have made art more expressive for us, to have shown us a passionate humanity lying behind line and colour.

☆

It is interesting to note that many of the most advanced modern ideas on the subject of the education of women are anticipated by Defoe in his wonderful *Essay on Projects,* where he proposes that a college for women should be erected in every county in England, and ten colleges of the kind in London . . . In its anticipations of many of our most modern inventions it shows how thoroughly practical all dreamers are.

☆

The health of a nation depends very largely on its mode of dress; the artistic feeling of a nation should find expression in its costume quite as much as in its architecture . . .

★　　★　　★

The Celtic element in literature is extremely valuable, but there is absolutely no excuse for shrieking 'Shillelagh!' and 'O'Gorrah!'

Review: *Pictures in the Fire,* by George Dalziel. *Pall Mall Gazette,*
20 January 1888

★　　★　　★

Warring Angels is a very sad and suggestive story. It contains no impossible heroine and no improbable hero, but is simply a faithful transcript from life, a truthful picture of men and women as they are. Darwin could not have enjoyed it, as it does not end happily.

'Literary and Other Notes', *Woman's World*, February 1888

★   ★   ★

As a general rule, his verse is full of pretty echoes of other writers, but in one sonnet he makes a distinct attempt to be original and the result is extremely depressing.

> Earth wears her grandest robe, by autumn spun,
> *Like some stout matron who of youth has run*
> *The course, . . .*

is the most dreadful simile we have ever come across, even in poetry. Mr Griffiths should beware of originality. Like beauty, it is a fatal gift.
Review: *Sonnets and Other Poems*, by William Griffiths. *Pall Mall Gazette*, 15 February 1888

★   ★   ★

The Chronicle of Mites is a mock-heroic poem about the inhabitants of a decaying cheese, who speculate about the origin of their species and hold learned discussions upon the meaning of Evolution and the Gospel according to Darwin. This cheese-epic is a rather unsavoury production, and the style is, at times, so monstrous and so realistic that the author should be called the Gorgon-Zola of literature.
Review: *The Chronicle of Mites*, by James Aitchison. *Ibid.*

★   ★   ★

It is a curious fact that the worst work is always done with the best intentions, and that people are never so trivial as when they take themselves very seriously.
Review: *The Story of the Cross*, by Charles Nash. *Pall Mall Gazette*, 6 April 1888

★   ★   ★

The late Professor of the Sorbonne could chatter charmingly about culture, and had all the fascinating insincerity of an accomplished phrase-maker; being an extremely superior person he had a great contempt for democracy and its doings, but he was always very popular with the Duchesses of the Faubourg, as there was nothing in history or in literature that he could not explain away for their edification; having never done anything remarkable he was naturally elected a member of the Academy, and he always remained loyal to the traditions of that thoroughly respectable and thoroughly pretentious institution. In fact, he was just the sort of man who should never have attempted to write a Life of George Sand or to interpret George Sand's genius . . . Madame Sand's doctrines are antediluvian, he tells us, her philosophy is quite dead and her ideas of social regeneration are Utopian, incoherent and absurd . . . Poor M. Caro! This spirit, which he treats with such airy flippancy, is the very leaven of modern life. It is remoulding the world for us, and fashioning our age anew. If it is antediluvian, it is so because the deluge is yet to come; if it is Utopian then Utopia must be added to our geographies.

Review: *George Sand*, by the late Elmé Marie Caro. *Pall Mall Gazette*, 14 April 1888

★　　★　　★

'He is as beautiful as a weathercock', remarked one of the Town Councillors who wished to gain a reputation for having artistic tastes; 'only not quite so useful', he added, fearing lest people should think him unpractical, which he really was not.

'The Happy Prince', *The Happy Prince and Other Tales*, May 1888

☆

'What a remarkable phenomenon!' said the Professor of Ornithology as he was passing over the bridge. 'A swallow in winter!' And he wrote a long letter about it to the local newspaper. Every one quoted it, it was full of so many words that they could not understand.

☆

'And here is actually a dead bird at his feet!' continued the Mayor. 'We must really issue a proclamation that birds are not to be allowed to die here.' And the Town Clerk made a note of the suggestion.

So they pulled down the statue of the Happy Prince. 'As he is no longer beautiful he is no longer useful', said the Art Professor at the University.

☆

'What a strange thing!' said the overseer of the workmen at the foundry. 'This broken lead heart will not melt in the furnace. We must throw it away.' So they threw it on a dust-heap where the dead Swallow was also lying.

'Bring me the two most precious things in the city', said God to one of His Angels; and the Angel brought Him the leaden heart and the dead bird.

★　　★　　★

'Here at last is a true lover', said the Nightingale. 'Night after night have I sung of him, though I knew him not: night after night have I told his story to the stars and now I see him. His hair is dark as the hyacinth-blossom, and his lips are red as the rose of his desire; but passion has made his face like pale ivory, and sorrow has set her seal upon his brow.'

'The Nightingale and the Rose'. *Ibid.*

90

☆

'Here indeed is the true lover', said the Nightingale. 'What I sing of, he suffers: what is joy to me, to him is pain. Surely Love is a wonderful thing. It is more precious than emeralds, and dearer than fine opals. Pearls and pomegranates cannot buy it, nor is it set forth in the market-place. It may not be purchased of the merchants, nor can it be weighed out in the balance for gold.'

☆

'Death is a great price to pay for a red rose', cried the Nightingale, 'and Life is very dear to all. It is pleasant to sit in the green wood, and to watch the Sun in his chariot of gold, and the Moon in her chariot of pearl. Sweet is the scent of the hawthorn, and sweet are the bluebells that hide in the valley, and the heather that blows on the hill. Yet Love is better than Life, and what is the heart of a bird compared to the heart of a man?'

☆

'Be happy', cried the Nightingale, 'be happy; you shall have your red rose. I will build it out of music by moonlight, and stain it with my own heart's-blood. All that I ask of you in return is that you will be a true lover, for Love is wiser than Philosophy, though he is wise, and mightier than Power, though he is mighty. Flame-coloured are his wings, and coloured like flame is his body. His lips are sweet as honey, and his breath is like frankincense.'

☆

'Look, look!' cried the Tree, 'the rose is finished now'; but the Nightingale made no answer, for she was lying dead in the long grass, with the thorn in her heart.

☆

'What a silly thing Love is!' said the Student as he walked away. 'It is not half as useful as Logic, for it does not prove anything, and it is always telling one of things that are not going to happen, and making one believe things that are not true. In fact, it is quite unpractical, and, as in this age to be practical is everything, I shall go back to Philosophy and study Metaphysics.'

So he returned to his room and pulled out a great dusty book, and began to read.

★   ★   ★

One day the Giant came back. He had been to visit his friend the Cornish ogre, and had stayed with him for seven years. After the seven years were over he had said all that he had to say, for his conversation was limited . . .

'The Selfish Giant'. *Ibid.*

☆

'I have many beautiful flowers', he said; 'but the children are the most beautiful flowers of all.'

☆

He hastened across the grass, and came near to the child. And when he came quite close his face grew red with anger, and he said, 'Who hath dared to wound thee?' For on the palms of the child's hands were the prints of two nails, and the prints of two nails were on the little feet.

'Who hath dared to wound thee?' cried the Giant; 'tell me, that I may take my big sword and slay him.'

'Nay!', answered the child; 'but these are the wounds of Love.'

'Who art thou?' said the Giant, and a strange awe fell on him, and he knelt before the little child.

And the child smiled on the Giant, and said to him, 'You let me play once in your garden, to-day you shall come with me to my garden, which is Paradise.'

And when the children ran in that afternoon, they found the Giant lying dead under the tree, all covered with white blossoms.

★   ★   ★

'You will never be in the best society unless you can stand on your heads', she kept saying to them; and every now and then she showed them how it was to be done. But the little ducks paid no attention to her. They were so young that they did not know what an advantage it is to be in society at all.

'The Devoted Friend'. *Ibid.*

☆

'There is no good in my going to see little Hans as long as the snow lasts', the Miller used to say to his wife, 'for when people are in trouble they should be left alone, and not be bothered by visitors. That at least is my idea about friendship, and I am sure I am right . . .'

☆

'. . . if little Hans came up here, and saw our warm fire, and our good supper, and our great cask of red wine, he might get envious, and envy is a most terrible thing, and would spoil anybody's nature. I certainly will not allow Hans's nature to be spoiled. I am his best friend, and I will always watch over him, and see that he is not led into any temptations. Besides, if Hans came here, he might ask me to let him have some flour on credit, and that I could not do. Flour is one thing, and friendship is another, and they should not be confused. Why, the words are spelled differently, and mean quite different things. Everybody can see that.'

☆

'Lots of people act well . . . but very few people talk well, which shows that talking is much the more difficult thing of the two, and much the finer thing also' . . .

☆

'Every good storyteller nowadays starts with the end, and then goes on to the beginning, and concludes with the middle. That is the new method. I heard all about it the other day from a critic who was walking round the pond with a young man. He spoke of the matter at great length, and I am sure he must have been right, for he had blue spectacles and a bald head, and whenever the young man made any remark, he always answered "Pooh!" . . .'

☆

'. . . what is the good of friendship if one cannot say exactly what one means? Anybody can say charming things and try to please and to flatter, but a true friend always says unpleasant things, and does not mind giving pain. Indeed, if he is a really true friend he prefers it, for he knows that then he is doing good.'

☆

'It is certainly a great privilege hearing you talk . . . a very great privilege. But I am afraid I shall never have such beautiful ideas as you have.'

'Oh! they will come to you', said the Miller, 'but you must take more pains. At present you have only the practice of friendship; some day you will have the theory also.'

☆

Everybody went to little Hans's funeral, as he was so popular, and the Miller was the chief mourner.

'As I was his best friend', said the Miller, 'it is only fair that I should have the best place . . .'

☆

'I am afraid you don't quite see the moral of the story', remarked the Linnet.

'The what?' screamed the Water-rat.

'The moral.'

93

'Do you mean to say that the story has a moral?'

'Certainly', said the Linnet.

'Well, really', said the Water-rat, in a very angry manner. 'I think you should have told me that before you began. If you had done so, I certainly would not have listened to you; in fact, I should have said "Pooh", like the critic. However, I can say it now'; so he shouted out 'Pooh', at the top of his voice, gave a whisk with his tail, and went back to his hole.

'The Devoted Friend'. *Ibid.*

☆

'. . . for my own part I have a mother's feelings, and I can never look at a confirmed bachelor without the tears coming into my eyes.'

☆

'The fact is that I told him a story with a moral.'

'Ah! that is always a very dangerous thing to do', said the Duck. And I quite agree with her.

★   ★   ★

. . . all our decorative arts in Europe at present have, at least, this element of strength – that they are in immediate relationship with the decorative arts of Asia. Wherever we find in European history a revival of decorative art, it has, I fancy, nearly always been due to Oriental influence and contact with Oriental nations.

'A Fascinating Book' (Review: *Embroidery and Lace,* by Ernest Lefébure). *Woman's World,* November 1888

☆

It is never with impunity that an art seeks to mirror life. If Truth has her revenge upon those who do not follow her, she is often pitiless to her worshippers.

☆

Now and then we find in the tomb of some dead Egyptian a piece of delicate work. In the treasury at Ratisbon is preserved a specimen of Byzantine embroidery on which the Emperor Constantine is depicted riding on a white palfrey, and receiving homage from the East and West. Metz has a red silk cope wrought with great eagles, the gift of Charlemagne, and Bayeux the needle-wrought epic of Queen Matilda. But where is the great crocus-coloured robe that was wrought for Athena, and on which the gods fought against the giants?

★   ★   ★

Poverty and misery . . . are terribly concrete things. We find their incarnation everywhere . . . the poet has admirable opportunities of drawing weird and dramatic contrasts between the purple of the rich and the rags of the poor. From Miss Nesbit's book comes not merely the voice of sympathy, but also the cry of revolution:

> This is our vengeance day. Our masters made fat with our fasting
> Shall fall before us like corn when the sickle for harvest is strong,
> Old wrongs shall give might to our arm, remembrance of wrong
>   shall make lasting
> The graves we will dig for our tyrants we bore with too much and
>   too long.

The poem from which we take this stanza is remarkably vigorous, and the only consolation that we can offer to the timid and the Tories is that as long as so much strength is employed in blowing the trumpet, the sword, so far as Miss Nesbit is concerned, will probably remain sheathed.

Review: *Lays and Legends*, by E. Nesbit. *Pall Mall Gazette*, 16 November 1888

★   ★   ★

Andiatorocté is the title of a volume of poems by the Rev. Clarence Walworth, of Albany, N.Y. It is a word borrowed from the Indians, and should, we think, be returned to them as soon as possible.

Review. *Ibid.*

★   ★   ★

The snow lies thick now upon Olympus, and its scarped sides are bleak and barren, but once, we fancy, the white feet of the Muses brushed the dew from the anemones in the morning, and at evening came Apollo to sing to the shepherds in the vale. But in this we are merely lending to other ages what we desire, or think we desire, for our own. Our historical sense is at fault. Every century that produces poetry is, so far, an artificial century, and the work that seems to us the most natural and simple product of its time is probably the result of the most deliberate and self-conscious effort. For Nature is always behind the age. It takes a great artist to be thoroughly modern.

'A Note on Some Modern Poets', *Woman's World*, December 1888

☆

Are we all to talk Scotch, and to speak of the moon as the 'mune', and the soul as the 'saul'? I hope not. And yet if this Renaissance is to be a vital, living thing, it must have its linguistic side. Just as the spiritual development of music, and the artistic development of painting, have always been accompanied, if not occasioned, by the discovery of some new instrument or some fresh medium, so, in the case of any important literary movement, half of its strength resides in its language. If it does not bring with it a rich and novel mode of expression, it is doomed either to sterility or to imitation. Dialect, archaisms and the like will not do.

'A Note on Some Modern Poets', *Woman's World*, December 1888

☆

Only those should sing of Death whose song is stronger than Death is.

★   ★   ★

. . . Sappho, who, to the antique world was a pillar of flame, is to us but a pillar of shadow. Of her poems, burnt with other most precious work by Byzantine Emperor and by Roman Pope, only a few fragments remain. Possibly they lie mouldering in the scented darkness of an Egyptian tomb, clasped in the withered hands of some long-dead lover. Some Greek monk at Athos may even now be poring over an ancient manuscript, whose crabbed characters conceal lyric or ode by her whom the Greeks spoke of as 'the Poetess' just as they termed Homer 'the Poet', who was to them the tenth Muse, the flower of the Graces, the child of Erōs, and the pride of Hellas – Sappho, with the sweet voice, the bright, beautiful eyes, the dark hyacinth-coloured hair. But, practically, the work of the marvellous singer of Lesbos is entirely lost to us.

'English Poetesses', *Queen*, 8 December 1888

☆

The fragile clay vases of the Greeks still keep for us pictures of Sappho, delicately painted in black and red and white; but of her song we have only the echo of an echo . . . She stirred the whole antique world . . . Never had Love such a singer. Even in the few lines that remain to us the passion seems to scorch and burn . . . unjust Time, who has crowned her with the barren laurels of fame, has twined with them the dull poppies of oblivion . . .

☆

Poetry is for our highest moods, when we wish to be with the gods, and in our poetry nothing but the very best should satisfy us; but prose is for our daily bread, and the lack of good prose is one of the chief blots on our culture. French prose, even in the hands of the most ordinary writers, is always readable, but English prose is detestable. We have a few, a very few, masters, such as they are. We have Carlyle, who should not be imitated; and Mr Pater, who, through the subtle perfection of form, is inimitable absolutely; and Mr Froude, who is useful; and Matthew Arnold, who is a model; and Mr George Meredith, who is a warning; and Mr Lang, who is the divine amateur; and Mr Stevenson, who is the humane artist; and Mr Ruskin, whose rhythm

96

and colour and fine rhetoric and marvellous music of words are entirely unattainable.

*   *   *

. . . poetry may be said to need far more self-restraint than prose. Its conditions are more exquisite. It produces its effects by more subtle means. It must not be allowed to degenerate into mere rhetoric, or mere eloquence. It is, in one sense, the most self-conscious of all the arts, as it is never a means to an end, but always an end in itself.

Pall Mall Gazette, 11 December 1888

*   *   *

Women seem to me to possess just what our literature wants – a light touch, a delicate hand, a graceful mode of treatment, and an unstudied felicity of phrase. We want some one who will do for our prose what Madame de Sévigné did for the prose of France. George Eliot's style was far too cumbrous, and Charlotte Brontë's too exaggerated.

'Some Literary Notes', *Woman's World,* January 1889

1889

Every country now has its own models, except America. In New York, and even in Boston, a good model is so great a rarity that most of the artists are reduced to painting Niagara and millionaires.

'London Models'. *English Illustrated Magazine*, January 1889

☆

As a rule the model, nowadays, is a pretty girl, from about twelve to twenty-five years of age, who knows nothing about art, cares less, and is merely anxious to earn seven or eight shillings a day without much trouble. English models rarely look at a picture, and never venture on any aesthetic theories. In fact they realise very completely Mr Whistler's idea of the function of an art critic, for they pass no criticisms at all.

☆

Intellectually, it must be acknowledged, they are Philistines, but physically they are perfect – at least some are. Though none of them can talk Greek, many can look Greek, which to a nineteenth-century painter is naturally of great importance.

☆

When they are tired a wise artist gives them a rest. Then they sit in a chair and read penny dreadfuls, till they are roused from the tragedy of literature to take their place again in the tragedy of art.

☆

. . . there is the true Academy model. He is usually a man of thirty, rarely good-looking, but a perfect miracle of muscles. In fact he is the apotheosis of anatomy, and is so conscious of his own splendour that he tells you of his tibia and his thorax, as if no one else had anything of the kind.

☆

. . . the Oriental models . . . are very much sought after as they can remain immobile for hours, and generally possess lovely costumes. However they have a very poor opinion of English art, which they regard as

something between a vulgar personality and a commonplace photo-
graph.

☆

. . . the Italian youth . . . is often quite charming with his large melancholy eyes, his crisp hair, and his slim brown figure. It is true he eats
garlic, but then he can stand like a faun and couch like a leopard, so he
is forgiven. He is always full of pretty compliments, and has been
known to have kind words of encouragement for even our greatest
artists.

☆

Sometimes an ex-model who has a son will curl his hair, and wash his
face, and bring him the round of the studios, all soap and shininess.
The young school don't like him, but the older school do, and when he
appears on the walls of the Royal Academy he is called *The Infant
Samuel*.

☆

Occasionally also an artist catches a couple of *gamins* in the gutter and
asks them to come to his studio. The first time they always appear, but
after that they don't keep their appointments. They dislike sitting still,
and have a strong and perhaps natural objection to looking pathetic.
Besides they are always under the impression that the artist is laughing at them. It is a sad fact, but there is no doubt that the poor are
completely unconscious of their own picturesqueness.

☆

A good acrobat is always graceful though grace is never his object; he
is graceful because he does what he has to do in the best way in which
it can be done – graceful because he is natural. If an ancient Greek
were to come to life now, which considering the probable severity of
his criticisms would be rather trying to our conceit, he would be found
far oftener at the circus than at the theatre. A good circus is an oasis of
Hellenism in a world that reads too much to be wise, and thinks too
much to be beautiful.

★   ★   ★

VIVIAN What Art really reveals to us is Nature's lack of design, her
curious crudities, her extraordinary monotony, her absolutely unfinished condition. Nature has good intentions, of course, but, as
Aristotle once said, she cannot carry them out. When I look at a
landscape I cannot help seeing all its defects. It is fortunate for us,
however, that Nature is so imperfect, as otherwise we should have

99

had no art at all. Art is our spirited protest, our gallant attempt to
teach Nature her proper place.

'The Decay of Lying: a Dialogue'. *Nineteenth Century*, January 1889

☆

VIVIAN I don't complain. If Nature had been comfortable, mankind
would never have invented architecture. . .

☆

VIVIAN Egotism itself, which is so necessary to a proper sense of human
dignity, is entirely the result of indoor life. Out of doors one
becomes abstract and impersonal. One's individuality absolutely
leaves one.

☆

VIVIAN Nothing is more evident than that Nature hates Mind. Thinking is the most unhealthy thing in the world, and people die of it
just as they die of any other disease. Fortunately, in England at
any rate, thought is not catching. Our splendid physique as a
people is entirely due to our national stupidity. I only hope we
shall be able to keep this historic bulwark of our happiness for
many years to come . . .

☆

VIVIAN . . . everybody who is incapable of learning has taken to teaching. . .

☆

CYRIL Lying! I should have thought that our politicians kept up that
habit.

VIVIAN I assure you that they do not. They never rise beyond the level
of misrepresentation, and actually condescend to prove, to discuss, to argue. How different from the temper of the true liar, with
his frank, fearless statements, his superb irresponsibility, his
healthy, natural disdain of proof of any kind!

☆

VIVIAN . . . what is a fine lie? Simply that which is its own evidence.

☆

VIVIAN They . . . have been known to wrest from reluctant juries trium-
phant verdicts of acquittal for their clients, even when those
clients, as often happens, were clearly and unmistakeably innocent.

☆

VIVIAN Newspapers . . . may now be absolutely relied upon. One feels it as one wades through their columns. It is always the unreadable that occurs.

☆

CYRIL Well, I should fancy you are all a good deal bored with each other.
VIVIAN We are. That is one of the objects of the club.

☆

VIVIAN People have a careless way of talking about a 'born liar', just as they talk about a 'born poet'. But in both cases they are wrong. Lying and poetry are arts – arts, as Plato saw, not unconnected with each other – and they require the most careful study, the most disinterested devotion. Indeed, they have their technique, just as the more material arts of painting and sculpture have, their subtle secrets of form and colour, their craft-mysteries, their deliberate artistic methods. As one knows the poet by his fine music, so one can recognise the liar by his rich rhythmic utterance, and in neither case will the casual inspiration of the moment suffice. Here, as elsewhere, practice must precede perfection.

☆

VIVIAN Many a young man starts in life with a natural gift for exaggeration which, if nurtured in congenial and sympathetic surroundings, or by the imitation of the best models, might grow into something really great and wonderful. But, as a rule, he comes to nothing. . . He either falls into careless habits of accuracy, or takes to frequenting the society of the aged and the well informed. Both things are equally fatal to his imagination. . .

☆

VIVIAN . . . novels which are so lifelike that no one can possibly believe in their probability.

☆

VIVIAN Even Mr Robert Louis Stevenson, that delightful master of delicate and fanciful prose, is tainted with this modern vice . . . There is such a thing as robbing a story of its reality by trying to make it too true, and *The Black Arrow* is so inartistic as not to contain a single anachronism to boast of, while the transformation of Dr Jekyll reads dangerously like an experiment out of the *Lancet*.

☆

VIVIAN Mr Henry James writes fiction as if it were a painful duty, and wastes upon mean motives and imperceptible 'points of view' his neat literary style, his felicitous phrases, his swift and caustic satire.

'The Decay of Lying: a Dialogue'. *Nineteenth Century*, January 1889

☆

VIVIAN Mr James Payn is an adept in the art of concealing what is not worth finding. He hunts down the obvious with the enthusiasm of a short-sighted detective. As one turns over the pages, the suspense of the author becomes almost unbearable.

☆

VIVIAN As for that great and daily increasing school of novelists for whom the sun always rises in the East-End, the only thing that can be said about them is that they find life crude, and leave it raw.

☆

VIVIAN M. Guy de Maupassant, with his keen mordant irony and his hard vivid style, strips life of the few poor rags that still cover her, and shows us foul sore and festering wound. He writes lurid little tragedies in which everybody is ridiculous; bitter comedies at which one cannot laugh for very tears.

☆

VIVIAN M. Zola, true to the lofty principle that he lays down in one of his pronunciamentos in literature, *'L'homme de génie n'a jamais d'esprit'*, is determined to show that, if he has not got genius, he can at least be dull. And how well he succeeds! . . . at times, as in *Germinal*, there is something almost epic in his work. . . From any ethical standpoint it is just what it should be. The author is perfectly truthful, and describes things exactly as they happen. What more can any moralist desire? We have no sympathy at all with the moral indignation of our time against M. Zola. It is simply the indignation of Tartuffe on being exposed. But from the standpoint of art, what can be said in favour of the author of *L'Assommoir*, *Nana* and *Pot-Bouille?* Nothing. Mr Ruskin once described the characters in George Eliot's novels as being like the sweepings of a Pentonville omnibus, but M. Zola's characters are much worse. They have their dreary vices, and their drearier virtues. The record of their lives is absolutely without interest.

☆

VIVIAN M. Daudet is better. He has wit, a light touch and an amusing style. But he has lately committed literary suicide. . . now that we have learned from *Vingts Ans de ma Vie littéraire* that . . . characters were taken directly from life . . . they seem to have suddenly lost all their vitality . . . The only real people are the people who never existed, and if a novelist is base enough to go to life for his personages, he should at least pretend that they are creations, and not boast of them as copies. The justification of a character in a novel is not that other persons are what they are, but that the author is what he is.

☆

VIVIAN . . . what is interesting about people in good society . . . is the mask that each one of them wears, not the reality that lies behind the mask. It is a humiliating confession, but we are all of made out of the same stuff. . . Where we differ from each other is purely in accidentals: in dress, manner, tone of voice, religious opinions, personal appearance, tricks of habit, and the like. The more one analyses people, the more all reasons for analysis disappear. Sooner or later one comes to that dreadful universal thing called human nature.

☆

VIVIAN Meredith! Who can define him? His style is chaos illumined by flashes of lightning. As a writer he has mastered everything except language: as a novelist he can do everything, except tell a story: as an artist he is everything, except articulate . . . he is a child of realism who is not on speaking terms with his father. By deliberate choice he has made himself a romanticist. He has refused to bow the knee to Baal, and after all, even if the man's fine spirit did not revolt against the noisy assertions of realism, his style would be quite sufficient of itself to keep life at a respectful distance. By its means he has planted round his garden a hedge full of thorns, and red with wonderful roses.

☆

VIVIAN A steady course of Balzac reduces our living friends to shadows, and our acquaintances to the shadows of shades. His characters have a kind of fervent fiery-coloured existence. They dominate us, and defy scepticism. One of the greatest tragedies of my life is the death of Lucien de Rubempré. It is a grief from which I have never been able to completely rid myself. It haunts me in my moments of pleasure. I remember it when I laugh. But Balzac is no more a realist than Holbein was. He created life, he did not copy it.

☆

VIVIAN The public imagine that, because they are interested in their immediate surroundings, Art should be interested in them also, and should take them as her subject-matter. But the mere fact that they are interested in these things makes them unsuitable subjects for Art. The only beautiful things, as somebody once said, are the things that do not concern us. . . It is exactly because Hecuba is nothing to us that her sorrows are such an admirable motive for a tragedy.

'The Decay of Lying: a Dialogue'. *Nineteenth Century*, January 1889

☆

VIVIAN . . . we are a degraded race, and have sold our birthright for a mess of facts.

☆

CYRIL . . . this is perhaps the best rough test of what is literature and what is not. If one cannot enjoy reading a book over and over again, there is no use reading it at all.

☆

VIVIAN The popular cry of our time is 'Let us return to Life and Nature; they will recreate Art for us, and send the red blood coursing through her veins; they will shoe her feet with swiftness and make her hand strong.' But, alas! we are mistaken in our amiable and well-meaning efforts. Nature is always behind the age. And as for Life, she is the solvent that breaks up Art, the enemy that lays waste her house.

☆

VIVIAN One touch of Nature may make the whole world kin, but two touches of Nature will destroy any work of Art.

☆

VIVIAN Wordsworth went to the lakes, but he was never a lake poet. He found in stones the sermons he had already hidden there. He went moralising about the district, but his good work was produced when he returned, not to Nature but to poetry. Poetry gave him 'Laodamia', and the fine sonnets, and the great Ode, such as it is. Nature gave him 'Martha Ray' and 'Peter Bell', and the address to Mr Wilkinson's spade.

☆

VIVIAN As the inevitable result of this substitution of an imitative for a creative medium, this surrender of an imaginative form, we have the modern English melodrama. The characters in these plays talk on the stage exactly as they would talk off it; they have neither aspirations nor aspirates; they are taken directly from life and reproduce its vulgarity down to the smallest detail; they present the gait, manner, costume and, accent of real people; they would pass unnoticed in a third-class railway carriage.

☆

VIVIAN . . . Carlyle, whose *French Revolution* is one of the most fascinating historical novels ever written. . .

☆

VIVIAN The crude commercialism of America, its materialising spirit, its indifference to the poetical side of things, and its lack of imagination and of high unattainable ideals, are entirely due to that country having adopted for its national hero a man, who according to his own confession, was incapable of telling a lie, and it is not too much to say that the story of George Washington and the cherry-tree has done more harm, and in a shorter space of time, than any other moral tale in the whole of literature.
CYRIL My dear boy!
VIVIAN I assure you it is the case, and the amusing part of the whole thing is that the story of the cherry-tree is an absolute myth.

☆

VIVIAN They will call upon Shakespeare – they always do – and will quote that hackneyed passage forgetting that this unfortunate aphorism about Art holding the mirror up to Nature, is deliberately said by Hamlet in order to convince the bystanders of his absolute insanity in all art-matters.

☆

VIVIAN A great artist invents a type, and Life tries to copy it, to reproduce it in a popular form, like an enterprising publisher.

☆

VIVIAN Schopenhauer has analysed the pessimism that characterises modern thought, but Hamlet invented it. The world has become sad because a puppet was once melancholy.

☆

VIVIAN The Nihilist, that strange martyr who has no faith, who goes to the stake without enthusiasm, and dies for what he does not believe in, is a purely literary product. He was invented by Tourgénieff, and completed by Dostoieffski.

☆

VIVIAN Scientifically speaking, the basis of life – the energy of life, as Aristotle would call it – is simply the desire for expression, and Art is always presenting various forms through which this expression can be attained.

'The Decay of Lying: a Dialogue'. *Nineteenth Century*, January 1889

☆

VIVIAN At present, people see fogs, not because there are fogs, but because poets and painters have taught them the mysterious loveliness of such effects. There may have been fogs for centuries in London. I dare say there were. But no one saw them, and so we do not know anything about them. They did not exist till Art had invented them. Now, it must be admitted, fogs are carried to excess. They have become the mere mannerism of a clique, and the exaggerated realism of their method gives dull people bronchitis. Where the cultured catch an effect, the uncultured catch cold.

☆

VIVIAN Art creates an incomparable and unique effect, and, having done so, passes on to other things. Nature, upon the other hand, forgetting that imitation can be made the sincerest form of insult, keeps on repeating this effect until we all become absolutely wearied of it.

☆

VIVIAN The sibyls and prophets of the Sistine may indeed serve to interpret for some that new birth of the emancipated spirit that we call the Renaissance; but what do the drunken boors and bawling peasants of Dutch art tell us about the great soul of Holland? The more abstract, the more ideal an art is, the more it reveals to us the temper of its age. If we wish to understand a nation by means of its art, let us look at its architecture or its music.

☆

VIVIAN The fact is that we look back on the ages entirely through the medium of Art, and Art, very fortunately, has never once told us the truth.

☆

VIVIAN Most of our modern portrait painters are doomed to absolute oblivion. They never paint what they see. They paint what the public sees, and the public never sees anything.

☆

VIVIAN The dreams of the great middle classes of this country, as recorded in Mr Myers's two bulky volumes on the subject, and in the Transactions of the Psychical Society, are the most depressing things that I have ever read. There is not even a fine nightmare among them. They are commonplace, sordid and tedious.

☆

VIVIAN . . . in the English Church a man succeeds, not through his capacity for belief, but through his capacity for disbelief. Ours is the only Church where the sceptic stands at the altar, and where St Thomas is regarded as the ideal apostle.

☆

VIVIAN . . . it is sufficient for some shallow uneducated passman out of either University to get up in his pulpit and express his doubts about Noah's ark, or Balaam's ass, or Jonah and the whale, for half of London to flock to hear him, and to sit open-mouthed in rapt admiration at his superb intellect.

☆

VIVIAN Man can believe the impossible, but man can never believe the improbable.

☆

VIVIAN Lying for the sake of the improvement of the young, which is the basis of home education, still lingers amongst us, and its advantages are so admirably set forth in the early books of Plato's *Republic* that it is unnecessary to dwell upon them here. It is a mode of lying for which all good mothers have peculiar capabilities, but it is capable of still further development. . .

☆

VIVIAN Lying for the sake of a monthly salary is of course well known in Fleet Street, and the profession of a political leader-writer is not without its advantages. But it is said to be a somewhat dull occupation, and it certainly does not lead to much beyond a kind of ostentatious obscurity.

☆

VIVIAN Art never expresses anything but itself. It has an independent life, just as Thought has, and develops purely on its own lines. It is not necessarily realistic in an age of realism, nor spiritual in an age of faith.

☆

VIVIAN To pass from the art of a time to the time itself is the great mistake that all historians commit.

'The Decay of Lying: a Dialogue'. *Nineteenth Century*, January 1889

☆

VIVIAN At twilight nature becomes a wonderfully suggestive effect, and
is not without loveliness, though perhaps its chief use is to illustrate quotations from the poets.

★   ★   ★

. . . Thomas Griffiths Wainewright. . . so powerful with 'pen, pencil
and poison' . . . if we set aside his achievements in the sphere of poison,
what he has actually left to us hardly justifies his reputation.

But then it is only the Philistine who seeks to estimate a personality
by the vulgar test of production. This young dandy sought to be somebody, rather than do something. He recognised that Life itself is an
art, and has its modes of style no less than the arts that seek to express
it.

'Pen, Pencil and Poison'. *Fortnightly Review*, January 1889

☆

He had that curious love of green, which in individuals is always the
sign of a subtle artistic temperament, and in nations is said to denote a
laxity, if not a decadence of morals.

☆

He saw that in decorating a room, which is to be, not a room for show,
but a room to live in, we should never aim at any archaeological recon-
struction of the past, nor burden ourselves with any fanciful necessity
for historical accuracy. In this artistic perception he was perfectly
right. All beautiful things belong to the same age.

☆

As an art-critic he concerned himself primarily with the complex impressions produced by a work of art, and certainly the first step in aesthetic criticism is to realise one's own impressions.

☆

The conception of making a prose-poem out of paint is excellent.
Much of the best modern literature springs from the same aim. In a
very ugly and sensible age, the arts borrow, not from life, but from
each other.

☆

To his fellow-contributors in the *London Magazine* he was always most
generous, and praises Barry Cornwall, Allan Cunningham, Hazlitt,

Elton, and Leigh Hunt without anything of the malice of a friend.

☆

To have a style so gorgeous that it conceals the subject is one of the highest achievements of an important and much admired school of Fleet Street leader-writers . . .

☆

He also saw that it was quite easy by continued reiteration to make the public interested in his own personality . . . This being the least valuable side of his work, is the one that has had the most obvious influence. A publicist, now-a-days, is a man who bores the community with the details of the illegalities of his private life.

☆

Like most artificial people he had a great love of nature.

☆

. . . we must not forget that the cultivated young man . . . who was so susceptible to Wordsworthian influences, was also . . . one of the most subtle and secret poisoners of this or any age. How he first became fascinated by this strange sin he does not tell us, and the diary in which he carefully noted the results of his terrible experiments and the methods that he adopted, has unfortunately been lost to us. Even in later days, too, he was always reticent on the matter, and preferred to speak about 'The Excursion', and the 'Poems founded on the Affections'. There is no doubt, however, that the poison that he used was strychnine.

☆

Why he murdered Mrs Abercrombie is not ascertained. It may have been for a caprice, or to quicken some hideous sense of power that was in him, or because she suspected something, or for no reason.

☆

De Quincey says that Mrs Wainewright was not really privy to the murder. Let us hope that she was not. Sin should be solitary, and have no accomplices.

☆

He knew that this forgery had been discovered, and that by returning to England he was imperilling his life. Yet he returned. Should one wonder? It was said that the woman was very beautiful. Besides, she did not love him.

☆

There is, however, something dramatic in the fact that this heavy punishment was inflicted on him for what, if we remember his fatal influence on the prose of modern journalism, was certainly not the worst of all his sins.

'Pen, Pencil and Poison', *Fortnightly Review*, January 1889

☆

Crime in England is rarely the result of sin. It is nearly always the result of starvation. There was probably no one on board in whom he would have found a sympathetic listener, or even a psychologically interesting nature.

☆

The fact of a man being a poisoner is nothing against his prose. The domestic virtues are not the true basis of art, though they may serve as an excellent advertisement for second-rate artists.

☆

There is no essential incongruity between crime and culture. We cannot rewrite the whole of history for the purpose of gratifying our moral sense of what should be.

☆

Of course he is far too close to our own time for us to be able to form an purely artistic judgement about him. It is impossible not to feel a strong prejudice against a man who might have poisoned Lord Tennyson, or Mr Gladstone, or the Master of Balliol.

☆

I know that there are many historians, or at least writers on historical subjects, who still think it necessary to apply moral judgments to history, and who distribute their praise or blame with the solemn complacency of a successful schoolmaster. This, however, is a foolish habit, and merely shows that the moral instinct can be brought to such a pitch of perfection that it will make its appearance wherever it is not required.

☆

... neither art nor science knows anything of moral approval or disapproval.

☆

To be suggestive for fiction is to be of more importance than a fact.

★   ★   ★

Literature is not much indebted to Mr Balfour for his sophistical

Defence of Philosophic Doubt, which is one of the dullest books we know, but it must be admitted that by sending Mr Blunt to gaol he has converted a clever rhymer into an earnest and deep-thinking poet. The narrow confines of the prison cell seem to suit the 'sonnet's scanty plot of ground', and an unjust imprisonment for a noble cause strengthens as well as deepens the nature.

Review: *In Vinculis*, by Wilfrid Scawen Blunt. *Pall Mall Gazette*,
3 January 1889

★   ★   ★

. . . in his very rejection of art Walt Whitman is an artist. He tried to produce a certain effect by certain means and he succeeded. . . He stands apart, and the chief value of his work is in its prophecy, not in its performance. He has begun a prelude to larger themes. He is the herald to a new erea. As a man he is the precursor of a fresh type. He is a factor in the heroic and spiritual evolution of the human being. If Poetry has passed him by, Philosophy will take note of him.

Review: *November Boughs*, by Walt Whitman. *Pall Mall Gazette*,
25 January 1889

★   ★   ★

Mr Whistler always spelt art, and we believe still spells it, with a capital 'I'. However, he was never dull. His brilliant wit, his caustic satire, and his amusing epigrams, or perhaps we should say epitaphs, on his contemporaries, made his views on art as delightful as they were misleading, and as fascinating as they were unsound. Besides, he introduced American humour into art criticism, and for this if for no other reason he deserves to be affectionately remembered.

Pall Mall Gazette, 26 January 1889

☆

Mr Whistler, for some reason or other, always adopted the phraseology of the minor prophets. Possibly it was in order to emphasise his well-known claims to verbal inspiration . . . The idea was clever enough at the beginning, but ultimately the manner became monotonous. The spirit of the Hebrews is excellent, but their mode of writing is not to be imitated, and no amount of American jokes will give it that modernity which is essential to a good literary style. Admirable as are Mr Whistler's fireworks on canvas, his fireworks in prose are abrupt, violent and exaggerated. However, oracles, since the days of the Pythia, have never been remarkable for style . . . [Mr Whistler], with all his faults, was never guilty of writing a line of poetry, and . . . is, indeed, quite incapable of doing anything of the kind.

☆

. . . if we want to understand the history of a nation through the medium of art, it is to the imaginative and ideal arts that we have to go and not to the arts that are definitely imitative. The visible aspect of life no longer contains for us the secret of life's spirit. Probably it never did contain it.

Pall Mall Gazette, 26 January 1889

★　　★　　★

Blake once saw a fairy's funeral. But this, as Mr Yeats points out, must have been an English fairy, for the Irish fairies never die; they are immortal.

Review: *Fairy and Folk Tales of the Irish Peasantry*, edited and selected by W. B. Yeats. 'Some Literary Notes', *Woman's World*, February 1889

☆

The banshee does not care much for our democratic levelling tendencies; she only loves old families, and despises the *parvenu* or the *nouveau riche*.

☆

A *Dullahan* is the most terrible thing in the world. In 1807 two of the sentries stationed outside St James's Park saw one climbing the railings, and died of fright. Mr Yeats suggests that they are possibly 'descended from that Irish giant who swam across the Channel with his head in his teeth'.

☆

It is delightful to come across the collection of purely imaginative work, and Mr Yeats has a very quick instinct in finding out the best and the most beautiful things in Irish folk-lore.

★　　★　　★

To be a fine social critic is no small thing, and to be able to incorporate in a work of fiction the results of such careful observation is to achieve what is out of reach of many. The difficulty under which the novelists of our day labour seems to me to be this: if they do not go into society, their books are unreadable; and if they do go into society, they have no time left for writing.

'Some Literary Notes', *Ibid.*

★　　★　　★

. . . I cannot say that I like the blending of the postman with St John the Baptist.

Review: *Dreams and Dream-Stories*, by Dr Anna Kingsford. *Ibid.*

★　　★　　★

. . . Socialism is not going to allow herself to be trammelled by any hard-and-fast creed or to be stereotyped into an iron formula. She welcomes many and multiform natures. She rejects none, and has room for all. She has the attraction of a wonderful personality and touches the heart of one and the brain of another, and draws this man by his hatred of injustice, and his neighbour by his faith in the future, and a third, it may be, by his love of art or by his wild worship of a lost and buried past. And all of this is well. For, to make men Socialists is nothing, but to make Socialism human is a great thing.

Review: *Chants of Labour: A Song-Book of the People*, edited by Edward
Carpenter. *Pall Mall Gazette*, 15 February 1889

☆

Nero fiddled while Rome was burning, at least, inaccurate historians say he did, but it is for the building up of an eternal city that the Socialists of our day are making music, and they have complete confidence in the art-instincts of the people... The Reformation gained much from the use of popular hymns and hymn-tunes, and the Socialists seem determined to gain by similar means a similar hold upon the people. However, they must not be too sanguine about the result. The walls of Thebes rose up to the sound of music, and Thebes was a very dull city indeed.

     ★   ★   ★

Like most of the distinctly national products of America, it seems to have been imported from abroad...

i.e. Poker. Review: Brander Matthews, *Pen and Ink: Papers on Subjects of
More or Less Importance. Pall Mall Gazette*, 27 February 1889

☆

... Mr Austin Dobson ... has produced work that is absolutely classical in its exquisite beauty of form. Nothing more artistically perfect in its way than the *Lines to a Greek Girl* has been written in our time. This little poem will be remembered in literature as long as *Thyrsis* is remembered, and *Thyrsis* will never be forgotten. Both had that note of distinction that is so rare in these days of violence, exaggeration and rhetoric.

     ★   ★   ★

The Wanderings of Oisin and Other Poems ... is, I believe, the first volume of poems that Mr Yeats has published, and it is certainly full of promise. It must be admitted that many of the poems are too fragmentary, too incomplete. They read like stray scenes out of unfinished plays, like things only half remembered, or, at best, but dimly seen. But the architectonic power of construction, the power to build up and make perfect a harmonious whole, is nearly always the latest, as it certainly is the highest, development of the artistic temperament. It is somewhat unfair to expect it in early work. One quality Mr Yeats has in a marked degree, a quality that is not uncommon in the work of our minor poets, and is therefore all the more welcome to us – I mean the romantic temper. He is essentially Celtic, and his verse, at its best, is Celtic also. Strongly influenced by Keats, he seems to study how to 'load every rift with ore', yet is more fascinated by the beauty of words than by the beauty of metrical music. . . It is impossible to doubt, after reading his present volume, that he will some day give us work of high import. Up to this he has been merely trying the strings of his instrument, running over the keys.

'Some Literary Notes'. *Woman's World*, March 1889

☆

Those who regard Hannah More as a prim maiden lady of the conventional type, with a pious and literary turn of mind, will be obliged to change their views should they read Mrs Walford's admirable sketch . . . Hannah More was a brilliant wit, a *femme d'esprit*, passionately fond of society, and loved by society in return. When the serious-minded little country girl, who at the age of eight had covered a whole quire of paper with letters seeking to reform imaginary depraved characters and with return epistles full of contrition and promises of amendment, paid her first visit to London, she became at once the intimate friend of Johnson, Burke, Sir Joshua Reynolds, Garrick, and most of the distinguished people of the day, delighting them by her charm, and grace, and wit . . . How incredible it all sounds!

★ ★ ★

When the result is beautiful, the method is justified, and no shrill insistence upon a supposed necessity for absolute modernity of form can prevail against the value of work that has the incomparable excellence of style. Certainly Mr Morris's work possesses this excellence. His fine harmonies and rich cadences create in the reader that spirit by which alone can its own spirit be interpreted, awake in him something of the temper of romance, and by taking him out of his own age, place him in a truer and more vital relation to the great masterpieces of all time. It is a bad thing for an age to be always looking in art for its own reflection . . . As we read Mr Morris's story with its fine alternations of verse and prose, its decorative and descriptive beauties, its wonderful handling of romantic and adventurous themes, we cannot but feel that we are as far removed from the ignoble fiction as we are from the ignoble facts of our day. We breathe a purer air, and have dreams of a time when life had a kind of poetical quality of its own, and was simple, and stately, and complete.

Review: *A Tale of the House of the Wolfings and all the Kindreds of the Mark*, written in Prose and Verse by William Morris. *Pall Mall Gazette*, 2 March 1889

★   ★   ★

... the social atmosphere of Melbourne was not favourable to poets, and the worthy colonials seem to have shared Audrey's doubts as to whether poetry was a true and honest thing.... Australia has converted many of our failures into prosperous and admirable mediocrities, but she certainly spoiled one of our poets for us. Ovid at Tomi is no more tragic than Gordon driving cattle or farming an unprofitable sheep-ranch.

Review: *Poems*, by Adam Lindsay Gordon. *Pall Mall Gazette*, 25 March 1889

★   ★   ★

That Australia, however, will some day make amends by producing a poet of her own we cannot doubt, and for him there will be new notes to sound and new wonders to tell of.... The aborigines aver that, when night comes, from the bottomless depth of some lagoon a mis-shapen monster rises, dragging his loathsome length along the ooze. From a corner of a silent forest rises a dismal chant, and around a fire dance natives painted like skeletons. All is fear-inspiring and gloomy. No bright fancies are linked with the memories of the mountains. Hopeless explorers have named them out of their sufferings – Mount Misery, Mount Dreadful, Mount Despair.... Here, certainly, is new material for the poet, here is a land that is waiting for its singer.

Ibid., with specific reference to Marcus Clarke's preface

★   ★   ★

Judges, like the criminal classes, have their lighter moments, and it was probably in one of his happiest and, certainly, in one of his most careless moods that Mr Justice Denman conceived the idea of putting the early history of Rome into doggerel verse for the benefit of a little boy of the name of Jack. Poor Jack! He is still, we learn from the preface, under six years of age, and it is sad to think of the future career of a boy who is being brought up on bad history and worse poetry.... The reign of Tullus Hostilius opens with a very wicked rhyme:

> As Numa, dying, only left
> A daughter, named Pompilia,
> The Senate had to choose a King.
> They choose one sadly *sillier*.

If Jack goes to the bad, Mr Justice Denman will have much to answer for.

Review: *The Story of the Kings of Rome in Verse*, by the Hon. G. Denman, Judge of the High Court of Justice. *Pall Mall Gazette*, 30 March 1889

*   *   *

The Smouse, by Fannin, had the modern merit of incomprehensibility. It reads like something out of *The Hunting of the Snark*:

> I'm a Smouse, I'm a Smouse in the wilderness wide,
> The veld is my home, and the wagon's my pride:
> The crack of my 'voerslag' shall sound o'er the lea,
> I'm a Smouse, I'm a Smouse, and the trader is free!
> I heed not the Governor, I fear not his law,
> I care not for 'civilisation' one straw
> And ne'er to 'Ompanda' – 'Umgazis' I'll throw
> While my arm carries fist, or my foot bears a toe!
> 'Trek', 'trek', ply the whip – touch the fore oxen's skin,
> I'll warrant we'll 'go it' through thick and through thin –
> 'Loop! loop ye oud skellums! ot Vigmaan trek jy.'
> I'm a Smouse, I'm a Smouse, and the trader is free!

The South African poets, as a class, are rather behind the age. They seem to think that 'Aurora' is a very novel and delightful epithet for the dawn. On the whole, they depress us.

Review: *The Poetry of South Africa*, coll. and arr. A. Wilmot. *Ibid.*

*   *   *

Mrs Cora M. Davis is eloquent about the splendours of what the authoress of *The Circle of Seasons* calls 'this earthly ball'.

'Let's sing of the beauties of this grand old earth', she cries, and proceeds to tell how

> Imagination paints old Egypt's former glory,
> Of mighty temples reaching heavenward,
> Of grim, colossal statues, whose barbaric story
> The caustic pens of erudition still record,
> Whose ancient cities of glittering minarets
> Reflect the gold of Afric's gorgeous sunsets.

'The caustic pens of erudition' is quite delightful and will be appreciated by all Egyptologists. There is also a charming passage in the same poem on the pictures of the Old Masters:

> the mellow richness of whose tints impart,
> By contrast, greater delicacy still to modern art.

This seems to us the highest form of optimism we have ever come across in art criticism. It is American in origin, Mrs Davis, as her biographer tells us, having been born in Alabama, Genesee co., N.Y.

Review: *The Circle of Seasons*, by K.E.V., and *Immortelles*, by Cora M.
Davis. *Ibid.*

*   *   *

Blue-books [Reports to Parliament] are generally dull reading, but Blue-Books on Ireland have always been interesting. They form the record of one of the great tragedies of modern Europe. In them England has written down her indictment against herself, and has given to the world the history of her shame. If in the last century she tried to govern Ireland with an insolence that was intensified by race, hatred and religious prejudice, she has sought to rule her in this century with a stupidity that is aggravated by good intentions.

Review: *The Two Chiefs of Dunboy: or an Irish Romance of the Last Century*,
by J. A. Froude. *Pall Mall Gazette*, 13 April 1889

☆

An entirely new factor has appeared in the social development of the country, and this factor is the Irish-American, and his influence. To mature its powers, to concentrate its action, to learn the secret of its own strength and of England's weakness, the Celtic intellect has had to cross the Atlantic. At home it had but learned the pathetic weakness of nationality; in a strange land it realised what indomitable forces nationality possesses. What captivity was to the Jews, exile has been to the Irish: America and American influence have educated them. Their first practical leader is an Irish-American.

☆

Mr Froude admits the martyrdom of Ireland, but regrets that the martyrdom was not more completely carried out. His ground of complaint against the executioner is not his trade, but his bungling. It is the bluntness, not the cruelty, of the sword that he objects to. Resolute government, that shallow shibboleth of those who do not understand how complex a thing the art of government is, is his posthumous panacea for past evils. His hero, Colonel Goring, has the words Law and Order ever on his lips, meaning by the one the enforcement of unjust legislation, and implying by the other the suppression of every fine national aspiration. That the Government should enforce iniquity and the governed submit to it, seems to be to Mr Froude, as it certainly is to many others, the true ideal of political science. Like most pen-men he overrates the power of the sword.

☆

There are some who will welcome with delight the idea of solving the

Irish question by doing away with the Irish people. There are others who will remember that Ireland has extended her boundaries, and that we have now to reckon with her not merely in the Old World but in the New.

Review: *The Two Chiefs of Dunboy: or an Irish Romance of the Last Century,*
by J. A. Froude. *Pall Mall Gazette,* 13 April 1889

★   ★   ★

Certainly dialect is dramatic. It is a vivid method of re-creating a past that never existed. It is something between 'A Return to Nature' and 'A Return to the Glossary'. It is so artificial that it is really *naïve.* From the point of view of mere music, much may be said for it. Wonderful diminutives lend new notes of tenderness to the song. There are possibilities of fresh rhymes, and in search for a fresh rhyme poets may be excused if they wander from the broad high-road of classical utterances into devious byways and less-trodden paths. Sometimes one is tempted to look on dialect as expressing simply the pathos of provincialisms, but there is more in it than mere mispronunciations. With the revival of an antique form, often comes the revival of an antique spirit. Through limitations that are sometime uncouth, and always narrow, comes Tragedy herself; and though she may stammer in her utterance, and deck herself in cast-off weeds and trammelling raiment, still we must hold ourselves in readiness to accept her, so rare are her visits to us now, so rare her presence in an age that demands a happy ending from every play, and that sees in the theatre merely a source of amusement.

'Some Literary Notes', *Woman's World,* June 1889

★   ★   ★

There is a great deal to be said in favour of reading a novel backwards. The last page is as a rule the most interesting, and when one begins with the catastrophe or the *dénouement* one feels on pleasant terms of equality with the author. It is like going behind the scenes of a theatre. One is no longer taken in, and the hair-breadth escapes of the hero and the wild agonies of the heroine leave one absolutely unmoved. One knows the jealously-guarded secret, and one can afford to smile at the quite unnecessary anxiety that the puppets of fiction always consider it their duty to display.

Pall Mall Gazette, 5 June 1889

★   ★   ★

Is Mr Alfred Austin among the Socialists? Has somebody converted the respectable editor of the respectable *National Review?* Has even dulness become revolutionary? From a poem in Mr Austin's last volume this would seem to be the case.

Review: *Love's Widowhood and Other Poems,* by Alfred Austin. *Pall Mall Gazette,* 24 June 1889

☆

... the log-rolling poet of the fifth stanza is an ideal that we have already realised, and in which we had but little comfort; and the fourth stanza leaves us in some doubt whether Mr Austin means that washerwomen are to take to reading Dante, or that students of Italian literature are to wash their own clothes. But, on the whole, though Mr Austin's vision of the *città divina* of the future is not very inspiriting, it is certainly extremely interesting as a sign of the times, and it is evident from the two concluding lines of the following stanzas that there will be no danger of the intellect being overworked:

> Age lorded not, nor rose the hectic
>   Up to the cheek of youth;
> But reigned throughout their dialectic
>   Sobriety of truth.
>
> And if a long-held contest tended
>   To ill-defined result,
> *It was by calm consent suspended*
>   *As over-difficult.*

★　　　★　　　★

Mr Swinburne ... has always been a great poet. But he has his limitations, the chief of which is, curiously enough, an entire lack of any sense of limit. His song is nearly always too loud for his subject. His magnificent rhetoric ... conceals rather than reveals. It has been said of him, and with truth, that he is a master of language, but with still greater truth it may be said that Language is his master. Words seem to dominate him. Alliteration tyrannises over him. Mere sound often becomes his lord. He is so eloquent that whatever he touches becomes unreal.

Review: *Poems and Ballads. Third Series*, by Algernon Charles
Swinburne. *Pall Mall Gazette*, 27 June 1889

☆

To be at one with the elements seems to be Mr Swinburne's aim. He seeks to speak with the breath of wind and wave. The roar of the fire is ever in his ears. He puts his clarion to the lips of Spring and bids her blow, and the Earth wakes from her dreams and tells him her secret. He is the first lyric poet who has tried to make an absolute surrender of his own personality, and he has succeeded. We hear the song, but we never know the singer. We never even get near to him. Out of the thunder and splendour of words he himself says nothing. We have often had man's interpretation of Nature; now we have Nature's interpretation of man, and she has curiously little to say. Force and Freedom form her vague message. She deafens us with her clangours.

Review: *Poems and Ballads. Third Series*, by Algernon Charles
Swinburne. *Pall Mall Gazette*, 27 June 1889

★　　★　　★

'. . . He was an extraordinary old aristocrat, who swore like a coster-
monger, and had the manners of a farmer. . .'

The Portrait of Mr W. H., originally published in shorter form,
Blackwood's Magazine, July 1889

☆

'. . . Freckles run in Scotch families just as gout does in English families . . .'

☆

'. . . People who did not like him, Philistines and college tutors, and
young men reading for the Church, used to say that he was merely
pretty. . .'

☆

'He was often wilful and petulant, and I used to think him dreadfully
insincere. It was due, I think, chiefly to his inordinate desire to please
. . .'

☆

'. . . All charming people, I fancy, are spoiled. It is the secret of their
attraction . . .'

☆

'. . . You will laugh at me, but I assure you that Cyril Graham was the
only perfect Rosalind I have ever seen. . . . the part might have been
written for him . . .'

☆

'. . . It is always a silly thing to give advice, but to give good advice is
absolutely fatal. I hope you will never fall into that error. If you do,
you will be sorry for it . . .'

☆

'. . . The only apostle who did not deserve proof was St Thomas, and
St Thomas was the only apostle who got it . . .'

☆

'. . . You forget that a thing is not necessarily true because a man dies
for it . . .'

☆

'. . . I am sorry I told you anything about it, and very sorry indeed that

I should have converted you to a thing in which I don't believe.'

☆

'. . . let me advise you not to waste your time over the Sonnets. . . what do they tell us about Shakespeare? Simply that he was the slave of beauty.'
'Well, that is the condition of being an artist!'

☆

The great events of life often leave one unmoved; they pass out of consciousness, and, when one thinks of them, become unreal. Even the scarlet flowers of passion seem to grow in the same meadow as the poppies of oblivion. We reject the burden of their memory, and have anodynes against them. But the little things, the things of no moment, remain with us. In some tiny ivory cell the brain stores the most delicate, and the most fleeting impressions.

☆

. . . in my Lord Pembroke days, if I may so term them, I must admit that it had always seemed to me very difficult to understand how the creator of Hamlet and Lear and Othello could have addressed in such extravagant terms of praise and passion one who was merely an ordinary young nobleman of the day.

☆

To have discovered the true name of Mr W. H. was comparatively nothing: others might have done that, had perhaps done it: but to have discovered his profession was a revolution in criticism.

☆

. . . Shakespeare himself was a player, and wrote for players. He saw the possibilities that lay hidden in an art that up to his time had expressed itself but in bombast or in clowning. He has left us the most perfect rules for acting that have ever been written. He has created parts that can be only truly revealed to us on the stage, wrote plays that need the theatre for their full realisation, and we cannot marvel that he so worshipped one who was the interpreter of his vision, as he was the incarnation of his dreams.

☆

'The fear of the Lord is the beginning of wisdom', said the stern Hebrew prophet. 'The beginning of wisdom is Love', was the gracious message of the Greek.

☆

It is no doubt true that to be filled with an absorbing passion is to surrender the security of one's lower life, and yet in such surrender there
may be gain, certainly there was for Shakespeare.

The Portrait of Mr W. H., originally published in shorter form,
Blackwoods Magazine, July 1889

☆

In Willie Hughes, Shakespeare found not merely a most delicate instrument for the presentation of his art, but the visible incarnation of
his idea of beauty, and it is not too much to say that to this young
actor, whose very name the dull writers of his age forgot to chronicle,
the Romantic Movement of English Literature is largely indebted.

☆

Of all the motives of dramatic curiosity used by our great playwrights,
there is none more subtle or more fascinating than the ambiguity of the
sexes.

☆

To say that only a woman can portray the passions of a woman, and
that therefore no boy can play Rosalind, is to rob the art of acting of all
claim to objectivity, and to assign to the mere accident of sex what properly belongs to imaginative insight and creative energy.

☆

Sincerity itself, the ardent, momentary sincerity of the artist, is often
the unconscious result of style, and in the case of those rare temperaments that are exquisitely susceptible to the influences of language, the
use of certain phrases and modes of expression can stir the very pulse
of passion, can send the red blood coursing through the veins, and can
transform into a strange sensuous energy what in its origin had been
mere aesthetic impulse, and desire of art.

☆

We become lovers when we see Romeo and Juliet, and Hamlet makes
us students. The blood of Duncan is upon our hands, with Timon we
rage against the world, and when Lear wanders out upon the heath the
terror of madness touches us. Ours is the white sinlessness of Des-
demona, and ours, also, the sin of Iago. Art, even the art of fullest
scope and widest vision, can never really show us the external world.
All that it shows us is our own soul, the one world of which we have
any real cognizance. . . . It is Art, and Art only, that reveals us to ourselves.

☆

The soul had a life of its own, and the brain its own sphere of action.

There was something within us that knew nothing of sequence or extension, and yet . . . was the spectator of all time and of all existence. It had senses that quickened, passions that came to birth, spiritual ecstasies of contemplation, ardours of fiery-coloured love. It was we who were unreal, and our conscious life was the least important part of our development. The soul, the secret soul, was the only reality.

☆

. . . once in Egypt I had been present at the opening of a frescoed coffin that had been found in one of the basalt tombs at Thebes. Inside there was the body of a young girl swathed in tight bands of linen, and with a gilt mask over her face. As I stooped down to look at it, I had seen that one of the little withered hands held a scroll of yellow papyrus covered with strange characters. How I wished now that I had it read to me! It might have told me something more about the soul that hid within me, and had its mysteries of passion of which I was kept in ignorance. . . Were we to look in tombs for our real life, and in art for the legend of our days?

☆

Martyrdom was to me merely a tragic form of scepticism, an attempt to realise by fire what one had failed to do by faith. No man dies for what he knows to be true. Men die for what they want to be true, for what some terror in their hearts tells them is not true.

★   ★   ★

Books of poetry by young writers are usually promissory notes that are never met. Now and then, however, one comes across a volume that is so far above the average that one can hardly resist the fascinating temptation of recklessly prophesying a fine future for its author. Such a book Mr Yeats's *Wanderings of Oisin* certainly is. Here we find nobility of treatment and nobility of subject matter, delicacy of poetic instinct and richness of imaginative resource. Unequal and uneven much of the work must be admitted to be. Mr Yeats does not try to 'out-baby' Wordsworth, we are glad to say, but he occasionally succeeds in 'out-glittering' Keats, and here and there in his book we come across strange crudities and irritating conceits. But when he is at his best he is very good. If he has not the grand simplicity of epic treatment, he has at least something of the largeness of vision that belongs to the epical temper. He does not rob of their stature the great heroes of Celtic mythology. He is very naïve and very primitive and speaks of his giants with the awe of a child.

Pall Mall Gazette, 12 July 1889

1890

It is clear that Chuang Tsū is a very dangerous writer, and the publication of his book in English, two thousand years after his death, is obviously premature, and may cause a great deal of pain to many thoroughly respectable and industrious persons. It may be true that the ideal of self-culture and self-development, which is the aim of his scheme of life, and the basis of his scheme of philosophy, is an ideal somewhat needed by an age like ours, in which most people are so anxious to educate their neighbours that they have actually no time left in which to educate themselves. But would it be wise to say so? It seems to me that if we once admitted the force of any one of Chuang Tsū's destructive criticisms we should have to put some check on our national habit of self-glorification; and the only thing that ever consoles man for the stupid things he does is the praise he always gives himself for doing them. There may, however, be a few who have grown wearied of that strange modern tendency that sets enthusiasm to do the work of the intellect. To these, and such as these, Chuang Tsū will be welcome. But let them only read him. Let them not talk about him. He would be disturbing at dinner-parties, and impossible at afternoon teas, and his whole life was a protest against platform speaking. 'The perfect man ignores self; the divine man ignores action; the true sage ignores reputation.' These are the principles of Chuang Tsū.

> Review: *Chuang Tsū: Mystic, Moralist, and Social Reformer*, trans. from
> the Chinese by Herbert A. Giles. *Speaker*, 8 February 1890

★   ★   ★

. . . where there is no exaggeration there is no love, and where there is no love there is no understanding. It is only about things that do not interest one, that one can give a really unbiassed opinion; and this is no doubt the reason why an unbiassed opinion is always valueless.

> Review: *Appreciations, with an Essay on Style*, by Walter Pater.
> *Speaker*, 22 March 1890

☆

. . . he to whom the present is the only thing that is present, knows nothing of the age in which he lives. To realise the nineteenth century one must realise every century that has preceded it, and that has contributed to its making. To know anything about oneself, one must know all about others. There must be no mood with which one cannot sympathise, no dead mode of life that one cannot make alive.

☆

. . . the true critic is he who bears within himself the dreams and ideas and feelings of myriad generations, and to whom no form of thought is alien, no emotional impulse obscure.

☆

The difference between the classical and romantic spirits in art has often, and with much over-emphasis, been discussed. But with what a light sure touch does Mr Pater write of it! How subtle and certain are his distinctions! If imaginative prose be really the special art of this century, Mr Pater must rank among our century's most characteristic artists. In certain things he stands almost alone. The age has produced wonderful prose styles, turbid with individualism, and violent with excess of rhetoric. But in Mr Pater, as in Cardinal Newman, we find the union of personality with perfection.

★　　　★　　　★

In the summer term Oxford teaches the exquisite art of idleness, one of the most important things that any University can teach, and possibly as the first-fruits of the dreaming in grey cloister and silent garden, which either makes or mars a man, there has just appeared in that lovely city a dainty and delightful volume of poems by four friends . . . On the whole *Primavera* is a pleasant little book, and we are glad to welcome it. It is charmingly 'got up', and undergraduates might read it with advantage during lecture-hours.

Review: *Primavera: Poems*, by [Laurence Binyon, Manmohan Ghose, Stephen Phillips, and Arthur Cripps], *Pall Mall Gazette*, 24 May 1890

★　　　★　　　★

ERNEST . . . modern memoirs . . . are generally written by people who have either entirely lost their memories, or have never done anything worth remembering; which, however, is, no doubt, the true explanation of their popularity, as the English public always feels perfectly at its ease when a mediocrity is talking to it.

'The Critic as Artist, Part I: with Some Remarks on the Importance of Doing Nothing', *Nineteenth Century*, July 1890, as 'The True Function and Value of Criticism'

☆

GILBERT . . . the public is wonderfully tolerant. It forgives everything except genius.

☆

GILBERT In literature mere egotism is delightful. It is what fascinates us in the letters of personalities so different as Cicero and Balzac, Flaubert and Berlioz, Byron and Madame de Sévigné. Whenever we come across it, and, strangely enough, it is rather rare, we cannot but welcome it, and do not easily forget it. Humanity will always love Rousseau for having confessed his sins, not to a priest, but to the world . . .

'The Critic as Artist, Part I: with Some Remarks on the Importance of Doing Nothing', *Nineteenth Century*, July 1890, as 'The True Function and Value of Criticism';

☆

GILBERT We are overrun by a set of people who, when poet or painter passes away, arrive at the house along with the undertaker, and forget that their one duty is to behave as mutes. But we won't talk about them. They are the mere body-snatchers of literature. The dust is given to one, and the ashes to another, and the soul is out of their reach.

☆

GILBERT I can fancy a man who had led a perfect commonplace life, hearing by chance some curious piece of music, and suddenly discovering that his soul, without his being conscious of it, had passed through terrible experiences, and known fearful joys, or wild romantic loves, or great renunciations.

☆

ERNEST If a man's work is easy to understand, an explanation is unnecessary –
GILBERT And if his work is incomprehensible, an explanation is wicked.
ERNEST I did not say that.
GILBERT Ah! but you should have. Nowadays, we have so few mysteries left to us that we cannot afford to part with one of them.

☆

GILBERT If Shakespeare could sing with myriad lips, Browning could stammer through a thousand mouths.

☆

GILBERT Yes, Browning was great. And as what will he be remembered? As a poet? Ah, not as a poet! He will be remembered as a writer of fiction, as the most supreme writer of fiction, it may be, that we have ever had. His sense of dramatic situation was unrivalled, and, if he could not answer his own problems, he could at least put problems forth, and what more should an artist do?

... Meredith is a prose Browning, and so is Browning. He used poetry as a medium for writing in prose.

☆

ERNEST ... in the best days of art there were no art-critics.
GILBERT I seem to have heard that observation before, Ernest. It has all the vitality of error and all the tediousness of an old friend.

☆

GILBERT I am afraid that you have been listening to the conversation of some one older than yourself. That is always a dangerous thing to do, and if you allow it to degenerate into a habit you will find it absolutely fatal to any intellectual development.

☆

GILBERT As for modern journalism, it is not my business to defend it. It justifies its own existence by the great Darwinian principle of the survival of the vulgarest.

☆

ERNEST But what is the difference between literature and journalism?
GILBERT Oh! journalism is unreadable, and literature is not read. That is all.

☆

GILBERT To give an accurate description of what has never occurred is not merely the proper occupation of the historian, but the inalienable privilege of any man of parts and culture.

☆

GILBERT Learned conversation is either the affectation of the ignorant or the profession of the mentally unemployed.

☆

GILBERT ... improving conversation ... is merely the foolish method by which the still more foolish philanthropist feebly tries to disarm the just rancour of the criminal classes.

☆

GILBERT I am but too conscious of the fact that we are born in an age when only the dull are treated seriously, and I live in terror of not being misunderstood.

☆

GILBERT Since the introduction of printing, and the fatal development of the habit of reading amongst the middle and lower classes of this country, there has been a tendency in literature to appeal more and more to the eye, and less and less to the ear which is really the sense which, from the standpoint of pure art, it should seek to please, and by whose canons of pleasure it should abide always.

'The Critic as Artist, Part I: with Some Remarks on the Importance of Doing Nothing', *Nineteenth Century*, July 1890, as 'The True Function and Value of Criticism';

☆

GILBERT We, in fact, have made writing a definite mode of composition, and have treated it as a form of elaborate design. The Greeks, upon the other hand, regarded writing simply as a method of chronicling. Their test was always the spoken word in its musical and metrical relations. The voice was the medium, and the ear the critic.

☆

GILBERT Yes: writing has done much harm to writers. We must return to the voice.

☆

GILBERT Whatever, in fact, is modern in our life we owe to the Greeks. Whatever is an anachronism is due to mediaevalism.

☆

ERNEST . . . the creative faculty is higher than the critical. There is really no comparison between them.
GILBERT The antithesis between them is entirely arbitrary. Without the critical faculty, there is no artistic creation at all, worthy of the name.

☆

GILBERT All fine imaginative work is self-conscious and deliberate. No poet sings because he must sing. At least, no great poet does. A great poet sings because he chooses to sing. It is so now, and it has always been so.

☆

GILBERT . . . there is no fine art without self-consciousness, and self-consciousness and the critical spirit are one.

☆

GILBERT . . . I am inclined to think that each myth and legend that seems to us to spring out of the wonder, or terror, or fancy of tribe and nation, was in its origin the invention of one single mind. The curiously limited number of the myths seems to me to point to this conclusion.

☆

GILBERT Mediocrity weighing mediocrity in the balance, and incompetence applauding its brother – that is the spectacle which the artistic activity of England affords us from time to time.

☆

GILBERT Anybody can write a three-volumed novel. It merely requires a complete ignorance of both life and literature.

☆

GILBERT The poor reviewers are apparently reduced to be the reporters of the police-court of literature, the chroniclers of the doings of the habitual criminals of art.

☆

GILBERT I am aware that there are many honest workers in painting as well as in literature who object to criticism entirely. They are quite right. Their work stands in no intellectual relation to their age. It brings us no new element of pleasure. It suggests no fresh departure of thought, or passion, or beauty. It should not be spoken of. It should be left to the oblivion that it deserves.

☆

GILBERT It is very much more difficult to talk about a thing than to do it. In the sphere of actual life that is of course obvious. Anybody can make history. Only a great man can write it.

☆

GILBERT . . . action . . . is a blind thing dependent on external influences, and moved by an impulse of whose nature it is unconscious. It is a thing incomplete in its essence, because limited by accident, and ignorant of its direction, being always at variance with its aim. Its basis is the lack of imagination. It is the last resource of those who know not how to dream.

☆

GILBERT The one duty we owe to history is to rewrite it.

☆

GILBERT It is because Humanity has never known where it was going that it has been able to find its way.

'The Critic as Artist, Part I: with Some Remarks on the Importance
of Doing Nothing', *Nineteenth Century*, July 1890, as 'The True
Function and Value of Criticism';

☆

GILBERT What is termed Sin is an essential element of progress. Without it the world would stagnate, or grow old, or become colourless. By its curiosity Sin increases the experience of the race.
Through its intensified assertion of individualism, it saves us from
monotony of type. In its rejection of the current notions about
morality, it is one with the higher ethics.

☆

GILBERT Nature, M. Renan tells us, cares little about chastity, and it
may be that it is to the shame of the Magdalen, and not to their
own purity, that the Lucretias of modern life owe their freedom
from stain.

☆

GILBERT Charity, as even those of whose religion it makes a formal part
have been compelled to acknowledge, creates a multitude of evils.
The mere existence of conscience, that faculty of which people
prate so much nowadays, and are so ignorantly proud, is a sign of
our imperfect development. It must be merged in instinct before
we become fine.

☆

GILBERT It is well for our vanity that we slay the criminal, for if we suffered him to live he might show us what we had gained by his
crime. It is well for his peace that the saint goes to his martyrdom.
He is spared the sight of the horror of his harvest.

☆

GILBERT Action! What is action? It dies at the moment of its energy. It
is a base concession to fact. The world is made by the singer for
the dreamer.

☆

GILBERT The critic occupies the same relation to the work of art that he
criticises as the artist does to the visible world of form and colour,
or the unseen world of passion and of thought. He does not even
require for the perfection of his art the finest materials. Anything
will serve his purpose.

☆

GILBERT That is what the highest criticism really is, the record of one's own soul. It is more fascinating than history, as it is concerned simply with oneself. It is more delightful than philosophy, as its subject is concrete and not abstract, real and not vague. It is the only civilised form of autobiography, as it deals not with the events, but with the thoughts of one's life; not with life's physical accidents of deed or circumstance, but with the spiritual moods and imaginative passions of the mind.

☆

GILBERT The best that one can say of most modern creative art is that it is just a little less vulgar than reality, and so the critic, with his fine sense of distinction and sure instinct of delicate refinement, will prefer to look into the silver mirror or through the woven veil, and will turn his eyes away from the chaos and clamour of actual existence, though the mirror be tarnished and the veil be torn. His sole aim is to chronicle his own impressions. It is for him that pictures are painted, books written, and marble hewn into form.

☆

GILBERT . . . Criticism's most perfect form . . . is in its essence purely subjective, and seeks to reveal its own secret and not the secret of another. For the highest Criticism deals with art not as expressive but as impressive purely.

☆

GILBERT Who cares whether Mr Ruskin's views on Turner are sound or not? What does it matter? That mighty and majestic prose of his, so fervid and so fiery-coloured in its noble eloquence, so rich in its elaborate symphonic music, so sure and certain, at its best, in subtle choice of word and epithet, is at least as great a work of art as any of those wonderful sunsets that bleach or rot on their corrupted canvases in England's Gallery . . .

☆

GILBERT It is sometimes said that the tragedy of an artist's life is that he cannot realise his ideal. But the true tragedy that dogs the steps of most artists is that they realise their ideal too absolutely. For, when the ideal is realised, it is robbed of its wonder and its mystery, and becomes simply a new starting-point for an ideal that is other than itself. That is the reason why music is the perfect type of art. Music can never reveal its ultimate secret.

☆

GILBERT It is through its very incompleteness that Art becomes complete in beauty, and so addresses itself, not to the faculty of recognition nor to the faculty of reason, but to the aesthetic sense alone . . .

'The Critic as Artist, Part I: with Some Remarks on the Importance of Doing Nothing', *Nineteenth Century*, July 1890, as 'The True Function and Value of Criticism';

☆

ERNEST Ah! you admit, then, that the critic may occasionally be allowed to see the object as in itself it really is.

GILBERT I am not quite sure. Perhaps I may admit it after supper. There is a subtle influence in supper.

★   ★   ★

GILBERT The critic will certainly be an interpreter, but he will not treat Art as a riddling Sphinx, whose shallow secret may be guessed and revealed by one whose feet are wounded and who knows not his name. Rather, he will look upon Art as a goddess whose mystery it is his province to intensify, and whose majesty his privilege to make more marvellous in the eyes of men.

'The Critic as Artist. Part II. With Some Remarks upon the Importance of Discussing Everything', *Nineteenth Century*, September 1890

☆

GILBERT . . . just as it is only by contact with the art of foreign nations that the art of a country gains that individual and separate life that we call nationality, so, by curious inversion, it is only by intensifying his own personality that the critic can interpret the personality and work of others . . .

☆

GILBERT The actor is a critic of the drama. He shows the poet's work under new conditions, and by a method special to himself. He takes the written word, and action, gesture and voice become the media of revelation. The singer, or the player on lute and viol, is the critic of music.

☆

GILBERT In point of fact, there is no such thing as Shakespeare's Hamlet. If Hamlet has something of the definiteness of a work of art, he has also all the obscurity that belongs to life. There are as many Hamlets as there are melancholies.

☆

GILBERT . . . as civilisation progresses and we become more highly organised, the elect spirits of each age, the critical and cultured spirits, will grow less and less interested in actual life, and *will seek to gain their impressions almost entirely from what Art has touched.* For Life is terribly deficient in form. Its catastrophes happen in the wrong way and to the wrong people. There is a grotesque horror about its comedies, and its tragedies seem to culminate in farce. One is always wounded when one approaches it. Things last either too long, or not long enough.

✩

GILBERT What are the unreal things, but the passions that once burned one like fire? What are the incredible things, but the things that one has faithfully believed?

✩

GILBERT . . . life cheats us with shadows, like a puppet-master. We ask it for pleasure. It gives it to us, with bitterness and disappointment in its train. We come across some noble grief that we think will lend the purple dignity of tragedy to our days, but it passes away from us, and things less noble take its place, and on some grey windy dawn, or odorous eve of silence and of silver, we find ourselves looking with callous wonder, or dull heart of stone, at the tress of gold-flecked hair that we had once so wildly worshipped and so madly kissed.

✩

GILBERT . . . the chief thing that makes life a failure from this artistic point of view is the thing that lends to life its sordid security, the fact that one can never repeat exactly the same emotion. How different it is in the world of Art! On a shelf of the bookcase behind you stands the *Divine Comedy*, and I know that, if I open it at a certain place, I shall be filled with a fierce hatred of some one who has never wronged me, or stirred by a great love for some one whom I shall never see.

✩

GILBERT Yes, we can put the earth back six hundred courses and make ourselves one with the great Florentine, kneel at the same altar with him, and share his rapture and his scorn. And if we grow tired of an antique time, and desire to realise our own age in all its weariness and sin, are there not books that can make us live more in one single hour than life can make us live in a score of shameful years?

✩

GILBERT It is a strange thing, this transference of emotion. We sicken

133

with the same maladies as the poets, and the singer lends us his pain. Dead lips have their message for us, and hearts that have fallen to dust can communicate their joy. We run to kiss the bleeding mouth of Fantine, and we follow Manon Lescaut over the whole world. Ours is the love-madness of the Tyrian, and the terror of Orestes is ours also. There is no passion that we cannot feel, no pleasure that we may not gratify, and we can choose the time of our initiation and the time of our freedom also.

'The Critic as Artist. Part II. With Some Remarks upon the Importance of Discussing Everything', *Nineteenth Century*, September 1890

☆

GILBERT Don't let us go to life for our fulfilment or our experience. It is a thing narrowed by circumstances, incoherent in its utterance, and without that fine correspondence of form and spirit which is the only thing that can satisfy the artistic and critical temperament. It makes us pay too high a price for its wares, and we purchase the meanest of its secrets at a cost that is monstrous and infinite.

ERNEST Must we go, then, to Art for everything?

GILBERT For everything. Because Art does not hurt us. The tears that we shed at a play are a type of the exquisite sterile emotions that it is the function of Art to awaken. We weep, but we are not wounded. We grieve, but our grief is not bitter.

☆

GILBERT It is through Art, and through Art only, that we can realise our perfection; through Art, and through Art only, that we can shield ourselves from the sordid perils of actual existence. . . One can feel so much, and no more. And how can it matter with what pleasure life tries to tempt one, or with what pain it seeks to maim and mar one's soul, if in the spectacle of the lives of those who have never existed one has found the true secret of joy, and wept away one's tears over their deaths who, like Cordelia and the daughter of Brabantio, can never die?

☆

GILBERT Society often forgives the criminal; it never forgives the dreamer.

☆

GILBERT . . . to do nothing at all is the most difficult thing in the world, the most difficult and the most intellectual.

☆

GILBERT The world through which the Academic philosopher becomes 'the spectator of all time and of all existence' is not really an ideal world, but simply a world of abstract ideal. When we enter it, we starve amidst the chill mathematics of thought. The courts of the city of God are not open to us now. Its gates are guarded by Ignorance, and to pass them we have to surrender all that in our nature is most divine. It is enough that our fathers believed. They have exhausted the faith-faculty of the species. Their legacy to us is the scepticism of which they were afraid. Had they put it into words, it might not live within us as thought.

☆

GILBERT By revealing to us the absolute mechanism of all action, and so freeing us from the self-imposed and trammelling burden of moral responsibility, the scientific principle of Heredity has become, as it were, the warrant for the contemplative life. It has shown us that we are never less free than when we try to act. It has hemmed us round with the nets of the hunter, and written upon the wall the prophecy of our doom. We may not watch it, for it is within us. We may not see it, save in a mirror that mirrors the soul. It is Nemesis without her mask. It is the last of the Fates, and the most terrible. It is the only one of the Gods whose real name we know.

☆

GILBERT . . . it is not our own life that we live, but the lives of the dead, and the soul that dwells within us is no single spiritual entity, making us personal and individual, created for our service, and entering into us for our joy. It is something that has dwelt in fearful places, and in ancient sepulchres has made its abode. It is sick with many maladies, and has memories of curious sins. It is wiser than we are, and its wisdom is bitter. It fills us with impossible desires, and makes us follow what we know we cannot gain.

☆

GILBERT There is no country in the world so much in need of unpractical people as this country of ours. With us, Thought is degraded by its constant association with practice.

☆

GILBERT Each of the professions means a prejudice.

☆

GILBERT The prig is a very interesting psychological study, and though

of all poses a moral pose is the most offensive, still to have a pose
at all is something.

'The Critic as Artist. Part II. With Some Remarks upon the
Importance of Discussing Everything', *Nineteenth Century*, September
1890

☆

GILBERT That Humanitarian Sympathy wars against Nature, by secur-
ing the survival of the failure, may make the man of science loathe
its facile virtues. The political economist may cry out against it for
putting the improvident on the same level as the provident, and
so robbing life of the strongest, because most sordid, incentive to
industry.

☆

GILBERT . . . when the revolution or crisis arrives, we shall be power-
less, because we shall know nothing.

☆

GILBERT England will never be civilised till she has added Utopia to
her dominions. There is more than one of her colonies that she
might with advantage surrender for so fair a land. What we want
are unpractical people who see beyond the moment, and think
beyond the day. Those why try to lead the people can only do so
by following the mob. It is through the voice of one crying in the
wilderness that the ways of the gods must be prepared.

☆

GILBERT It takes a thoroughly selfish age, like our own, to deify self-
sacrifice. It takes a thoroughly grasping age, such as that in which
we live, to set above the fine intellectual virtues, those shallow
and emotional virtues that are an immediate practical benefit to
itself.

☆

GILBERT How appalling is that ignorance which is the inevitable result
of the fatal habit of imparting opinions! How limited in range the
creature's mind proves to be! How it wearies us, and must weary
himself, with its endless repetitions and sickly reiteration! How
lacking it is in any element of intellectual growth! In what a
vicious circle it always moves!

☆

GILBERT People say that the schoolmaster is abroad. I wish to goodness
he were.

☆

GILBERT . . . the real weakness of England lies, not in incomplete arma-
ments or unfortified coasts, not in the poverty that creeps through
sunless lanes, or the drunkenness that brawls in loathsome courts,
but simply in the fact that her ideals are emotional and not intellectual.

☆

GILBERT An idea that is not dangerous is unworthy of being called an
idea at all.

☆

GILBERT The security of society lies in custom and unconscious instinct, and the basis of the stability of society, as a healthy organism, is in the complete absence of any intelligence amongst its
members. The great majority of people being fully aware of this,
rank themselves naturally on the side of that splendid system that
elevates them to the dignity of machines, and rage so wildly
against the intrusion of the intellectual faculty into any question
that concerns life, that one is tempted to define man as a rational
animal who always loses his temper when he is called upon to act
in accordance with the dictates of reason.

☆

GILBERT . . . out of ourselves we can never pass, nor can there be in
creation what in the creator was not . . . Shakespeare might have
met Rosencrantz and Guildenstern in the white streets of London,
or seen the serving-men of rival houses bite their thumbs at each
other in the open square; but Hamlet came out of his soul, and
Romeo out of his passion.

☆

GILBERT Action being limited would have left Shakespeare unsatisfied
and unexpressed; and, just as it is because he did nothing that he
has been able to achieve everything, so it is because he never
speaks to us of himself in his plays that his plays reveal him to us
absolutely, and show us his true nature and temperament far
more completely than do those strange and exquisite sonnets,
even, in which he bares to crystal eyes the secret closet of his
heart.

☆

GILBERT Man is least himself when he talks in his own person. Give
him a mask, and he will tell you the truth.

☆

GILBERT . . . each mode of criticism is, in its highest development, simply a mood, and . . . we are never more true to ourselves than when we are inconsistent.

> 'The Critic as Artist. Part II. With Some Remarks upon the Importance of Discussing Everything', *Nineteenth Century*, September 1890

☆

GILBERT What other people call one's past has, no doubt, everything to do with them, but has absolutely nothing to do with oneself. The man who regards his past is a man who deserves to have no future to look forward to. When one has found expression for a mood, one has done with it.

☆

GILBERT Dialogue . . . that wonderful literary form which . . . the creative critics of the world have always employed, can never lose for the thinker its attraction as a mode of expression. By its means he can both reveal and conceal himself, and give form to every fancy, and reality to every mood . . .

ERNEST By its means, too, he can invent an imaginary antagonist, and convert him when he chooses by some absurdly sophistical argument.

☆

GILBERT . . . it is so easy to convert others. It is so difficult to convert oneself. To arrive at what one really believes, one must speak through lips different from one's own.

☆

GILBERT . . . what is Truth? In matters of religion, it is simply the opinion that has survived. In matters of science, it is the ultimate sensation. In matters of art, it is one's last mood.

☆

GILBERT There are two ways of disliking art, Ernest. One is to dislike it. The other, to like it rationally.

☆

GILBERT A little sincerity is a dangerous thing, and a great deal of it is absolutely fatal. The true critic . . . will not consent to be the slave of his own opinions. For what is mind but motion in the intellectual sphere? The essence of thought, as the essence of life, is growth.

☆

GILBERT . . . there is much to be said in favour of modern journalism. By giving us the opinions of the uneducated, it keeps us in touch with the ignorance of the community. By carefully chronicling the current events of contemporary life, it shows us of what very little importance such events really are. By invariably discussing the unnecessary, it makes us understand what things are requisite for culture, and what are not.

☆

GILBERT . . . though the mission of the aesthetic movement is to lure people to contemplate, not to lead them to create, yet, as the creative instinct is strong in the Celt, and it is the Celt who leads in art, there is no reason why in future years this strange Renaissance should not become almost as mighty in its way as was that new birth of Art that woke many centuries ago in the cities of Italy.

☆

GILBERT Modern pictures are, no doubt, delightful to look at. At least, some of them are. But they are quite impossible to live with, they are too clever, too assertive, too intellectual. Their meaning is too obvious, and their method too clearly defined. One exhausts what they have to say in a very short time, and then they become as tedious as one's relations.

☆

GILBERT Forms are the food of faith, cried Newman in one of those great moments of sincerity that make us admire and know the man. He was right, though he may not have known how terribly right he was. The Creeds are believed, not because they are rational, but because they are repeated.

☆

GILBERT It is always with the best intentions that the worst work is done. And besides, my dear Ernest, when a man reaches the age of forty, or becomes a Royal Academician, or is elected a member of the Athenaeum Club, or is recognised as a popular novelist, whose books are in great demand at suburban railway stations, one may have the amusement of exposing him, but one cannot have the pleasure of reforming him.

☆

GILBERT That very concentration of vision that makes a man an artist, limits by its sheer intensity his faculty of fine appreciation. The energy of creation hurries him blindly on to his own goal. The wheels of his chariot raise the dust as a cloud around him. The gods are hidden from each other. They can recognise their worshippers. That is all.

'The Critic as Artist. Part II. With Some Remarks upon the Importance of Discussing Everything', *Nineteenth Century*, September 1890

☆

GILBERT An idea that is not dangerous is unworthy of being called an idea at all.

☆

GILBERT Bad artists always admire each other's work. They call it being large-minded and free from prejudice. But a truly great artist cannot conceive of life being shown, or beauty fashioned, under any conditions other than those that he has selected. Creation employs all its critical faculty within its own sphere. It may not use it in the sphere that belongs to others. It is exactly because a man cannot do a thing that he is the proper judge of it.

☆

GILBERT Technique is really personality. That is the reason why the artist cannot teach it, why the pupil cannot learn it, and why the aesthetic critic can understand it. To the great poet, there is only one method of music – his own. To the great painter, there is only one manner of painting – that which he himself employs. The aesthetic critic, and the aesthetic critic alone, can appreciate all forms and modes. It is to him that Art makes her appeal.

☆

GILBERT The subject-matter at the disposal of creation becomes every day more limited in extent and variety. Providence and Mr Walter Besant have exhausted the obvious.

☆

GILBERT As one turns over the pages of his *Plain Tales from the Hills*, one feels as if one were seated under a palm-tree reading life by superb flashes of vulgarity. The bright colours of the bazaars dazzle one's eyes. The jaded, second-rate Anglo-Indians are in exquisite incongruity with their surroundings. The mere lack of style in the story-teller gives an odd journalistic realism to what he tells us. From the point of view of literature Mr Kipling is a genius who drops his aspirates. From the point of view of life, he is a reporter who knows vulgarity better than any one has ever known it. Dickens knew its clothes and its comedy. Mr Kipling knows its essence and its seriousness. He is our first authority on the second-rate, and has seen marvellous things through keyholes, and his backgrounds are real works of art.

☆

GILBERT . . . there is still much to be done in the sphere of introspection. People sometimes say that fiction is getting too morbid. As far as psychology is concerned, it has never been morbid enough. We have merely touched the surface of the soul, that is all. In one single ivory cell of the brain there are stored away things more marvellous and more terrible than even they have dreamed of, who, like the author of *Le Rouge et le Noir*, have sought to track the soul into its most secret places, and to make life confess its dearest sins.

☆

GILBERT It is Criticism . . . that makes the mind a fine instrument. We, in our educational system, have burdened the memory with a load of unconnected facts, and laboriously striven to impart our laboriously-acquired knowledge. We teach people how to remember, we never teach them how to grow.

☆

GILBERT England has done one thing; it has invented and established Public Opinion, which is an attempt to organise the ignorance of the community, and to elevate it to the dignity of physical force.

☆

GILBERT . . . where there is no record, and history is either lost or was never written, Criticism can recreate the past for us from the very smallest fragment of language or art, just as surely as the man of science can from some tiny bone, or the mere impress of a foot upon a rock, recreate for us the winged dragon or Titan lizard that once made the earth shake beneath its tread, can call Behemoth out of his cave, and make Leviathan swim once more across the startled sea.

☆

GILBERT . . . philological criticism . . . can give us the exact science of mind in the process of becoming. It can do for us what History cannot do. It can tell us what man thought before he learned how to write.

☆

GILBERT There is only one thing worse than Injustice, and that is

Justice without her sword in her hand. When Right is not Might, it is Evil. . . the emotions will not make us cosmopolitan, any more than the greed for gain could do so. It is only by the cultivation of the habit of intellectual criticism that we shall be able to rise superior to race-prejudices.

'The Critic as Artist. Part II. With Some Remarks upon the
Importance of Discussing Everything', *Nineteenth Century*, September
1890

☆

GILBERT Criticism will annihilate race-prejudices, by insisting upon the unity of the human mind in the variety of its forms. If we are tempted to make war upon another nation, we shall remember that we are seeking to destroy an element of our own culture, and possibly its most important element. As long as war is regarded as wicked, it will always have its fascination. When it is looked upon as vulgar, it will cease to be popular.

☆

GILBERT Intellectual criticism will bind Europe together in bonds far closer than those that can be forged by shopman or sentimentalist. It will give us the peace that springs from understanding.

☆

GILBERT The English mind is always in a rage. The intellect of the race is wasted in the sordid and stupid quarrels of second-rate politicians or third-rate theologians.

☆

GILBERT To be good, according to the vulgar standard of goodness, is obviously quite easy. It merely requires a certain amount of sordid terror, a certain lack of imaginative thought, and a certain low passion for middle-class respectability.

☆

GILBERT Yes: I am a dreamer. For a dreamer is one who can only find his way by moonlight, and his punishment is that he sees the dawn before the rest of the world.
ERNEST His punishment?
GILBERT And his reward.

142

1891

'Is it your best work, Basil, the best thing you have ever done', said Lord Henry, languidly. 'You must certainly send it next year to the Grosvenor. The Academy is too large and too vulgar. Whenever I have gone there, there have been either so many people that I have not been able to see the pictures, which was dreadful, or so many pictures that I have not been able to see the people, which was worse. The Grosvenor is really the only place.'

The Picture of Dorian Gray. Lippincott's Magazine, July 1890. Book (revised and enlarged), April 1891 Chapter 1

☆

'. . . there is only one thing in the world worse than being talked about, and that is not being talked about. A portrait like this would set you far above all the young men in England, and make the old men quite jealous, if old men are ever capable of any emotion.'

☆

'. . . beauty, real beauty, ends where an intellectual expression begins. Intellect is in itself a model of exaggeration, and destroys the harmony of any face. The moment one sits down to think, one becomes all nose, or all forehead, or something horrid. Look at the successful men in any of the learned professions. How perfectly hideous they are! Except, of course, in the Church. But then in the Church they don't think. A bishop keeps on saying at the age of eighty what he was told to say when he was a boy of eighteen, and as a natural consequence he always looks absolutely delightful . . .'

☆

'. . . There is a fatality about all physical and intellectual distinction, the sort of fatality that seems to dog through history the faltering steps of kings. It is better not to be different from one's fellows. The ugly and the stupid have the best of it in this world. They can sit at their ease and gape at the play. If they know nothing of victory, they are at least spared the knowledge of defeat . . .'

☆

143

'. . . I have grown to love secrecy. It seems to be the one thing that can make modern life mysterious or marvellous to us. The commonest thing is delightful if only one hides it. When I leave town now I never tell my people where I am going. If I did, I would lose all my pleasure . . .'

The Picture of Dorian Gray. Lippincott's Magazine, July 1890. Book (revised and enlarged), April 1891 Chapter 1

☆

'. . . the one charm of marriage is that it makes a life of deception absolutely necessary for both parties . . .'

☆

'. . . You never say a moral thing, and you never do a wrong thing. Your cynicism is simply a pose.'
   'Being natural is simply a pose, and the most irritating pose I know'.

☆

'. . . every portrait that is painted with feeling is a portrait of the artist, not of the sitter. The sitter is merely the accident, the occasion . . .'

☆

'. . . I can believe anything, provided that it is quite incredible.'

☆

'. . . With an evening coat and a white tie, as you told me once, anybody, even a stockbroker, can gain a reputation for being civilised . . .'

☆

'Conscience and cowardice are really the same things, Basil. Conscience is the trade-name of the firm. That is all.'

☆

'Laughter is not at all a bad beginning for a friendship, and it is far the best ending for one', said the young lord, plucking another daisy.
. . . 'You don't understand what friendship is, Harry . . . or what enmity is, for that matter. You like every one; that is to say, you are indifferent to every one.'

☆

'. . . I choose my friends for their good looks, my acquaintances for their good characters, and my enemies for their good intellects. A man cannot be too careful in the choice of his enemies . . .'

☆

'Oh, brothers! I don't care for brothers. My elder brother won't die, and my younger brothers seem never to do anything else.'

☆

'. . . I quite sympathise with the rage of the English democracy against what they call the vices of the upper orders. The masses feel that drunkenness, stupidity, and immorality should be their own special property, and that if any of us makes an ass of himself he is poaching on their preserves . . . And yet I don't suppose that ten per cent of the proletariat live correctly.'

☆

'. . . If one puts forward an idea to a true Englishman – always a rash thing to do – he never dreams of considering whether the idea is right or wrong. The only thing he considers of any importance is whether one believes in it oneself. Now, the value of an idea has nothing whatsoever to do with the sincerity of the man who expresses it. Indeed, the probabilities are that the more insincere the man is, the more purely intellectual will the idea be, as in that case it will not be coloured by either his wants, his desires, or his prejudices . . .'

☆

'. . . I like persons better than principles, and I like persons with no principles better than anything else in the world . . .'

☆

'Poets are not so scrupulous as you are. They know how useful passion is for publication. Nowadays a broken heart will run to many editions.'

☆

'. . . An artist should create beautiful things, but should put nothing of his own life into them. We live in an age when men treat art as if it were meant to be a form of autobiography. We have lost the abstract sense of beauty . . .'

☆

'. . . I won't argue with you. It is only the intellectually lost who ever argue . . .'

☆

'. . . It is a sad thing to think of, but there is no doubt that Genius lasts longer than Beauty. This accounts for the fact that we all take such pains to over-educate ourselves. In this wild struggle for existence, we want to have something that endures, and so we fill our minds with rubbish and facts, in the silly hope of keeping our place. The thoroughly well-informed man – that is the modern ideal. And the mind of the thoroughly well-informed man is a dreadful thing. It is like a bric-à-brac shop, all monsters and dust, with everything priced above its proper value . . .'

The Picture of Dorian Gray. Lippincott's Magazine, July 1890. Book
(revised and enlarged), April 1891 Chapter 1

☆

'. . . the worst of having a romance of any kind is that it leaves one so unromantic.'

☆

'. . . Those who are faithful know only the trivial side of love; it is the faithless who know love's tragedies.'

☆

. . . the whole conversation would have been about the feeding of the poor, and the necessity for model lodging-houses. Each class would have preached the importance of those virtues, for whose exercise there was no necessity in their own lives. The rich would have spoken on the value of thrift, and the idle grown eloquent over the dignity of labour.

★   ★   ★

'There is no such thing as a good influence, Mr Gray. All influence is immoral – immoral from the scientific point of view . . . to influence a person is to give him one's own soul. He does not think his natural thoughts or burn with his natural passions. His virtues are not real to him. His sins, if there are such things as sins, are borrowed. He becomes an echo of some one else's music, an actor of a part that has not been written for him. The aim of life is self-development. To realise one's nature perfectly – that is what each of us is here for. People are afraid of themselves, nowadays . . . their own souls starve, and are naked . . .'

The Picture of Dorian Gray, Chapter 2

☆

'. . . the bravest man amongst us is afraid of himself. The mutilation of the savage has its tragic survival in the self-denial that mars our lives . . . The only way to get rid of a temptation is to yield to it. Resist it, and your soul grows sick with longing for the things it has forbidden to itself, with desire for what its monstrous laws have made monstrous and unlawful. It has been said that the great events of the world take place in the brain. It is in the brain, and the brain only, that the great sins of the world take place also . . .'

☆

'Nothing can cure the soul but the senses, just as nothing can cure the senses but the soul.'

☆

'. . . Beauty is a form of Genius – is higher, indeed than Genius, as it needs no explanation . . . It cannot be questioned. It has its divine right of sovereignty . . . People say sometimes that Beauty is only superficial. That may be so. But at least it is not so superficial as Thought is. To me Beauty is the wonder of wonders. It is only shallow people who do not judge by appearances. The true mystery of the world is the visible, not the invisible . . .'

☆

'. . . The pulse of joy that beats in us at twenty, becomes sluggish. Our limbs fail, our senses rot. We degenerate into hideous puppets, haunted by the memory of the passions of which we were too much afraid, and the exquisite temptations that we had not the courage to yield to. Youth! Youth! There is nothing in the world but youth!'

☆

'Always! That is a dreadful word. It makes me shudder when I hear it. Women are so fond of using it. They spoil every romance by trying to make it last for ever. It is a meaningless word, too. The only difference between a caprice and a life-long passion is that the caprice lasts a little longer.'

☆

'. . . If the picture could change, and I could be always what I am now! Why did you paint it? It will mock me some day – mock me horribly!'

☆

'I adore simple pleasures', said Lord Henry. 'They are the last refuge of the complex. But I don't like scenes, except on the stage . . . I wonder who was it defined man as a rational animal. It was the most premature definition ever given. Man is many things, but he is not rational. I am glad he is not, after all . . .'

☆

'. . . I have promised to dine at White's but it is only with an old friend, so I can send him a wire to say that I am ill, or that I am prevented from coming in consequence of a subsequent engagement. I think that would be a rather nice excuse: it would have all the surprise of candour.'

☆

147

'What a fuss people make about fidelity!' exclaimed Lord Henry.
'Why, even in love it is purely a question for physiology. It has nothing
to do with our own will. Young men want to be faithful, and are not;
old men want to be faithless, and cannot: that is all one can say.'

The Picture of Dorian Gray, Chapter 2

★   ★   ★

He paid some attention to the management of his collieries in the
Midland counties, excusing himself for this taint of industry on the
ground that the one advantage of having coal was that it enabled a
gentleman to afford the decency of burning wood on his own hearth.
In politics he was a Tory, except when the Tories were in office, during
which period he roundly abused them for being a pack of Radicals . . .
Only England could have produced him, and he always said that the
country was going to the dogs. His principals were out of date, but
there was a good deal to be said for his prejudices.

The Picture of Dorian Gray, Chapter 3

☆

'. . . When I was in the Diplomatic, things were much better. But I
hear they let them in now by examination. What can you expect?
Examinations, sir, are pure humbug from beginning to end. If a man is
a gentleman, he knows quite enough, and if he is not a gentleman,
whatever he knows is bad for him.'

☆

'American girls are as clever at concealing their parents as English
women are at concealing their past'.

☆

'. . . I am told that pork-packing is the most lucrative profession in
America, after politics.'

☆

'She behaves as if she was beautiful. Most American women do. It is
the secret of their charm.'
   'Why can't these American women stay in their own country? They
are always telling us that it is the Paradise for women.'
   'It is. That is why, like Eve, they are so excessively anxious to get
out of it'.

☆

'. . . I always like to know everything about my new friends, and
nothing about my old ones.'

☆

'. . . Philanthropic people lose all sense of humanity. It is their distinguishing characteristic.'

☆

. . . Sir Thomas Burden, a Radical member of Parliament, . . . followed his leader in public life, and in private life followed the best cooks, dining with the Tories, and thinking with the Liberals, in accordance with a wise and well-known rule . . . Mr Erskine of Treadley, an old gentleman of considerable charm and culture, had fallen, however, into bad habits of silence, having, as he explained once to Lady Agatha, said everything that he had to say before he was thirty . . . Mrs Vandeleur, one of his aunt's oldest friends, a perfect saint amongst women, but so dreadfully dowdy that she reminded one of a badly bound hymn-book . . . was conversing in that intensely earnest manner which is the one unpardonable error . . . that all really good people fall into, and from which none of them ever quite escape.

☆

'Do you think he will really marry this fascinating young person?'
   'I believe she has made up her mind to propose to him, Duchess.'
   . . . 'I am told, on excellent authority, that her father keeps an American dry-goods store', said Sir Thomas Burden, looking super-cilious.
   'Dry-goods! What are American dry-goods?' asked the Duchess, raising her large hands in wonder, and accentuating the verb.
   'American novels', answered Lord Henry, helping himself to some quail.

☆

Like all people who try to exhaust a subject, he exhausted his listeners.

☆

'Perhaps, after all, America never has been discovered', said Mr Erskine. 'I myself would say that it had merely been detected.'

☆

'. . . They get all their dresses in Paris. I wish I could afford to do the same.'
   'They say that when good Americans die they go to Paris', chuckled Sir Thomas, who had a large wardrobe of Humour's cast-off clothes.
   'Really! And where do bad Americans go to when they die?' in-quired the Duchess.
   'They go to America', murmured Lord Henry.

☆

'. . . Yes, Mr Erskine, an absolutely reasonable people. I assure you there is no nonsense about the Americans.'

'How dreadful!' cried Lord Henry. 'I can stand brute force, but brute reason is quite unbearable. There is something unfair about its use. It is hitting below the intellect.'

The Picture of Dorian Gray, Chapter 3

☆

'. . . the way of paradoxes is the way of truth. To test Reality we must see it on the tight-rope. When the Verities become acrobats we can judge them.'

☆

'I can sympathise with everything, except suffering . . . I cannot sympathise with that. It is too ugly, too horrible, too distressing. There is something terribly morbid in the modern sympathy with pain. One should sympathise with the colour, the beauty, the joy of life. The less said about life's sores the better.'

'Still the East End is a very important problem', remarked Sir Thomas, with a grave shake of the head.

'Quite so', answered the young lord. 'It is the problem of slavery, and we try to solve it by amusing the slaves.'

☆

'Humanity takes itself too seriously. It is the world's original sin. If the caveman had known how to laugh, History would have been different.'

☆

'To get back one's youth, one has merely to repeat one's follies.'

☆

'. . . Nowadays most people die of a sort of creeping common sense, and discover when it is too late that the only things one never regrets are one's mistakes.'

☆

'. . . If I am late, he is sure to be furious, and I couldn't have a scene in this bonnet. It is far too fragile. A harsh word would ruin it . . .'

☆

'. . . I am due at the Athenaeum. It is the hour when we sleep there.'

'All of you, Mr Erskine?'

'Forty of us, in forty arm-chairs. We are practising for an English Academy of Letters.'

★   ★   ★

He was always late on principle, his principle being that punctuality is the thief of time.

The Picture of Dorian Gray, Chapter 4

☆

She was a curious woman, whose dresses always looked as if they had been designed in a rage and put on in a tempest. She was usually in love with somebody, and, as her passion was never returned, she had kept all her illusions. She tried to look picturesque, but only succeeded in being untidy. Her name was Victoria, and she had a perfect mania for going to church.

☆

'. . . I like Wagner's music better than anybody's. It is so loud that one can talk the whole time without other people hearing what one says. That is a great advantage . . .'

☆

'. . . I have simply worshipped pianists – two at a time, sometimes, Harry tells me. I don't know what it is about them. Perhaps it is that they are foreigners. They all are, ain't they? Even those that are born in England become foreigners after a time, don't they? It is so clever of them, and such a compliment to art. Makes it quite cosmopolitan, doesn't it? . . .'

☆

'. . . Men marry because they are tired; women, because they are curious; both are disappointed.'

☆

'. . . no woman is a genius. Women are a decorative sex. They never have anything to say, but they say it charmingly. Women represent the triumph of matter over mind, just as men represent the triumph of mind over morals.'

☆

'. . . As long as a woman can look ten years younger than her own daughter, she is perfectly satisfied. As for conversation, there are only five women in London worth talking to, and two of these can't be admitted into decent society . . .'

☆

'. . . But you should not say the greatest romance of your life. You should say the first romance of your life. You will always be loved, and you will always be in love with love. A *grande passion* is the privilege of people who have nothing to do. That is the one use of the idle classes of a country . . .'

The Picture of Dorian Gray, Chapter 4

☆

'My dear boy, the people who love only once in their lives are really the shallow people. What they call their loyalty, and their fidelity, I call either the lethargy of custom or their lack of imagination. Faithfulness is to the emotional life was consistency is to the life of the intellect – simply a confession of failures. Faithfulness! I must analyse it some day. The passion for property is in it. There are many things that we would throw away if we were not afraid that others would pick them up . . .'

☆

'. . . The longer I live, Dorian, the more keenly I feel that whatever was good enough for our fathers is not good enough for us. In art, as in politics, *les grandpères ont toujours tort.*'

☆

'Then he asked if I wrote for any of the newspapers. I told him I never even read them. He seemed terribly disappointed at that, and confided to me that all the dramatic critics were in a conspiracy against him, and that they were every one of them to be bought.'
'I should not wonder if he was quite right there. But, on the other hand, judging from their appearance, most of them cannot be at all expensive.'

☆

'. . . He was a most offensive brute, though he had an extraordinary passion for Shakespeare. He told me once, with an air of pride, that his five bankruptcies were entirely due to "The Bard" as he insisted on calling him. He seemed to think it a distinction.'
'It was a distinction, my dear Dorian – a great distinction. Most people become bankrupt through having invested too heavily in the prose of life. To have ruined one's self over poetry is an honour . . .'

☆

'. . . There is always something infinitely mean about other people's tragedies.'

☆

'Basil, my dear boy, puts everything that is charming in him into his work. The consequence is that he had nothing left for life but his prejudices, his principles, and his common-sense. The only artists I have ever known, who are personally delightful, are bad artists. Good artists exist simply in what they make, and consequently are perfectly uninteresting in what they are. A great poet, a really great poet, is the most unpoetical of all creatures. But inferior poets are absolutely fascinating. The worse their rhymes are, the more picturesque they look. The mere fact of having published a book of second-rate sonnets makes a man quite irresistible. He lives the poetry he cannot write. The others write the poetry that they dare not realise.'

☆

And so he had begun by vivisecting himself, as he had ended by vivisecting others. Human life – that appeared to him the one thing worth investigating.

★   ★   ★

Children begin by loving their parents; as they grow older they judge them; sometimes they forgive them.
The Picture of Dorian Gray, Chapter 5

★   ★   ★

'. . . There is hardly a single person in the House of Commons worth painting; though many of them would be the better for a little white-washing.'
The Picture of Dorian Gray, Chapter 6

☆

'Dorian is far too wise not to do foolish things now and then, my dear Basil.'
 'Marriage is hardly a thing that one can do now and then, Harry.'
 'Except in America', rejoined Lord Henry, languidly.

☆

'I never approve, or disapprove, of anything new. It is an absurd attitude to take towards life. We are not sent into the world to air our moral prejudices. I never take any notice of what common people say, and I never interfere with what charming people do. If a personality fascinates me, whatever mode of expression that personality selects is absolutely delightful to me . . .'

☆

'. . . The real drawback to marriage is that it makes one unselfish. And unselfish people are colourless. They lack individuality. Still, there are certain temperaments that marriage makes more complex. They retain their egotism, and add to it many other egos. They are forced to have more than one life. They become more highly organised, and to

be highly organised is, I should fancy, the object of man's existence
. . .'

The Picture of Dorian Gray, Chapter 6

☆

'The reason we all like to think so well of others is that we are all afraid
for ourselves. The basis of optimism is sheer terror. We think that we
are generous because we credit our neighbour with the possession of
those virtues that are likely to be a benefit to us. We praise the banker
that we may overdraw our account, and find good qualities in the
highwayman in the hope that he may spare our pockets . . .'

☆

'. . . As for a spoiled life, no life is spoiled but one whose growth is
arrested. If you want to mar a nature, you have merely to reform it . . .'

☆

'Women are wonderfully practical', murmured Lord Henry – 'much
more practical than we are. In situations of that kind we often forget to
say anything about marriage, and they always remind us.'

☆

'Pleasure is the only thing worth having a theory about . . . But I am
afraid I cannot claim my theory as my own. It belongs to Nature, not
to me. Pleasure is Nature's test, her sign of approval. When we are
happy we are always good, but when we are good we are not always
happy.'

☆

'To be good is to be in harmony with one's self . . . Discord is to be
forced to be in harmony with others . . . Modern morality consists in
accepting the standard of one's age. I consider that for any man of
culture to accept the standard of his age is a form of the grossest immorality.'

☆

'. . . surely, if one lives merely for one's self . . . one pays a terrible price
for doing so?' . . .
    'Yes, we are overcharged for everything nowadays . . .'

☆

'. . . mediaeval art is charming, but mediaeval emotions are out of
date. One can use them in fiction, of course. But then the only things
that one can use in fiction are the things that one has ceased to use in
fact . . . no civilised man ever regrets a pleasure, and no uncivilised
man ever knows what a pleasure is.'

☆

'Being adored is a nuisance. Women treat us just as Humanity treats its gods. They worship us, and are always bothering us to do something for them.'

☆

'You must admit . . . that women give to men the very gold of their lives.'
   'Possibly . . . but they invariably want it back in such very small change . . .'

☆

'. . . A cigarette is the perfect type of a perfect pleasure. It is exquisite, and it leaves one unsatisfied. What more can one want? . . .'

☆

'. . . I love acting. It is so much more real than life . . .'

★   ★   ★

'. . . It is not good for one's morals to see bad acting . . .'
                    The Picture of Dorian Gray, Chapter 7

☆

'. . . There are only two kinds of people who are really fascinating – people who know absolutely everything, and people who know absolutely nothing . . .'

☆

'. . . How little you can know of love, if you say it mars your art! Without your art you are nothing . . .'

☆

There is always something ridiculous about the emotions of people whom one has ceased to love.

☆

Besides, women were better suited to bear sorrow than men. They lived on their emotions. They only thought of their emotions. When they took lovers, it was merely to have some one with whom they could have scenes. Lord Henry had told him that, and Lord Henry knew what women were.

★   ★   ★

When we blame ourselves we feel that no one else has a right to blame us. It is the confession, not the priest, that gives us absolution.
                    The Picture of Dorian Gray, Chapter 8

☆

'. . . There will have to be an inquest, of course, and you must not be
mixed up in it. Things like that make a man fashionable in Paris. But
in London people are so prejudiced. Here, one should never make
one's *début* with a scandal. One should reserve that to give an interest
to one's old age . . .'

The Picture of Dorian Gray, Chapter 8

☆

'. . . the only way a woman can ever reform a man is by boring him so
completely that he loses all possible interest in life. . . .'

☆

'Good resolutions are useless attempts to interfere with scientific laws.
Their origin is pure vanity. Their result is absolutely *nil*. They give us,
now and then, some of those luxurious sterile emotions that have a certain charm for the weak. That is all that can be said for them. They are
simply cheques that men draw on a bank where they have no account.'

☆

'. . . It often happens that the real tragedies of life occur in such an inartistic manner that they hurt us by their crude violence, their absolute incoherence, their absurd want of meaning, their entire lack of
style . . .'

☆

'. . . One should absorb the colour of life, but one should never remember its details. Details are always vulgar.'

☆

'. . . I once wore nothing but violets all through one season, as a form
of artistic mourning for a romance that would not die. Ultimately,
however, it did die. I forget what killed it. I think it was her proposing
to sacrifice the whole world for me. That is always a dreadful moment.
It fills one with the terror of eternity . . .'

☆

'. . . The one charm of the past is that it is the past. But women never
know when the curtain has fallen. They always want a sixth act, and
as soon as the interest of the play is entirely over they propose to continue it. If they were allowed their own way, every comedy would have
a tragic ending, and every tragedy would culminate in a farce. They
are charmingly artificial, but they have no sense of art . . .'

☆

156

'. . . Never trust a woman who wears mauve, whatever her age may be, or a woman over thirty-five who is fond of pink ribbons. It always means that they have a history . . .'

☆

'. . . nothing makes one so vain as being told that one is a sinner. Conscience makes egotists of us all . . .'

☆

'. . . the obvious consolation. Taking some one else's admirer when one loses one's own. In good society that always whitewashes a woman . . .'

☆

'. . . you must keep your good looks. We live in an age that reads too much to be wise, and that thinks too much to be beautiful. We cannot spare you . . .'

★   ★   ★

'. . . It is only shallow people who require years to get rid of an emotion. A man who is master of himself can end a sorrow as easily as he can invent a pleasure . . .'

The Picture of Dorian Gray, Chapter 9

☆

'. . . To become the spectator of one's own life . . . is to escape the suffering of life . . .'

☆

'. . . You people who go in for being consistent have just as many moods as others have. The only difference is that your moods are rather meaningless . . .'

☆

'. . . it is a mistake to think that the passion one feels in creation is ever really shown in the work one creates. Art is always more abstract than we fancy. Form and colour tell us of form and colour – that is all . . . art conceals the artist far more completely than it ever reveals him.'

☆

'Harry spends his days in saying what is incredible, and his evenings in doing what is improbable . . .'

★   ★   ★

. . . Mr Hubbard . . . had the true tradesman's spirited dislike of seeing
a gentleman doing anything useful . . .

The Picture of Dorian Gray, Chapter 10

★   ★   ★

. . . perhaps in nearly every joy, as certainly in every pleasure, cruelty
has its place . . .

The Picture of Dorian Gray, Chapter 11

☆

As he looked back upon man moving through History, he was haunted
by a feeling of loss. So much had been surrendered! And to such little
purpose!

☆

Society, civilised society at least, is never very ready to believe anything to the detriment of those who are both rich and fascinating. It
feels instinctively that manners are of more importance that morals,
and, in its opinion, the highest respectability is of much less value than
the possession of a good *chef.* And, after all, it is a very poor consolation
to be told that the man who has given one a bad dinner, or poor wine,
is irreproachable in his private life.

☆

. . . the canons of good society are, or should be, the same as the canons
of art. Form is absolutely essential to it. It should have the dignity of a
ceremony, as well as its unreality, and should combine the insincere
character of a romantic play with the wit and beauty that make such
plays delightful to us.

☆

. . . insincerity . . . is merely a method by which we can multiply our
personalities.

★   ★   ★

'. . . I love scandals about other people, but scandals about myself
don't interest me. They have not got the charm of novelty.'

The Picture of Dorian Gray, Chapter 12

☆

'. . . I know how people chatter in England. The middle classes air
their moral prejudices over their gross dinner-tables, and whisper
about what they call the profligacies of their betters in order to try and
pretend that they are in smart society, and on intimate terms with the
people they slander. In this country it is enough for a man to have dis-

tinction and brains for every common tongue to wag against him. And what sort of lives do these people, who pose as being moral, lead themselves? My dear fellow, you forget that we are in the native land of the hypocrite.'

★   ★   ★

. . . youth smiles without any reason. It is one of its chiefest charms.
The Picture of Dorian Gray, Chapter 14

☆

Time seemed to him to be crawling with feet of lead, while he by monstrous winds was being swept towards the jagged edge of some black cleft of precipice. He knew what was waiting for him there; saw it indeed, and, shuddering, crushed with dank hands his burning lids as though he would have robbed the very brain of sight, and driven the eyeballs back into their cave. It was useless. The brain had its own food on which it battened, and the imagination, made grotesque by terror, twisted and distorted as a living thing by pain, danced like some foul puppet on a stand, and grinned through moving masks. Then, suddenly, Time stopped for him. Yes: that blind, slow-breathing thing crawled no more, and horrible thoughts, Time being dead, raced nimbly on in front, and dragged a hideous future from its grave, and showed it to him.

☆

'. . . without my stirring in the matter, you are certain to be arrested. Nobody ever commits a crime without doing something stupid . . .'

☆

'. . . We were friends once, Alan.'
  'Don't speak of those days, Dorian: they are dead.'
  'The dead linger sometimes . . .'

☆

The ticking of the clock on the mantelpiece seemed to him to be dividing Time into separate atoms of agony, each of which was too terrible to be borne. He felt as if an iron ring was being slowly tightened round his forehead, as if the disgrace with which he was threatened had already come upon him. The hand upon his shoulder weighed like a hand of lead. It was intolerable. It seemed to crush him.

★   ★   ★

Perhaps one never seems so much at one's ease as when one has to play a part.
The Picture of Dorian Gray, Chapter 15

☆

159

He himself could not help wondering at the calm of his demeanour, and for a moment felt keenly the terrible pleasure of a double life.
The Picture of Dorian Gray, Chapter 15

☆

. . . Lady Narborough . . . was a very clever woman, with what Lord Henry used to describe as the remains of really remarkable ugliness.

☆

'I know, my dear, I should have fallen madly in love with you . . . and thrown my bonnet right over the mills for your sake. It is most fortunate that you were not thought of at the time. As it was, our bonnets were so unbecoming, and the mills were so occupied in trying to raise the wind, that I never had even a flirtation with anybody. However, that was all Narborough's fault. He was dreadfully short-sighted, and there is no pleasure in taking in a husband who never sees anything.'

☆

'. . . They get up early, because they have so much to do, and go to bed early because they have so little to think about. There has not been a scandal in the neighbourhood since the time of Queen Elizabeth, and consequently they all fall asleep after dinner . . .'

☆

. . . Ernest Harrowden, one of those middle-aged mediocrities so common in London clubs who have no enemies, but are thoroughly disliked by their friends; Lady Ruxton, an over-dressed woman of forty-seven, with a hooked nose, who was always trying to get herself compromised, but was so peculiarly plain that to her great disappointment no one would ever believe anything against her; Mrs Erlynne, a pushing nobody, with a delightful lisp, and Venetian-red hair; Lady Alice Chapman, his hostess's daughter, a dowdy dull girl, with one of those characteristic British faces, that, once seen, are never remembered; and her husband, a red-cheeked, white-whiskered creature who, like so many of his class, was under the impression that inordinate joviality can atone for an entire lack of ideas.

☆

'. . . when she is in a very smart gown she looks like an *édition de luxe* of a bad French novel . . .'

☆

'The husbands of very beautiful women belong to the criminal classes . . .'

☆

Lady Narborough hit him with her fan. 'Lord Henry, I am not at all surprised that the world says that you are extremely wicked.'

'But what world says that? . . . It can only be the next world. This world and I are on excellent terms.'

'Everybody I know says you are very wicked . . .'

Lord Henry looked serious for some moments. 'It is perfectly monstrous,' he said at last, 'the way people go about nowadays saying things against one behind one's back that are absolutely and entirely true.'

☆

'. . . When a woman marries again it is because she detested her first husband. When a man marries again, it is because he adored his first wife. Women try their luck; men risk theirs.'

☆

'. . . Women love us for our defects. If we have enough of them they will forgive us everything, even our intellects . . .'

☆

'. . . Nowadays all the married men live like bachelors, and all the bachelors like married men.'

☆

'. . . don't tell me that you have exhausted Life. When a man says that one knows that life has exhausted him . . .'

☆

'Moderation is a fatal thing. Enough is as bad as a meal. More than enough is as good as a feast.'

☆

An alliterative prefix served as an ornament of oratory. He hoisted the Union Jack on the pinnacles of Thought. The inherited stupidity of the race – sound English common sesnse he jovially termed it – was shown to be the proper bulwark for Society.

☆

'. . . She is very clever, too clever for a woman. She lacks the indefinable charm of weakness. It is the feet of clay that makes the gold of the image precious . . .'

★ ★ ★

Ugliness that had once been hateful to him because it made things real, became dear to him now for that very reason. Ugliness was the one reality. The coarse brawl, the loathsome den, the crude violence of disordered life, the very vileness of thief and outcast, were more vivid, in their intense actuality of impression, then all the gracious shapes of Art, the dreamy shadows of Song. They were what he needed for forgetfulness.

The Picture of Dorian Gray, Chapter 16

☆

He knew in what strange heavens they were suffering, and what dull hells were teaching them the secret of some new joy. They were better off than he was. He was prisoned in thought. Memory, like a horrible malady, was eating his soul away.

☆

One's days were too brief to take the burden of another's errors on one's shoulders. Each man lived his own life, and paid his own price for living it. The only pity was one had to pay so often for a single fault. One had to pay over and over again, indeed. In her dealings with man Destiny never closed her accounts.

☆

There are moments . . . when the passion for sin, or for what the world calls sin, so dominates a nature, that every fibre of the body, as every cell of the brain, seems to be instinct with fearful impulses. Men and women at such moments lose the freedom of their will. They move to their terrible end as automatons move. Choice is taken from them, and conscience is either killed, or, if it lives at all, lives but to give rebellion its fascination, and disobedience its charm. For all sins, as theologians weary of reminding us, are sins of disobedience. When that high spirit, that morning-star of evil, fell from heaven, it was as a rebel that he fell.

★   ★   ★

'. . . It is a sad truth, but we have lost the faculty of giving lovely names to things. Names are everything. I never quarrel with actions. My one quarrel is with words. That is the reason I hate vulgar realism in literature. The man who could call a spade a spade should be compelled to use one. It is the only thing he is fit for.'

The Picture of Dorian Gray, Chapter 17

☆

'. . . I admit that I think that it is better to be beautiful than to be good. But on the other hand no one is more ready than I am to acknowledge that it is better to be good than to be ugly.'

☆

'... Beer, the Bible, and the seven deadly virtues have made our England what she is.'

☆

'... the verdict of Europe on it? ... That Tartuffe has emigrated to England and opened a shop.'

☆

'Our countrymen ... are more cunning than practical. When they make up their ledger, they balance supidity by wealth, and vice by hypocrisy.'
'Still, we have done great things.'
'Great things have been thrust on us ...'
'We have carried their burden.'
'Only as far as the Stock Exchange.

☆

'... Scepticism is the beginning of Faith.'

☆

'... All good hats are made out of nothing.'
'Like all good reputations ... every effect that one produces gives one an enemy. To be popular one must be a mediocrity.'

☆

'... Romance lives by repetition, and repetition converts an appetite into an art ...'

☆

'... each time that one loves is the only time one has ever loved. Difference of object does not alter singleness of passion. It merely intensifies it. We can have in life but one great experience at best, and the secret of life is to reproduce that experience as often as possible ... Especially when one has been wounded by it.'

★　　★　　★

Actual life was chaos, but there was something logical in the imagination. It was the imagination that set remorse to dog the feet of sin. It was the imagination that made each crime bear its misshapen brood. In the common world of fact the wicked were not punished, nor the good rewarded. Success was given to the strong, failure thrust upon the weak. That was all.

The Picture of Dorian Gray, Chapter 18

☆

What sort of life would his be, if day and night, shadows of his crime were to peer at him from silent corners, to mock him from secret places, to whisper in his ear as he sat at the feast, to wake him with icy fingers as he lay asleep!

The Picture of Dorian Gray, Chapter 18

☆

His own nature had revolted against the excess of anguish that had sought to maim and mar the perfection of its calm. With subtle and finely-wrought temperaments it is always so. Their strong passions must either bruise or bend. They either slay the man, or themselves die. Shallow sorrows and shallow loves live on. The loves and sorrows that are great are destroyed by their own plenitude.

☆

. . . as the hare bounded into the thicket he fired. There were two cries heard, the cry of a hare in pain, which is dreadful, the cry of a man in agony, which is worse.

☆

'He must have got the whole charge of shot in his chest. He must have died almost simultaneously . . . It was the man's own fault. Why did he get in front of the guns? Besides, it's nothing to us. It is rather awkward for Geoffrey, of course. It does not do to pepper beaters. It makes people think that one is a wild shot. And Geoffrey is not; he shoots very straight. But there is no use talking about the matter.'

☆

'. . . there is no such thing as an omen. Destiny does not send us heralds. She is too wise or too cruel for that . . .'

☆

'. . . I have no terror of Death. It is the coming of Death that terrifies me . . .'

☆

'. . . A woman will flirt with anybody in the world as long as other people are looking on.'

☆

'. . . I like the Duchess very much, but I don't love her.'

'And the Duchess loves you very much, but she likes you less, so you are excellently matched.'

☆

'The basis for every scandal is an immoral certainty.'

☆

'. . . I am sorry they told you about the man. It is a hideous subject.'

'It is an annoying subject', broke in Lord Henry. 'It has no psychological value at all. Now, if Geoffrey had done the thing on purpose, how interesting he would be! I should like to know some one who has committed a real murder.'

★   ★   ★

'. . . anybody can be good in the country. There are no temptations there. That is the reason why people who live out of town are so absolutely uncivilised. Civilisation is not by any means an easy thing to attain to. There are only two ways by which man can reach it. One is by being cultured, the other by being corrupt. Country people have no opportunity of being either, so they stagnate.'

The Picture of Dorian Gray, Chapter 19

☆

'. . . You gave her good advice, and broke her heart. That was the beginning of your reformation.'

☆

'. . . the British public are really not equal to the mental strain of having more than one topic every three months . . .'

☆

'. . . I suppose in about a fortnight we shall be told that he has been seen in San Francisco. It is an odd thing, but everyone who disappears is said to be seen at San Francisco. It must be a delightful city, and possess all the attractions of the next world.'

☆

'. . . Death and vulgarity are the only two facts in the nineteenth century that one cannot explain away . . .'

☆

'. . . You must play Chopin to me. The man with whom my wife ran away played Chopin exquisitely . . .'

☆

'. . . married life is merely a habit, a bad habit. But then one regrets the loss even of one's worst habits. Perhaps one regrets them the most.

They are such an essential part of one's personality.'
The Picture of Dorian Gray, Chapter 19

☆

'Basil was very popular, and always wore a Waterbury watch. Why should he have been murdered? He was not clever enough to have enemies . . .'

☆

'. . . I know there are dreadful places in Paris, but Basil was not the sort of man to have gone to them. He had no curiosity. It was his chief defect.'

☆

'. . . All crime is vulgar, just as all vulgarity is crime . . . Crime belongs exclusively to the lower orders. I don't blame them in the smallest degree. I should fancy that crime was to them what art is to us, simply a method of procuring extraordinary sensations.'

☆

'. . . anything becomes a pleasure if one does it too often . . . That is one of the most important secrets of life. I should fancy, however, that murder is always a mistake. One should never do anything that one cannot talk about after dinner . . .'

☆

'. . . I suppose he bored you. If so, he never forgave you. It's a habit bores have . . .'

☆

'. . . It belonged to Basil's best period. Since then, his work was that curious mixture of bad painting and good intentions that always entitles a man to be called a representative British artist . . .'

☆

'If a man treats life artistically, his brain is his heart'.

☆

'. . . The things one feels absolutely certain about are never true. That is the fatality of faith, and the lesson of Romance . . .'

☆

'. . . To get back my youth I would do anything in the world, except take exercise, get up early, or be respectable . . .'

☆

'. . . The only people to whose opinions I listen now with any respect are people much younger than myself. They seem in front of me. Life has revealed to them her latest wonder . . .'

☆

'. . . The tragedy of old age is not that one is old, but that one is young . . .'

☆

'. . . Art has no influence upon action. It annihilates the desire to act. It is superbly sterile. The books that the world calls immoral are books that show the world its own shame. That is all . . .'

★ ★ ★

It would kill the past, and when that was dead he would be free.
The Picture of Dorian Gray, Chapter 20

★ ★ ★

The sphere of art and the sphere of ethics are absolutely distinct and separate; and it is to the confusion between the two that we owe the appearance of Mrs Grundy, that amusing old lady who represents the only original form of humour that the middle classes of this country have been able to produce.
To the Editor, *St James's Gazette*, printed 26 June 1890

☆

I wrote this book entirely for my own pleasure, and it gave me very great pleasure to write it. Whether it becomes popular or not is a matter of absolute indifference to me.

★ ★ ★

The English public, as a mass, takes no interest in a work of art until it is told that the work in question is immoral, and your *réclame* will, I have no doubt, largely increase the sale of the magazine; in which sale, I may mention with some regret, I have no pecuniary interest.
To the Editor, *St James's Gazette*, printed 27 June 1890

☆

To say that such a book as mine should be 'chucked into the fire' is silly. That is what one does with newspapers.

☆

. . . your writer . . . begins by assailing me with much ridiculous virulence because the chief personages in my story are 'puppies'. They *are* puppies. Does he think that literature went to the dogs when Thackeray wrote about puppydom?

To the Editor, *St James's Gazette*, printed 28 June 1890

☆

The poor public, hearing, from an authority so high as your own, that this is a wicked book that should be coerced and suppressed by a Tory Government, will, no doubt, rush to it and read it. But alas! they will find that it is a story with a moral. And the moral is this: All excess, as well as all renunciation, brings its own punishment . . . Yes; there is a terrible moral in *Dorian Gray* – a moral which the prurient will not be able to find in it, but which will be revealed to all whose minds are healthy. Is this an artistic error? I fear it is. It is the only error in the book.

★   ★   ★

A Government might just as well try to teach painters how to paint, or sculptors how to model, as attempt to interfere with the style, treatment, and subject-matter of the literary artist; and no writer, however eminent or obscure, should ever give his sanction to a theory that would degrade literature far more than any didactic or so-called immoral book could possibly do.

To the Editor, *St James's Gazette*, printed 28 June 1890

☆

A critic should be taught to criticise a work of art without making any reference to the personality of the author. This, in fact, is the beginning of criticism.

☆

. . . if I were criticising my book, which I have some thoughts of doing, I think I would consider it my duty to point out that it is far too crowded with sensational incident, and far too paradoxical in style, as far, at any rate, as the dialogue goes. I feel that from a standpoint of art these are two defects in the book.

☆

It is proper that limitations should be placed on action. It is not proper that limitations should be placed on art. To art belong all things that are and all things that are not, and even the editor of a London paper has no right to restrain the freedom of art in the selection of subject-matter.

★   ★   ★

No publisher should ever express an opinion on the value of what he publishes. That is a matter entirely for the literary critic to decide . . . I can quite understand how any ordinary critic would be strongly pre-judiced against a work that was accompanied by a premature and un-necessary panegyric from the publisher. A publisher is simply a useful middle-man. It is not for him to anticipate the verdict of criticism.

To the Editor, *St James's Gazette*, printed 30 June 1890

☆

What my story is, is an interesting problem. What my story is not, is a 'novelette', a term which you have more than once applied to it. There is no such word in the English language as novelette. It should never be used. It is merely part of the slang of Fleet street.

☆

You then gravely ask me what rights I imagine literature possesses. That is really an extraordinary question for the editor of a newspaper such as yours to ask. The rights of literature, Sir, are the rights of intellect.

☆

You say that a work of art is a form of action. It is not. It is the highest mode of thought.

☆

. . . leave my book I beg you, to the immortality that it deserves.

★　　　★　　　★

It is poisonous if you like, but you cannot deny that it is also perfect, and perfection is what we artists aim at.

To the Editor, *Daily Chronicle*, printed 2 July 1890

★　　　★　　　★

Your reviewer, sir, while admitting that the story in question is 'plainly the work of a man of letters', the work of one who has 'brains, and art, and style', yet suggests, and apparently in all seriousness, that I have written it in order that it should be read by the most depraved members of the criminal and illiterate classes. Now, sir, I do not sup-pose that the criminal and illiterate classes ever read anything except newspapers.

To the Editor, *Scots Observer*, printed 12 July 1890

☆

As for the mob, I have no desire to be a popular novelist. It is far too easy.

☆

Each man sees his own sin in Dorian Gray. What Dorian Gray's sins are no one knows. He who finds them has brought them.

To the Editor, *Scots Observer*, printed 12 July 1890

*   *   *

. . . if a work of art is rich, and vital, and complete, those who have artistic instincts will see its beauty, and those to whom ethics appeal more strongly than aesthetics will see its moral lesson. It will fill the cowardly with terror, and the unclean will see in it their own shame. It will be to each man what he is himself. It is the spectator, and not life, that art really mirrors.

To the Editor, *Scots Observer*, printed 2 August 1890

*   *   *

It takes a Goethe to see a work of art fully, completely, and perfectly, and I thoroughly agree with Mr Whibley when he says that it is a pity that Goethe never had an opportunity of reading *Dorian Gray*. I feel quite certain that he would have been delighted by it, and I only hope that some ghostly publisher is even now distributing shadowy copies in the Elysian fields, and that the cover of Gautier's copy is powdered with gilt asphodels.

To the Editor, *Scots Observer*, printed 16 August 1890

☆

The critic has to educate the public; the artist has to educate the critic.

☆

. . . Mr Whibley . . . ends his letter with the statement that I have been indefatigable in my public appreciation of my own work. I have no doubt that in saying this he means to pay me a compliment, but he really overrates my capacity, as well as my inclination, for work. I must frankly confess that, by nature and by choice, I am extremely indolent. Cultivated idleness seems to me to be the proper occupation for man.

☆

I am afraid that writing to newspapers has a deteriorating influence on style. People get violent, and abusive, and lose all sense of proportion, when they enter that curious journalistic arena in which the race is always to the noisiest.

☆

A comedy ends when the secret is out. Drop your curtain, and put your dolls to bed. I love Don Quixote, but I do not wish to fight any longer with marionettes, however cunning may be the master-hand that works the wires.

* * *

The artist is the creator of beautiful things.

To reveal art and conceal the artist is art's aim.

The critic is he who can translate into another manner or a new material his impression of beautiful things.

The highest as the lowest form of criticism is a mode of auto-biography.

'A Preface to *Dorian Gray*', *Fortnightly Review*, March 1891

☆

Those who find ugly meanings in beautiful things are corrupt without being charming. This is a fault.

Those who find beautiful meanings in beautiful things are the culti-vated. For these there is hope.

They are the elect to whom beautiful things mean only Beauty.

There is no such thing as a moral or an immoral book. Books are well written, or badly written. That is all.

☆

The nineteenth century dislike of Realism is the rage of Caliban seeing his own face in a glass.

The nineteenth century dislike of Romanticism is the rage of Caliban not seeing his own face in a glass.

☆

The moral life of man forms part of the subject-matter of the artist, but the morality of art consists in the perfect use of an imperfect medium.

No artist desires to prove anything. Even things that are true can be proved.

No artist has ethical sympathies. An ethical sympathy in an artist is an unpardonable mannerism of style.

No artist is ever morbid. The artist can express everything.

Thought and language are to the artist instruments of an art.

Vice and virtue are to the artist materials for an art.

☆

From the point of view of form, the type of all arts is the art of the musician. From the point of view of feeling, the actor's craft is the type.

All art is at once surface and symbol.

Those who go beneath the surface do so at their peril.

Those who read the symbol do so at their peril.

☆

It is the spectator, and not life, that art really mirrors.

Diversity of opinion about a work of art shows that the work is new, complex, and vital.

When critics disagree the artist is in accord with himself.

'A Preface to *Dorian Gray*', *Fortnightly Review*, March 1891

☆

We can forgive a man for making a useful thing as long as he does not admire it. The only excuse for making a useless thing is that one admires it intensely.

All art is quite useless.

★   ★   ★

The proper aim is to try and reconstruct society on such a basis that poverty will be impossible. And the altruistic virtues have really prevented the carrying out of this aim . . . Charity creates a multitude of sins.

'The Soul of Man Under Socialism', *Fortnightly Review*, February 1891

☆

It is immoral to use private property in order to alleviate the horrible evils that result from the institution of private property. It is both immoral and unfair.

☆

Under Socialism . . . The security of society will not depend, as it does now, on the state of the weather.

☆

If a frost comes we shall not have a hundred thousand men out of work, tramping about the streets in a state of disgusting misery, or whining to their neighbours for alms, or crowding round the doors of loathsome shelters to try and secure a hunch of bread and a night's unclean lodging. Each member of the society will share in the general prosperity and happiness of the society, and if a frost comes no one will practically be anything the worse.

☆

Upon the other hand, Socialism itself will be of value simply because it will lead to Individualism.

☆

Socialism, Communism, or whatever one chooses to call it, by converting private property into public wealth, and substituting co-operation for competition, will restore society to its proper condition of a thoroughly healthy organism, and ensure the material well-being of each member of the community. It will, in fact, give Life its proper basis and its proper environment.

☆

If the Socialism is Authoritarian; if there are Governments armed with economic power as they are now with political power; if, in a word, we are to have Industrial Tyrannies, then the last state of man will be worse than the first.

☆

... there are a great many people who, having no private property of their own, and being always on the brink of sheer starvation, are compelled to do the work of beasts of burden, to do work that is quite uncongenial to them, and to which they are forced by the peremptory, unreasonable, degrading Tyranny of want. These are the poor ... From their collective force Humanity gains much in material prosperity. But it is only the material result that it gains, and the man who is poor is in himself absolutely of no importance. He is merely the infinitesimal atom of a force that, so far from regarding him, crushes him: indeed, prefers him crushed, as in that case he is far more obedient.

☆

The possession of private property is very often extremely demoralising, and that is, of course, one of the reasons why Socialism wants to get rid of the institution.

☆

Property not merely has duties, but has so many duties that its possession to any large extent is a bore. It involves endless claims upon one, endless attention to business, endless bother. If property had simply pleasures, we could stand it; but its duties make it unbearable. In the interest of the rich we must get rid of it.

☆

We are often told that the poor are grateful for charity. Some of them are, no doubt, *but the best amongst the poor are never grateful*. They are ungrateful, discontented, disobedient, and rebellious. They are quite right to be so.

☆

Why should they be grateful for the crumbs that fall from the rich man's table? They should be seated at the board, and are beginning to know it.

☆

173

As for being discontented, a man who would not be discontented with such surroundings and such a low mode of life would be a perfect brute.

'The Soul of Man Under Socialism', *Fortnightly Review*, February 1891

☆

Disobedience, in the eyes of any one who has read history, is man's original virtue. It is through disobedience that progress has been made, through disobedience and through rebellion.

☆

. . . to recommend thrift to the poor is both grotesque and insulting. It is like advising a man who is starving to eat less.

☆

Man should not be ready to show that he can live like a badly-fed animal. He should decline to live like that, and should either steal or go on the rates, which is considered by many to be a form of stealing. As for begging, it is safer to beg than to take, but it is finer to take than to beg.

☆

As for the virtuous poor, one can pity them, of course, but one cannot possibly admire them. They have made private terms with the enemy, and sold their birthright for very bad pottage. They must also be extraordinarily stupid . . . it is almost incredible to me how a man whose life is marred and made hideous by such laws can possibly acquiesce in their continuance.

☆

Misery and poverty are so absolutely degrading, and exercise such a paralysing effect over the nature of men, that no class is ever really conscious of its own suffering.

☆

Agitators are a set of interfering, meddling people, who come down to some perfectly contented class of the community, and sow the seeds of discontent amongst them. That is the reason why agitators are so absolutely necessary. Without them, in our incomplete state, there would be no advance towards civilisation.

☆

To the thinker, the most tragic fact in the whole of the French Revolution is not that Marie Antoinette was killed for being a queen, but that the starved peasant of the Vendée voluntarily went out to die for the hideous cause of feudalism.

☆

It is to be regretted that a portion of our community should be practically in slavery, but to propose to solve the problem by enslaving the entire community is childish. Every man must be left quite free to choose his own work. No form of compulsion must be exercised over him. If there is, his work will not be good for him, will not be good in itself, and will not be good for others.

☆

Of course, authority and compulsion are out of the question. All association must be quite voluntary. *It is only in voluntary associations that man is fine.*

☆

. . . the recognition of private property has really harmed Individualism, and obscured it, by confusing a man with what he possesses . . . It has made gain not growth its aim. So that man thought that the important thing was to have, and did not know that the important thing is to be. *The true perfection of man lies, not in what man has, but in what man is.*

☆

Private property has crushed true Individualism. and set up an Individualism that is false. It has debarred one part of the community from being individual by starving them. It has debarred the other part of the community from being individual by putting them on the wrong road, and encumbering them.

☆

In a community like ours, where property confers immense distinction, social position, honour, respect, titles, and other pleasant things of the kind, man, being naturally ambitious, makes it his aim to accumulate this property, and goes on wearily and tediously accumulating it long after he has got far more than he wants, or can use, or enjoy, or perhaps even know of.

☆

One's regret is that society should be constructed on such a basis that man has been forced into a groove in which he cannot freely develop what is wonderful, and fascinating, and delightful in him – in which, in fact, he misses the true pleasure and joy of living. He is also, under existing conditions, very insecure. An enormously wealthy merchant may be – often is – at every moment of his life at the mercy of things that are not under his control.

'The Soul of Man Under Socialism', *Fortnightly Review*, February 1891

☆

Nothing should be able to rob a man at all. What a man really has, is what is in him. What is outside of him should be a matter of no importance.

☆

With the abolition of private property, then, we shall have true, beautiful, healthy Individualism. Nobody will waste his life in accumulating things, and the symbols for things. One will live. To live is the rarest thing in the world. Most people exist, that is all.

☆

When Jesus talks about the poor he simply means personalities, just as when he talks about the rich he simply means people who have not developed their personalities.

☆

There is only one class in the community that thinks more about money than the rich, and that is the poor. The poor can think of nothing else. That is the misery of being poor.

☆

There was a woman who was taken in adultery. We are not told the history of her love, but that love must have been very great; for Jesus said that her sins were forgiven her, not because she repented, but because her love was so intense and wonderful.

☆

And so he who would lead a Christ-like life is he who is perfectly and absolutely himself. He may be a great poet, or a great man of science, or a young student at a University, or one who watches sheep upon a moor; or a maker of dramas, like Shakespeare, or a thinker about God, like Spinoza; or a child who plays in a garden, or a fisherman who throws his net into the sea.

☆

Father Damien was Christ-like when he went out to live with the lepers, because in such service he realised fully what was best in him. But he was not more Christ-like than Wagner, when he realised his soul in music; or than Shelley, when he realised his soul in song.

☆

And while to the claims of charity a man may yield and yet be free, to the claims of conformity no man may yield and remain free at all.

☆

. . . the State must give up all idea of government . . . *All modes of govern-ment are failures.*

☆

Despotism is unjust to everybody, including the despot, who was probably made for better things.

☆

High hopes were once formed of democracy; but democracy means simply the bludgeoning of the people by the people for the people. It has been found out.

☆

. . . all authority is quite degrading. It degrades those who exercise it, and degrades those over whom it is exercised . . . authority, by bribing people to conform, produces a very gross kind of over-fed barbarism amongst us.

☆

As one reads history . . . one is absolutely sickened, not by the crimes that the wicked have committed, but by the punishment that the good have inflicted; *and a community is infinitely more brutalised by the habitual employment of punishment than it is by the occasional occurrence of crime.*

☆

The less punishment, the less crime. When there is no punishment at all, crime will either cease to exist, or, if it occurs, will be treated by physicians as a very distressing form of dementia, to be cured by care and kindness.

☆

When private property is abolished there will be no necessity for crime, no demand for it; it will cease to exist . . . though a crime may not be against property, it may spring from the misery and rage and depression produced by our wrong system of property-holding, and so, when that system is abolished, will disappear.

☆

Jealousy, which is an extraordinary source of crime in modern life, is an emotion closely bound up with our conceptions of property, and under Socialism and Individualism will die out.

☆

177

The State is to make what is useful. The individual is to make what is beautiful.
'The Soul of Man Under Socialism', *Fortnightly Review*, February 1891

☆

. . . a great deal of nonsense is being written and talked nowadays about the dignity of manual labour. There is nothing necessarily dignified about manual labour at all, and most of it is absolutely degrading . . . To sweep a slushy crossing for eight hours on a day when the east wind is blowing is a disgusting occupation. To sweep it with mental, moral, or physical dignity seems to me to be impossible. To sweep it with joy would be appalling. Man is made for something better than disturbing dirt.
'The Soul of Man Under Socialism', *Fortnightly Review*, February 1891

☆

Up to the present, man has been, to a certain extent, the slave of machinery, and there is something tragic in the fact that as soon as man had invented a machine to do his work he began to starve. This, however, is, of course, the result of our property system and our system of competition.

☆

All unintellectual labour, all monotonous, dull labour, all labour that deals with dreadful things, and involves unpleasant conditions, must be done by machinery . . . *At present machinery competes against man. Under proper conditions machinery will serve man* . . . Human slavery is wrong, insecure, and demoralising. On mechanical slavery, on the slavery of the machine, the future of the world depends.

☆

Progress is the realisation of Utopias.

☆

In England, the arts that have escaped best are the arts in which the public take no interest . . . We have been able to have fine poetry in England because the public do not read it, and consequently do not influence it. The public like to insult poets because they are individual, but once they have insulted them they leave them alone.

☆

In Art, the public accept what has been, because they cannot alter it, not because they appreciate it. They swallow their classics whole, and never taste them.

☆

. . . in the case of Shakespeare it is quite obvious that the public see neither the beauties nor the defects of his plays. If they saw the beauties, they would not object to the development of the drama; and if they saw the defects, they would not object to the development of the drama either.

☆

. . . the public . . . degrade the classics into authorities. They use them as bludgeons for preventing the free expression of Beauty in new forms. They are always asking a writer why he does not write like somebody else, or a painter why he does not paint like somebody else, quite oblivious of the fact that if either of them did anything of the kind he would cease to be an artist.

☆

When they say a work is grossly unintelligible, they mean that the artist has said or made a beautiful thing that is new; when they describe a work as grossly immoral, they mean that the artist has said or made a beautiful thing that is true.

☆

But I can fancy that if an artist produced a work of art in England that immediately on its appearance was recognised by the public, through the medium, which is the public Press, as a work that was quite intelligible and highly moral, he would begin to seriously question whether in its creation he had really been himself at all, and consequently whether the work was not quite unworthy of him, and either of a thoroughly second-rate order, or of no artistic value whatsoever.

☆

On the whole, an artist in England gains something by being attacked. His individuality is intensified. He becomes more completely himself.

☆

Vulgarity and stupidity are two very vivid facts in modern life. One regrets them, naturally. But there they are. They are subjects for study, like everything else. And it is only fair to state, with regard to modern journalists, that they always apologise to one in private for what they have written against one in public.

☆

The very violence of a revolution may make the public grand and splendid for a moment. It was a fatal day when the public discovered that the pen is mightier than the paving-stone, and can be made as offensive as the brickbat.

☆

In old days men had the rack. Now they have the press. That is an improvement certainly. But still it is very bad, and wrong, and demoralising . . . at the present moment it really is the only estate. It has eaten up the other three. The Lords Temporal say nothing, the Lords Spiritual have nothing to say, and the House of Commons has nothing to say and says it. We are dominated by Journalism.

'The Soul of Man Under Socialism', *Fortnightly Review*, February 1891

☆

In America the President reigns for four years, and Journalism governs for ever and ever.

☆

In England, Journalism . . . is still . . . a really remarkable power. The tyranny that it proposes to exercise over people's private lives seems to me to be quite extraordinary. *The fact is that the public have an insatiable curiosity to know everything, except what is worth knowing.* Journalism, conscious of this, and having tradesmanlike habits, supplies their demands.

☆

In centuries before ours the public nailed the ears of journalists to the pump. That was quite hideous. In this century journalists have nailed their own ears to the keyhole. That is much worse.

☆

The harm is done by the serious, thoughtful, earnest journalists, who solemnly, as they are doing at present, will drag before the eyes of the public some incident in the private life of a great statesman [Parnell], of a man who is a leader of political thought as he is a creator of political force, and invite the public to discuss the incident, to exercise authority in the matter, to give their views, and not merely to give their views, but to carry them into action, to dictate to the man upon all other points, to dictate to his party, to dictate to his country, in fact, to make themselves ridiculous, offensive, and harmful.

☆

The private lives of men and women should not be told to the public. The public have nothing to do with them at all.

☆

English public opinion . . . tries to constrain and impede and warp the man who makes things that are beautiful in effect, and compels the journalist to retail things that are ugly, or disgusting, or revolting in fact, so that we have the most serious journalists in the world, and the most indecent newspapers.

☆

There are possibly some journalists who take a real pleasure in publishing horrible things, or who, being poor, look to scandals as forming a sort of permanent basis for an income. But there are other journalists, I feel certain, men of education and cultivation, who really dislike publishing these things, who know that it is wrong to do so, and only do it because the unhealthy conditions under which their occupation is carried on oblige them to supply the public with what the public wants, and to compete with other journalists in making that supply as full and satisfying to the gross popular appetite as possible. It is a very degrading position for any body of educated men to be placed in, and I have no doubt that most of them feel it acutely.

☆

No spectator of art needs a more perfect mood of receptivity than the spectator of a play. The moment he seeks to exercise authority he becomes the avowed enemy of Art and of himself. Art does not mind. It is he who suffers.

☆

The form of government that is most suitable to the artist is no government at all. Authority over him and his art is ridiculous.

☆

One who is an Emperor and King may stoop down to pick up a brush for a painter, but when the democracy stoops down it is merely to throw mud. And yet the democracy have not so far to stoop as the emperor. In fact, when they want to throw mud they have not to stoop at all. But there is no necessity to separate the monarch from the mob; all authority is equally bad.

☆

The bad Popes loved Beauty, almost as passionately, nay, with as much passion as the good Popes hated Thought. To the wickedness of the Papacy humanity owes much. The goodness of the Papacy owes a terrible debt to humanity.

☆

The People bribe and brutalise. Who told them to exercise authority? They were made to live, to listen, and to love. Some one has done them a great wrong. They have marred themselves by imitation of their inferiors. They have taken the sceptre of the Prince. How should they use it? They have taken the triple tiar of the Pope. How should they carry its burden? They are as a clown whose heart is broken. They are as a priest whose soul is not yet born. Let all who love Beauty pity them. Though they themselves love not Beauty, yet let them pity themselves. Who taught them the trick of tyranny?

'The Soul of Man Under Socialism', *Fortnightly Review*, February 1891

☆

But the past is of no importance. The present is of no importance. It is with the future that we have to deal. For the past is what man should not have been. The present is what man ought not to be. The future is what artists are.

☆

The only thing that one really knows about human nature is that it changes . . . The systems that fail are those that rely on the permanency of human nature, and not on its growth and development. The error of Louis XIV was that he thought human nature would always be the same. The result of his error was the French Revolution. It was an admirable result. All the results of the mistakes of governments are quite admirable.

☆

It is grossly selfish to require of one's neighbour that he should think in the same way, and hold the same opinions. Why should he? If he can think, he will probably think differently. If he cannot think, it is monstrous to require thought of any kind from him.

☆

Anybody can sympathise with the sufferings of a friend, but it requires a very fine nature – it requires, in fact, that nature of a true Individualist – to sympathise with a friend's success.

☆

And when Socialism has solved the problem of poverty, and Science solved the problem of disease, the area of the sentimentalists will be lessened, and the sympathy of man will be large, healthy and spontaneous. Man will have joy in the contemplation of the joyous lives of others.

☆

A Russian who lives happily under the present system of government in Russia must either believe that man has no soul, or that, if he has, it is not worth developing.

☆

Pain is not the ultimate mode of perfection. It is merely provisional and a protest. It has reference to wrong, unhealthy, unjust surroundings. When the wrong, and the disease, and the injustice are removed, it will have no further place. It will have done its work. It was a great work, but it is almost over. Its sphere lessens every day.

★　　★　　★

. . . there is no truth whatsoever in the statement made in one of my essays that 'Providence and Mr Walter Besant have exhausted the obvious'. The public need be under no misapprehension. One has merely to read the ordinary English newspapers and the ordinary English novels of our day to become conscious of the fact that it is only the obvious that occurs, and only the obvious that is written about. Both facts are much to be regretted.

To the Editor, *Pall Mall Gazette*, printed 29 August 1891

★　　★　　★

The writer of a letter signed 'An Indian Civilian' . . . says I have described Anglo-Indians as being vulgar. This is not the case. Indeed, I have never met a vulgar Anglo-Indian. There may be many, but those whom I have had the pleasure of meeting here have been chiefly scholars, men interested in art and thought, men of cultivation; nearly all of them have been exceedingly brilliant talkers; some of them have been exceedingly brilliant writers.

What I did say – I believe in the pages of the *Nineteenth Century* – was that vulgarity is the distinguishing note of those Anglo-Indians whom Mr Rudyard Kipling loves to write about, and writes about so cleverly. This is quite true, and there is no reason why Mr Rudyard Kipling should not select vulgarity as his subject-matter, or as part of it. For a realistic artist, certainly, vulgarity is a most admirable subject.

To the Editor, *The Times*, printed 26 September 1891

★　　★　　★

. . . more often he would be alone, feeling through a certain quick instinct, which was almost a divination, that the secrets of art are best learned in secret, and that Beauty, like Wisdom, loves the lonely worshipper.

'The Young King'. *A House of Pomegranates*, November 1891

☆

'The land is free', said the young King, 'and thou art no man's slave.'

'In war', answered the weaver, 'the strong make slaves of the weak, and in peace the rich make slaves of the poor. We must work to live, and they give us such mean wages that we die. We toil for them all day long, and they heap up gold in their coffers, and our children fade away before their time, and the faces of those we love become hard and evil. We tread out the grapes, and another drinks the wine. We sow the corn, and our own board is empty. We have chains, though no eye beholds them; and we are slaves, though men call us free.'

'The Young King'. *A House of Pomegranates*, November 1891

☆

'. . . Through our sunless lanes creeps Poverty with her hungry eyes, and Sin with his sodden face follows close behind her. Misery wakes us in the morning, and Shame sits with us at night. But what are these things to thee? Thou art not one of us. Thy face is too happy.'

☆

'Take these things away, and hide them from me. Though it be the day of my coronation, I will not wear them. For on the loom of sorrow, and by the white hands of Pain, has this my robe been woven. There is Blood in the heart of the ruby, and Death in the heart of the pearl.'

☆

'. . . what have we to do with the lives of those who toil for us? Shall a man not eat bread till he has seen the sower, nor drink wine till he has talked with the vinedresser?'

☆

'Sir, knowest thou not that out of the luxury of the rich cometh the life of the poor? By your pomp we are nurtured, and your vices give us bread. To toil for a master is bitter, but to have no master to toil for is more bitter still. Thinkest thou that the ravens will feed us? And what cure hast thou for these things? Wilt thou say to the buyer, "Thou shalt buy for so much", and to the seller, "Thou shalt sell at this price"? I trow not. Therefore go back to the Palace and put on thy purple and fine linen. What hast thou to do with us, and what we suffer?'

'Are not the rich and the poor brothers?' asked the young King.

'Ay', answered the man, 'and the name of the rich brother is Cain.'

☆

'. . . The burden of this world is too great for one man to bear, and the world's sorrow too heavy for one heart to suffer.'

'Sayest thou that in this house?' said the young King, and he strode past the Bishop, and climbed up the steps of the altar, and stood before the image of Christ.

*   *   *

Perhaps the most amusing thing about him was his complete unconsciousness of his own grotesque appearance. Indeed he seemed quite happy and full of the highest spirits. When the children laughed, he laughed as freely and as joyously as any of them, and at the close of each dance he made them each the funniest of bows, smiling and nodding at them just as if he was really one of themselves, and not a little misshapen thing that Nature, in some humourous mood, had fashioned for others to mock at.

'The Birthday of the Infanta'. *Ibid.*

☆

'. . . birds and lizards have no sense of repose, and indeed birds have not even a permanent address. They are mere vagrants like the gipsies, and should be treated in exactly the same manner.'

☆

'His dancing was funny', said the Infanta; 'but his acting is funnier still. Indeed, he is almost as good as the puppets, only of course not quite so natural.'

☆

'*Mi bella Princesa,* your funny little dwarf will never dance again. It is a pity, for he is so ugly that he might have made the King smile.'

'But why will he not dance again', asked the Infanta, laughing.

'Because his heart is broken', answered the Chamberlain.

And the Infanta frowned, and her dainty rose-leaf lips curled in pretty disdain. 'For the future let those who come to play with me have no hearts', she cried, and she ran out into the garden.

★   ★   ★

And the young Fisherman said to himself: 'How strange a thing this is! The priest telleth me that the soul is worth all the gold in the world, and the merchants say that it is not worth a clipped piece of silver.'

'The Fisherman and his Soul'. *Ibid.*

☆

'Once every year I will come to this place, and call to thee', said the Soul. 'It may be that thou wilt have need of me.'

☆

'Love is better than Wisdom', he cried, 'and the little Mermaid loves me.'

'Nay, but there is nothing better than Wisdom', said the Soul.

'Love is better', answered the young Fisherman, and he plunged into the deep, and the Soul went weeping away over the marshes.

☆

'. . . I would not that the Sun, who is my father, should see that there is in my city a man whom I cannot slay.'

'The Fisherman and his Soul'. *Ibid*.

☆

'. . . Naked were her feet, and they moved over the carpet like little white pigeons. Never have I seen anything so marvellous, and the city in which she dances is but a day's journey from this place.'

Now when the young Fisherman heard the words of his Soul, he re-membered that the little Mermaid had no feet and could not dance.

☆

And his Soul answered him, 'When thou didst send me forth into the world thou gavest me no heart, so I learned to do all these things and love them.'

☆

'. . . Once in his life may a man send his Soul away, but he who re-ceiveth back his Soul must keep it with him for ever, and this is his punishment and his reward.'

☆

'. . . what is this trouble of thine about the things of sin? Is that which is pleasant to eat not made for the eater? Is there poison in that which is sweet to drink? Trouble not thyself, but come with me to another city . . .'

☆

And after the year was over, the Soul thought within himself, 'I have tempted my master with evil, and his love is stronger than I am. I will tempt him now with good, and it may be that he will come with me.'

☆

And his Soul besought him to depart, but he would not, so great was his love. And the sea came nearer, and sought to cover him with its waves, and when he knew that the end was at hand he kissed with mad lips the cold lips of the Mermaid, and the heart that was within him brake. And as through the fullness of his love his heart did break, the Soul found an entrance and entered in, and was one with him even as before. And the sea covered the young Fisherman with its waves.

☆

But the beauty of the white flowers troubled him, and their odour was sweet in his nostrils, and there came another word into his lips, and he spake not of the wrath of God, but of the God whose name is Love.

186

And why he so spake, he knew not.

    ★   ★   ★

'Nonsense!' growled the Wolf. 'I tell you that it is all the fault of the Government, and if you don't believe me I shall eat you.' The Wolf had a thoroughly practical mind, and was never at a loss for a good argument.

 'Well, for my own part', said the Woodpecker, who was a born philosopher, 'I don't care an atomic theory for explanations. If a thing is so, it is so, and at present it is terribly cold.'

        'The Star-Child.' *Ibid.*

       ☆

'Why did we make merry, seeing that life is for the rich, and not for such as we are? Better that we had died of cold in the forest, or that some wild beast had fallen on us and slain us.'

       ☆

'This is a bitter ending to our hope, nor have we any good fortune, for what doth a child profit to a man?'

       ☆

For the space of three years he wandered over the world, and in the world there was neither love nor loving-kindness nor charity for him, but it was even such a world as he had made for himself in the days of his great pride.

       ☆

'Mother, I denied thee in the hour of my pride. Accept me in the hour of my humility. Mother, I gave thee hatred. Do thou give me love. Mother, I rejected thee. Receive thy child now . . . Mother, my suffering is greater than I can bear. Give me thy forgiveness, and let me go back to the forest.'

       ☆

Yet ruled he not long, so great had been his suffering, and so bitter the fire of his testing, for after the space of three years he died. And he who came after him ruled evilly.

    ★   ★   ★

. . . the decorative designs that make lovely my book *A House of Pomegranates* . . . may suggest, as they do sometimes to me, peacocks and pomegranates and splashing fountains of gold water, or, as they do to your critic, sponges and Indian clubs and chimney-pot hats. Such suggestions and evocations have nothing whatsoever to do with the aesthetic quality and value of the design. A thing in Nature becomes much lovelier if it reminds us of a thing in Art, but a thing in Art gains no real beauty through reminding us of a thing in Nature. The primary aesthetic impression of a work of art borrows nothing from recognition or resemblance. These belong to a later and less perfect stage of apprehension. Properly speaking, they are not part of a real aesthetic impression at all, and the constant preoccupation with subject-matter that characterises nearly all our English art-criticism is what makes our art-criticism, especially as regards literature, so sterile, so profitless, so much beside the mark, and of such curiously little account.

To the Editor, Speaker, printed 5 December 1891

★   ★   ★

The writer of this review ... starts by asking an extremely silly question, and that is, whether or not I have written this book for the purpose of giving pleasure to the British child ... he proceeds, apparently quite seriously, to make the extremely limited vocabulary at the disposal of the British child the standard by which the prose of an artist is to be judged! Now in building this *House of Pomegranates* I had about as much intention of pleasing the British child as I had of pleasing the British public. Mamilius is as entirely delightful as Caliban is entirely detestable, but neither the standard of Mamilius nor the standard of Caliban is my standard.

To the Editor, Pall Mall Gazette, printed 11 December 1891

☆

1892

LORD DARLINGTON Oh, now-a-days so many conceited people go about Society pretending to be good, that I think it shows rather a sweet and modest disposition to pretend to be bad. Besides, there is this to be said. If you pretend to be good, the world takes you very seriously. If you pretend to be bad, it doesn't. Such is the astounding stupidity of optimism.

Lady Windermere's Fan, February 1892; Act I

☆

LORD DARLINGTON I can resist everything except temptation.
LADY WINDERMERE You have the modern affectation of weakness.
LORD DARLINGTON It's only an affectation, Lady Windermere.

☆

LORD DARLINGTON As a wicked man I am a complete failure. Why, there are lots of people who say I have never really done anything wrong in the whole course of my life. Of course they only say it behind my back.

☆

DUCHESS OF BERWICK We have just had tea at Lady Markby's. Such bad tea, too. It was quite undrinkable. I wasn't at all surprised. Her own son-in-law supplies it.

☆

DUCHESS OF BERWICK Our husbands would really forget our existence if we didn't nag at them from time to time, just to remind them that we have a perfect legal right to do so.
LORD DARLINGTON It's a curious thing, Duchess, about the game of marriage – a game, by the way, that is going out of fashion – the wives hold all the honours, and invariably lose the odd trick.
DUCHESS OF BERWICK The odd trick? Is that the husband, Lord Darlington?

☆

LADY WINDERMERE Why do you *talk* so trivially about life, then?

LORD DARLINGTON Because I think that life is far too important a thing
ever to talk seriously about it.

Lady Windermere's Fan, February 1892; Act I

☆

LORD DARLINGTON Now-a-days to be intelligible is to be found out.

☆

DUCHESS OF BERWICK Many a woman has a past, but I am told that she
has at least a dozen, and that they all fit.

☆

DUCHESS OF BERWICK My dear nieces – you know the Saville girls, don't
you? – such nice domestic creatures – plain, dreadfully plain, but
so good – well, they're always at the window doing fancy work,
and making ugly things for the poor, which I think so useful of
them in these dreadful socialistic days . . .

☆

DUCHESS OF BERWICK I assure you, my dear, that on several occasions
after I was first married, I had to pretend to be very ill, and was
obliged to drink the must unpleasant mineral waters, merely to
get Berwick out of town. He was so extremely susceptible.
Though I am bound to say he never gave away any large sums of
money to anybody. He is far too high-principled for that!

☆

DUCHESS OF BERWICK It was only Berwick's brutal and incessant
threats of suicide that made me accept him at all, and before the
year was out, he was running after all kinds of petticoats, every
colour, every shape, every material. In fact, before the honey-
moon was over, I caught him winking at my maid, a most pretty,
respectable girl. I dismissed her at once without a character. –
No, I remember I passed her on to my sister; poor dear Sir
George is so short-sighted, I thought it wouldn't matter. But it
did, though – it was most unfortunate.

☆

DUCHESS OF BERWICK Yes, dear, these wicked women get our husbands
away from us, but they always come back, slightly damaged, of
course.

☆

DUCHESS OF BERWICK His father made a great fortune by selling some
kind of food in circular tins – most palatable, I believe – I fancy it

is the thing the servants always refuse to eat.

*　　*　　*

DUCHESS OF BERWICK Do you know, Mr Hopper, dear Agatha and I are so much interested in Australia. It must be so pretty with all the dear little kangaroos flying about. Agatha has found it on the map. What a curious shape it is! Just like a large packing case. However, it is a very young country, isn't it?

HOPPER Wasn't it made at the same time as the others, Duchess?

DUCHESS OF BERWICK How clever you are, Mr Hopper. You have a cleverness quite of your own.

Lady Windermere's Fan, Act II

☆

CECIL GRAHAM Why don't you ask me how I am? I like people to ask me how I am. It shows a wide-spread interest in my health. Now, to-night I am not at all well. Been dining with my people. Wonder why it is one's people are always so tedious? My father would talk morality after dinner. I told him he was old enough to know better. But my experience is that as soon as people are old enough to know better, they don't know anything at all.

☆

CECIL GRAHAM By the way, Tuppy, which is it? Have you been twice married and once divorced, or twice divorced and once married? I say you've been twice divorced and once married. It seems so much more probable.

LORD AUGUSTUS I have a very bad memory. I really don't remember which.

☆

LADY WINDERMERE London is full of women who trust their husbands. One can always recognise them. They look so thoroughly unhappy.

☆

MRS ERLYNNE I am so much interested in his political career. I think he's sure to be a 'wonderful success. He thinks like a Tory, and talks like a Radical, and that's so important now-a-days.

☆

LADY PLYMDALE It takes a thoroughly good woman to do a thoroughly stupid thing.

☆

LADY PLYMDALE . . . my husband . . . has been so attentive lately, that he has become a perfect nuisance. Now, this woman is just the thing for him. He'll dance attendance upon her as long as she lets him, and won't bother me. I assure you, women of that kind are most useful. They form the basis of other people's marriages.

Lady Windermere's Fan, Act II

☆

DUMBY I am the only person in the world I should like to know thoroughly; but I don't see any chance of it just at present.

☆

DUCHESS OF BERWICK There are lots of vulgar people live in Grosvenor Square, but at least there are no horrid kangaroos crawling about.

☆

DUCHESS OF BERWICK I'm afraid it's the old, old story, dear. Love – well, not love at first sight, but love at the end of the season, which is so much more satisfactory.

☆

CECIL GRAHAM Hopper is one of Nature's gentlemen, the worst type of gentleman I know.

☆

CECIL GRAHAM . . . nothing looks so like innocence as an indiscretion.

★　　★　　★

LORD WINDERMERE Well, that's no business of yours, is it, Cecil?
CECIL GRAHAM None! That is why it interests me. My own business always bores me to death. I prefer other people's.

Lady Windermere's Fan, Act III

☆

DUMBY Awfully commercial, women nowadays. Our grandmothers threw their caps over the mills, of course, but, by Jove, their granddaughters only throw their caps over mills that can raise the wind for them.

☆

CECIL GRAHAM Wicked women bother one. Good women bore one. That is the only difference between them.

☆

DUMBY The youth of the present day are quite monstrous. They have absolutely no respect for dyed hair.

☆

DUMBY It is perfectly brutal the way most women now-a-days behave to men who are not their husbands.

☆

CECIL GRAHAM Oh! gossip is charming! History is merely gossip. But scandal is gossip made tedious by morality. Now, I never moralise. A man who moralises is usually a hypocrite, and a woman who moralises is invariably plain. There is nothing in the whole world so unbecoming to a woman as a Nonconformist conscience. And most women know it, I'm glad to say.

☆

CECIL GRAHAM . . . whenever people agree with me, I always feel I must be wrong.

☆

DUMBY Good heavens! how marriage ruins a man! It's as demoralising as cigarettes, and far more expensive.

☆

LORD DARLINGTON . . . we are all in the gutter, but some of us are looking at the stars.

☆

CECIL GRAHAM Well, there's nothing in the world like the devotion of a married woman. It's a thing no married man knows anything about.

☆

CECIL GRAHAM [*who wears a green carnation*] My dear fellow, what on earth should we men do going about with purity and innocence? A carefully thought-out buttonhole is much more effective.

☆

DUMBY In this world there are only two tragedies. One is not getting what one wants, and the other is getting it. The last is much the worst, the last is a real tragedy!

☆

DUMBY I have been wildly, madly adored. I am sorry I have. It has been an immense nuisance. I should like to be allowed a little time to myself now and then.

LORD AUGUSTUS Time to educate yourself, I suppose.

DUMBY No, time to forget all I have learned. That is so much more important, dear Tuppy.

Lady Windermere's Fan, Act III

☆

CECIL GRAHAM What is a cynic?

LORD DARLINGTON A man who knows the price of everything and the value of nothing.

CECIL GRAHAM And a sentimentalist, my dear Darlington, is a man who sees an absurd value in everything, and doesn't know the market price of any single thing.

☆

DUMBY It's no use talking to Tuppy. You might just as well talk to a brick wall.

CECIL GRAHAM But I like talking to a brick wall – it's the only thing in the world that never contradicts me!

★   ★   ★

MRS ERLYNNE The English climate doesn't suit me. My – heart is affected here, and that I don't like. I prefer living in the south. London is too full of fogs and – and serious people, Lord Windermere. Whether the fogs produce the serious people or whether the serious people produce the fogs, I don't know, but the whole thing rather gets on my nerves . . .

Lady Windermere's Fan, Act IV

☆

MRS ERLYNNE I suppose, Windermere, you would like me to retire into a convent, or become a hospital nurse, or something of that kind, as people do in silly modern novels. That is stupid of you, Arthur; in real life we don't do such things – not as long as we have any good looks left, at any rate. No – what consoles one now-a-days is not repentance, but pleasure. Repentance is quite out of date. And besides, if a woman really repents, she has to go to a bad dressmaker, otherwise no one believes in her. And nothing in the world would induce me to do that.

☆

LADY WINDERMERE We all have ideals in life. At least we all should have. Mine is my mother.

MRS ERLYNNE Ideals are dangerous things. Realities are better. They wound, but they're better.

LADY WINDERMERE If I lost my ideals, I should lose everything.

MRS ERLYNNE Everything?
LADY WINDERMERE Yes.

★　　★　　★

. . . it is quite true that I hold that the stage is to a play no more than a picture-frame is to a painting, and that the actable value of a play has nothing whatsoever to do with its value as a work of art . . . It is, sir, not by the mimes that the muses are to be judged.

To the Editor, *Daily Telegraph*, printed 20 February 1892

☆

. . . the writer of the article in question . . . goes wrong . . . in saying that I describe this frame – the stage – as being furnished 'with a set of puppets'. He admits that he speaks only by report; but he should have remembered, sir, that report is not merely a lying jade, which I personally would readily forgive her, but a jade who lies without lovely invention – a thing that I, at any rate, can forgive her never.

☆

. . . the personality of the actor is often a source of danger in the perfect presentation of a work of art. It may distort. It may lead astray. It may be a discord in the tone or symphony. For anybody can act. Most people in England do nothing else. To be conventional is to be a comedian. To act a particular part, however, is a very different thing, and a very difficult thing as well.

☆

The actor's aim is, or should be, to convert his own accidental personality into the real and essential personality of the character he is called upon to impersonate, whatever that character may be; or perhaps I should say that there are two schools of actors – the school of those who attain their effect by exaggeration of personality, and the school of those who attain it by suppression. It would be too long to discuss these schools, or to decide which of them the dramatist loves best.

☆

There are many advantages in puppets. They never argue. They have no crude views about art. They have no private lives. We are never bothered by accounts of their virtues, or bored by recitals of their vices; and when they are out of an engagement they never do good in public or save people from drowning; nor do they speak more than is set down for them. They recognise the presiding intellect of the dramatist, and have never been known to ask for their parts to be written up. They are admirably docile, and have no personalities at all.

☆

All artists in this vulgar age need protection certainly. Perhaps they have always needed it. But the nineteenth-century artist finds it not in Prince, or Pope, or patron, but in high indifference of temper, in the pleasures of creation of beautiful things, and the long contemplation of them in disdain of what in life is common and ignoble, and in such felicitous sense of humour as enables one to see how vain and foolish is all popular opinion, and popular judgment, upon the wonderful things of art.

To the Editor, *Daily Telegraph*, printed 20 February 1892

★   ★   ★

When criticism becomes in England a real art, as it should be, and when none but those of artistic instinct and artistic cultivation are allowed to write about works of art, artists will no doubt read criticisms with a certain amount of intellectual interest. As things are at present, the criticisms of ordinary newspapers are of no interest whatsoever, except in so far as they display in its crudest form the extraordinary Bœotianism of a country that has produced some Athenians, and in which other Athenians have come to dwell.

To the Editor, *St James's Gazette*, printed 27 February 1892

1893

SALOMÉ Je ne resterai pas. Je ne peux pas rester. Pourquoi le tétrarque me regarde-t-il toujours avec ses yeux de taupe sous ses paupières tremblantes? – C'est étrange que le mari de ma mère me regarde comme cela. Je ne sais pas ce que cela veut dire. – Au fait, si, je le sais.

Salomé
☆

SALOMÉ Comme l'air est frais ici! Enfin, ici on respire! Là-dedans il y a des Juifs de Jérusalem qui se déchirent à cause de leurs ridicules cérémonies, et des barbares qui boivent toujours et jettent leur vin sur les dalles, et des Grecs de Smyrne avec leurs yeux peints et leurs joues fardées, et leurs cheveux frisés en spirales, et des Egyptiens, silencieux, subtils, avec leurs ongles de jade et leurs manteaux bruns, et des Romains avec leur brutalité, leur lourdeur, leurs gros mots. Ah! que je déteste les Romains! Ce sont des gens communs, et ils se donnent des airs de grands seigneurs.

☆

SALOMÉ Que c'est bon de voir la lune! Elle ressemble à une petite pièce de monnaie. On dirait une toute petite fleur d'argent. Elle est froide et chaste, la lune – Je suis sûre qu'elle est vierge. Elle a la beauté d'une vierge – Oui, elle est vierge. Elle ne s'est jamais souillée. Elle ne s'est jamais donnée aux hommes, comme les autres Déesses.

☆

SALOMÉ Qui a crié cela?

☆

SALOMÉ Ah! le prophète. Celui dont le tétrarque a peur?

☆

SALOMÉ Il dit des choses monstrueuses, à propos de ma mère, n'est-ce pas?

☆

SALOMÉ Oui, il dit des choses monstrueuses d'elle.

☆

197

SALOMÉ Je n'y retournerai pas.

☆

SALOMÉ Est-ce un vieillard, le prophète?

☆

SALOMÉ Le prophète – est-ce un vieillard?

☆

SALOMÉ Qui est Elie?

☆

SALOMÉ Quelle étrange voix! Je voudrais bien lui parler.

☆

SALOMÉ Je veux lui parler.

☆

SALOMÉ Je le veux.

☆

SALOMÉ Faîtes sortir le prophète. ·

☆

SALOMÉ [*s'approchant de la citerne et y regardant*] Comme il fait noir là-dedans! Cela doit être terrible d'être dans un trou si noir! Cela ressemble à une tombe [*aux soldats*] – Vous ne m'avez pas entendue? Faîtes-le sortir. Je veux le voir.

☆

SALOMÉ Vous me faîtes attendre.

☆

SALOMÉ [*regardant le jeune syrien*] Ah!

☆

SALOMÉ [*s'approchant du jeune syrien*] Vous ferez cela pour moi, n'est-ce pas, Narraboth? Vous ferez cela pour moi? J'ai toujours été douce pour vous. N'est-ce pas que vous ferez cela pour moi? Je veux seulement le regarder, cet étrange prophète. On a tant parlé de lui. J'ai si souvent entendu le tétrarque parler de lui. Je pense qu'il a peur de lui, le tétrarque. Je suis sûre qu'il a peur de lui – Est-ce que vous aussi, Narraboth, est-ce que vous aussi vous en avez peur?

☆

SALOMÉ Vous ferez cela pour moi, Narraboth, et demain quand je passerai dans ma litière sous la porte des vendeurs d'idoles, je laisserai tomber une petite fleur pour vous, une petite fleur verte.

☆

SALOMÉ [*souriant*] Vous ferez cela pour moi, Narraboth. Vous savez bien que vous ferez cela pour moi. Et demain quand je passerai dans ma litière sur le pont des acheteurs d'idoles je vous regarderai à travers les voiles de mousseline, je vous regarderai, Narraboth, je vous sourirai, peut-être. Regardez-moi, Narraboth. Regardez-moi. Ah! vous savez bien que vous allez faire ce que je vous demande. Vous le savez bien, n'est-ce pas? – Moi, je sais bien.

☆

SALOMÉ Ah!... [*Le prophète sort de la citerne. Salomé le regarde et recule.*]

☆

SALOMÉ De qui parle-t-il?

☆

SALOMÉ C'est de ma mère qu'il parle.

☆

SALOMÉ Si, c'est de ma mère.

☆

SALOMÉ Mais il est terrible, il est terrible.

☆

SALOMÉ Ce sont les yeux surtout qui sont terribles. On dirait des trous noirs laissés par des flambeaux sur une tapisserie de Tyr. On dirait des cavernes noires où demeurent des dragons, des cavernes noires d'Égypte où les dragons trouvent leur asile. On dirait des lacs noirs troublés par des lunes fantastiques – Pensez-vous qu'il parlera encore?

☆

SALOMÉ Comme il est maigre aussi! il ressemble à une mince image d'ivoire. On dirait une image d'argent. Je suis sûre qu'il est chaste, autant que la lune. Il ressemble à un rayon de lune. Sa chair doit être très froide, comme de l'ivoire – Je veux le regarder de près.

☆

SALOMÉ Il faut que je le regarde de près.

☆

SALOMÉ Je suis Salomé, fille d'Herodias, princesse de Judée.

☆

SALOMÉ Parle encore, Iokanaan. Ta voix m'enivre.

☆

SALOMÉ Mais parle encore. Parle encore, Iokanaan, et dis-moi ce qu'il faut que je fasse.

☆

SALOMÉ Qui est-ce, le fils de l'Homme? Est-il aussi beau que toi, Iokanaan?

☆

SALOMÉ Iokanaan!

☆

SALOMÉ Iokanaan! Je suis amoureuse de ton corps. Ton corps est blanc comme le lis d'un pré que le faucheur n'a jamais fauché. Ton corps est blanc comme les neiges qui couchent sur les montagnes, comme les neiges qui couchent sur les montagnes de Judée, et descendent dans les vallées. Les roses du jardin de la reine d'Arabie ne sont pas aussi blanches que ton corps. Ni les roses du jardin de la reine d'Arabie, ni les pieds de l'aurore qui trépignent sur les feuilles, ni le sein de la lune quand elle couche sur le sein de la mer – Il n'y a rien au monde d'aussi blanc que ton corps. – Laisse-moi toucher ton corps!

☆

SALOMÉ Ton corps est hideux. Il est comme le corps d'un lepreux. Il est comme un mur de plâtre ou les vipères sont passées, comme un mur de plâtre ou les scorpions ont fait leur nid. Il est comme un sépulcre blanchi, et qui est plein de choses dégoûtantes. Il est horrible, il est horrible ton corps! – C'est de tes cheveux que je suis amoureuse, Iokanaan. Tes cheveux ressemblent à des grappes de raisins, à des grappes de raisins noirs qui pendent des vignes d'Edom dans le pays des Edomites. Tes cheveux sont comme les cèdres du Liban, comme les grands cèdres du Liban qui donnent de l'ombre aux lions et aux voleurs qui veulent se cacher pendant la journée. Les longues nuits noires, les nuits où la lune ne se montre pas, où les étoiles ont peur, ne sont pas aussi noires. Le silence qui demeure dans les forêts n'est pas aussi noir. Il n'y a rien au monde d'aussi noir que tes cheveux. – Laisse-moi toucher tes cheveux.

☆

SALOMÉ Tes cheveux sont horribles. Ils sont couverts de boue et de poussière. On dirait une couronne d'épines qu'on a placée sur ton front. On dirait un nœud de serpents noirs qui se tortillent autour de ton cou. Je n'aime pas tes cheveux. – C'est de ta bouche que je suis amoureuse, Iokanaan. Ta bouche est comme une bande d'écarlate sur une tour d'ivoire. Elle est comme une pomme de grenade coupé par un couteau d'ivoire. Les fleurs de grenade qui fleurissent dans les jardins de Tyr et sont plus rouges que les roses, ne sont pas aussi rouges. Les cris rouges des trompettes qui annoncent l'arrivée des rois, et font peur à l'ennemi ne sont pas aussi rouges. Ta bouche est plus rouge que les pieds de ceux qui foulent le vin dans les pressoirs. Elle est plus rouge que les pieds des colombes qui demeurent dans les temples et sont nourries par les prêtres. Elle est plus rouge que les pieds de celui qui revient d'une forêt ou il a tué un lion et vu des tigres dorés. Ta bouche est comme une branche de corail que des pêcheurs ont trouvée dans le crépuscule de la mer et qu'ils réservent pour les rois – ! Elle est comme le vermillon que les Moabites trouvent dans les mines de Moab et que les rois leur prennent. Elle est comme l'arc du roi des Perses qui est peint avec du vermillon et qui a des cornes de corail. Il n'y a rien au monde d'aussi rouge que ta bouche – laisse-moi baiser ta bouche.

☆

SALOMÉ Je baiserai ta bouche, Iokanaan. Je baiserai ta bouche.

☆

SALOMÉ Je baiserai ta bouche, Iokanaan.

☆

SALOMÉ Laisse-moi baiser ta bouche, Iokanaan.

☆

SALOMÉ Laisse-moi baiser ta bouche.

☆

SALOMÉ Laisse-moi baiser ta bouche.

☆

SALOMÉ Je baiserai ta bouche, Iokanaan.

☆

SALOMÉ Je baiserai ta bouche, Iokanaan, je baiserai ta bouche. [*Il descend dans la citerne.*]

☆

SALOMÉ Je n'ai pas soif, tétrarque.

☆

SALOMÉ Je n'ai pas faim, tétrarque.

☆

SALOMÉ Je ne suis pas fatiguée, tétrarque.

☆

SALOMÉ Je n'ai aucune envie de danser, tétrarque.

☆

SALOMÉ Je ne danserai pas, tétrarque.

☆

SALOMÉ [*se levant*] Vous me donnerez tout ce que je demanderai, tétrarque?

☆

SALOMÉ Vous le jurez, tétrarque?

☆

SALOMÉ Sur quoi jurez-vous, tétrarque?

☆

SALOMÉ Vous avez juré, tétrarque.

☆

SALOMÉ Tout ce que je vous demanderai, fût-ce la moitié de votre royaume?

☆

SALOMÉ Je danserai pour vous, tétrarque.

☆

SALOMÉ Vous avez juré, têtrarque.

☆

SALOMÉ J'attends que mes esclaves m'apportent des parfums et les sept voiles et m'ôtent mes sandales. [*Les esclaves apportent des parfums et les sept voiles et ôtent les sandales de Salomé.*]

☆

SALOMÉ Je suis prête, tétrarque. [*Salomé danse la danse des sept voiles.*]

☆

SALOMÉ [*s'agenouillant*] Je veux qu'on m'apporte présentement dans un bassin d'argent –

☆

SALOMÉ [*se levant*] La tête d'Iokanaan.

☆

SALOMÉ Je n'écoute pas ma mère. C'est pour mon propre plaisir que je demande la tête d'Iokanaan dans un bassin d'argent. Vous avez juré, Hérode. N'oubliez pas que vous avez juré.

☆

SALOMÉ Je vous demande la tête d'Iokanaan.

☆

SALOMÉ Vous avez juré, Hérode.

☆

SALOMÉ Je demande la tête d'Iokanaan.

☆

SALOMÉ La tête d'Iokanaan.

☆

SALOMÉ Donnez-moi la tête d'Iokanaan.

☆

SALOMÉ Donnez-moi la tête d'Iokanaan.

☆

SALOMÉ Donne-moi la tête d'Iokanaan.

☆

SALOMÉ [*Elle se penche sur la citerne et écoute*] Il n'y a pas de bruit. Je n'entends rien. Pourquoi ne crie-t-il pas, cet homme? Ah! si quelqu'un cherchait à me tuer, je crierais, je me débattrais, je ne voudrais pas souffrir –

Frappe, frappe, Naaman. Frappe, je te dis –

Non. Je n'entends rien. Il y a un silence affreux. Ah! quelque chose est tombé par terre. J'ai entendu quelque chose tomber. C'était l'épée du bourreau. Il a peur, cet esclave! Il a laissé tomber son épée. Il n'ose pas le tuer. C'est un lâche, cet esclave! Il faut envoyer des soldats. [*Elle voit le page d'Herodias et s'adresse à lui.*]

Viens ici. Tu as été l'ami de celui qui est mort, n'est-ce pas? Eh bien, il n'y a pas en assez de morts. Dîtes aux soldats qu'ils descendent et m'apportent ce que je demande, ce que le tétrarque m'a promis, ce qui m'appartient. [*Le page recule. Elle s'adresse aux soldats.*]

Venez ici, soldats. Descendez dans cette citerne, et apportez-moi le tête de cet homme. [*Les soldats reculent.*]

Tétrarque, tétrarque, commandez a vos soldats de m'apporter la tête d'Iokanaan. [*Un grand bras noir, le bras du bourreau, sort de la citerne apportant sur un bouclier d'argent la tête d'Iokanaan. Salomé la saisit.*]

Ah! tu n'as pas voulu me laisser baiser ta bouche, Iokanaan. Eh bien! je la baiserai maintenant. Je la mordrai avec mes dents comme on mord un fruit mûr. Oui, je baiserai ta bouche, Iokanaan. Je te l'ai dit, n'est-ce pas? je te l'ai dit. Eh bien! je la baiserai maintenant –

Mais pourquoi ne me regardes-tu pas, Iokanaan? Tes yeux qui étaient si terribles, qui étaient si pleins de colère et de mépris, ils sont fermés maintenant. Pourquoi sont-ils fermés? Ouvre tes yeux! Soulève tes paupières, Iokanaan. Pourquoi ne me regardes-tu pas? As-tu peur de moi, Iokanaan, que tu ne veux pas me regarder? –

Et ta langue qui était comme un serpent rouge dardant des poisons, elle ne dit rien maintenant, Iokanaan, cette vipère rouge qui a vomi son venin sur moi. C'est étrange, n'est-ce pas? Comment se fait-il que la vipère rouge ne remue plus? –

Tu n'as pas voulu de moi, Iokanaan. Tu m'as rejetée. Tu m'as dit des choses infâmes. Tu m'as traitée comme une courtisane, comme une prostituée, moi, Salomé, fille d'Herodias, Princesse de Judée! Eh bien, Iokanaan, moi je vis encore, mais toi tu es mort et ta tête m'appartient. Je puis en faire ce que je veux. Je puis la jeter aux chiens et aux oiseaux de l'air. Ce que laisseront les chiens, les oiseaux de l'air le mangeront –

Ah! Iokanaan, tu as été le seul homme que j'ai aimé. Tous les autres hommes m'inspirent du dégoût. Mais, toi, tu étais beau. Ton corps était une colonne d'ivoire sur un socle d'argent. C'était un jardin plein de colombes et de lis d'argent. C'était une tour d'argent ornée de boucliers d'ivoire. Il n'y avait rien au monde d'aussi blanc que ton corps. Il n'y avait rien au monde d'aussi noir que tes cheveux. Dans le monde tout entier il n'y avait rien d'aussi rouge que ta bouche. Ta voix était un encensoir qui répandait d'étranges parfums, et quand je te regardais j'entendais une musique étrange! Ah! pourquoi ne m'as-tu pas regardée, Iokanaan? Derrière tes mains et tes blasphèmes tu as caché ton visage. Tu as mis sur tes yeux le bandeau de celui qui veut voir son Dieu. Eh bien, tu l'as vu, ton Dieu, Iokanaan, mais moi, moi – tu ne m'as jamais vue. Si tu m'avais vue, tu m'aurais aimée. Moi, je t'ai vu, Iokanaan, et je t'ai aimé. Oh! comme je t'ai aimé. Je t'aime encore, Iokanaan. Je n'aime que toi –

J'ai soif de ta beauté. J'ai faim de ton corps. Et ni le vin, ni les fruits ne peuvent apaiser mon désir. Que ferai-je, Iokanaan, maintenant? Ni les fleuves ni les grandes eaux, ne pourraient éteindre ma passion. J'étais une Princesse, tu m'as dédaignée.

J'étais une vierge, tu m'as déflorée. J'étais chaste, tu as rempli
mes veines de feu –

Ah! Ah! pourquoi ne m'as-tu pas regardée, Iokanaan? Si tu
m'avais regardée tu m'aurais aimée. Je sais bien que tu m'aurais
aimée, et le mystère de l'amour est plus grand que le mystère de la
mort. Il ne faut regarder que l'amour.

☆

LA VOIX DE SALOMÉ Ah! j'ai baisé ta bouche, Iokanaan, j'ai baisé ta
bouche. Il y avait une âcre saveur sur tes lèvres. Était-ce la saveur
du sang? –

Mais, peut-être est-ce la saveur de l'amour. On dit que l'amour
a une âcre saveur –

Mais, qu'importe? Qu'importe? J'ai baisé ta bouche, Iokanaan,
j'ai baisé ta bouche.

[Un rayon de lune tombe sur Salomé et l'éclaire.]
HERODE *[se retournant et voyant Salomé]*: Tuez cette femme!

*[Les soldats s'élancent et écrasent sous leurs boucliers Salomé, fille d'Héro-
dias, Princesse de Judée.]*

★   ★   ★

My attention has been drawn to a review of *Salomé* which was
published in your columns last week. The opinions of English critics
on a French work of mine have, of course, little, if any, interest for me.

To the Editor, *The Times*, printed 2 March 1893

☆

The fact that the greatest tragic actress of any stage now living saw in
my play such beauty that she was anxious to produce it, to take herself
the part of the heroine, to lend the entire poem the glamour of her personality, and to my prose the music of her flute-like voice – this was
naturally, and always will be, a source of pride and pleasure to me,
and I look forward with delight to seeing Mme Bernhardt present my
play in Paris, that vivid centre of art, where religious dramas are often
performed. But my play was in no sense of the words written for this
great actress. I have never written a play for any actor or actress, nor
shall I ever do so. Such work is for the artisan in literature, not for the
artist.

★   ★   ★

LADY CAROLINE And that member of Parliament, Mr Kettle –
SIR JOHN Kelvil, my love, Kelvil.
LADY CAROLINE He must be quite respectable. One has never heard his
name before in the course on one's life, which speaks volumes for
a man, now-a-days.

A Woman of No Importance, April 1893, Act I

204

✩

LADY CAROLINE It is not customary in England, Miss Worsley, for a young lady to speak with such enthusiasm for any person of the opposite sex. English women conceal their feelings till after they are married. They show them then.

✩

LADY HUNSTANTON . . . Lord Illingworth may marry any day. I was in hopes he would have married Lady Kelso. But I believe he said her family was too large. Or was it her feet? I forget which.

✩

LADY HUNSTANTON Nobody likes to be asked favours. I remember poor Charlotte Pagden making herself quite unpopular one season, because she had a French governess she wanted to recommend to every one.
LADY CAROLINE I saw the governess, Jane. Lady Pagden sent her to me. It was before Eleanor came out. She was far too good-looking to be in any respectable household. I don't wonder Lady Pagden was so anxious to get rid of her.

✩

MRS ALLONBY But somehow, I feel sure that if I lived in the country for six months, I should become so unsophisticated that no one would take the slightest notice of me.
LADY HUNSTANTON I assure you, dear, that the country has not that effect at all. Why, it was from Melthorpe, which is only two miles from here, that Lady Belton eloped with Lord Fethersdale. I remember the occurrence perfectly. Poor Lord Belton died three days afterwards of joy, or gout. I forget which.

✩

LADY HUNSTANTON I am afraid, dear, you like making fools out of men.
LADY CAROLINE That is never necessary.
LADY HUNSTANTON The modern education of woman is certainly wonderful. I am told that now-a-days every wife knows more than her husband does.
MRS ALLONBY Much more, Lady Hunstanton, man as a sex has been found out.
LADY HUNSTANTON Ah, we found them out too, dear, but in a different way.
> Not used. Not cancelled. Ultimately replaced by Lady Hunstanton's line 'I don't know how the world would get on with such a theory as that, dear Mrs Allonby.'

✩

LADY STUTFIELD Ah! The world was made for men and not for women.
MRS ALLONBY Oh, don't say that, Lady Stutfield. We have a much better time than they have. There are far more things forbidden to us than are forbidden to them.

☆

LADY STUTFIELD And what have you been writing about this morning, Mr Kelvil?
KELVIL On the usual subject, Lady Stutfield. On Purity.
LADY STUTFIELD That must be such a very, very interesting thing to write about.
KELVIL It is the one subject of really national importance, now-a-days, Lady Stutfield. I purpose addressing my constituents on the question before Parliament meets. I find that the poorer classes of this country display a marked desire for a higher ethical standard.
LADY STUTFIELD How quite, quite nice of them.

Originally followed last item, but retained.

☆

LORD ILLINGWORTH The youth of America is their oldest tradition. It has been going on now for three hundred years. To hear them talk one would imagine they were in their first childhood. As far as civilisation goes they are in their second.

☆

LORD ILLINGWORTH One should never take sides in anything, Mr Kelvil. Taking sides is the beginning of sincerity, and earnestness follows shortly afterwards, and the human being becomes a bore.

☆

LORD ILLINGWORTH As for the two sides in our politics, what are they? A Radical is merely a man who has never dined, and a Tory simply a gentleman who has never thought.

Not used. Not cancelled. Originally followed previous item.

☆

KELVIL Still our East End is a very important problem.
LORD ILLINGWORTH Quite so. It is the problem of slavery. And we are trying to solve it by amusing the slaves.
LADY HUNSTANTON Certainly, a great deal may be done by means of cheap entertainments, as you say, Lord Illingworth. Dear Dr Daubeny, our rector here, provides, with the assistance of his curates, really admirable recreations for the poor during the winter. And much good may be done by means of a magic lantern, or a missionary, or some popular amusement of that kind.

206

LADY CAROLINE I am not at all in favour of amusements for the poor, Jane. Blankets and coals are sufficient. There is too much love of pleasure amongst the upper classes as it is. Health is what we want in modern life. The tone is not healthy, not healthy at all.

KELVIL You are quite right, Lady Caroline.

LADY CAROLINE I believe I am usually right.

MRS ALLONBY Horrid word 'health'.

LORD ILLINGWORTH Silliest word in our language, and one knows so well the popular idea of health. The English country gentleman galloping after a fox – the unspeakable in full pursuit of the uneatable.

☆

KELVIL Surely the opinion of the majority is what is to be followed?

LORD ILLINGWORTH Majorities are always wrong, and minorities are never right.

Not used. Cancelled. Originally preceded next item.

☆

KELVIL Are you serious in putting forward such a view?

LORD ILLINGWORTH Quite serious, Mr Kelvil. (*To* MRS ALLONBY) Vulgar habit that is people have now-a-days of asking one, after one has given them an idea, whether one is serious or not. Nothing is serious except passion. The intellect is not a serious thing, and never has been. It is an instrument on which one plays, that is all. The only serious form of intellect I know is the British intellect. And on the British intellect the illiterates play the drum.

☆

LADY HUNSTANTON Are you going, Mrs Allonby?

MRS ALLONBY Just as far as the conservatory. Lord Illingworth told me this morning that there was an orchid there as beautiful as the seven deadly sins.

LADY HUNSTANTON My dear, I hope there is nothing of the kind. I will certainly speak to the gardener.

☆

LADY CAROLINE You believe good of every one, Jane. It is a great fault.

LADY STUTFIELD Do you really, really think, Lady Caroline, that one should believe evil of every one?

LADY CAROLINE I think it is much safer to do so, Lady Stutfield. Until, of course, people are found out to be good. But that requires a great deal of investigation nowadays.

LADY STUTFIELD But there is so much unkind scandal in modern life.

LADY CAROLINE Lord Illingworth remarked to me last night at dinner that the basis of every scandal is an absolutely immoral certainty.

A Woman of No Importance, April 1893, Act I

☆

MRS ALLONBY Curious thing, plain women are always jealous of their husbands, beautiful women never are!

LORD ILLINGWORTH Beautiful women never have time. They are always so occupied in being jealous of other people's husbands.

☆

LORD ILLINGWORTH Twenty years of romance make a woman look like a ruin; but twenty years of marriage make her something like a public building.

☆

LORD ILLINGWORTH Nothing spoils a romance so much as a sense of humour in the woman.

MRS ALLONBY Or the want of it in the man.

LORD ILLINGWORTH You are quite right. In a Temple every one should be serious, except the thing that is worshipped.

MRS ALLONBY And that should be man?

LORD ILLINGWORTH Women kneel so gracefully; men don't.

☆

MRS ALLONBY Don't you find yourself longing for a London dinner-party?

HESTER WORSLEY I dislike London dinner-parties.

MRS ALLONBY I adore them. The clever people never listen, and the stupid people never talk.

HESTER WORSLEY I think the stupid people talk a great deal.

MRS ALLONBY Ah, I never listen!

☆

LORD ILLINGWORTH One should never trust a woman who tells one her real age. A woman who would tell one that would tell one anything.

☆

LORD ILLINGWORTH I don't mind plain women being Puritans. It is the only excuse they have for being plain.

☆

LORD ILLINGWORTH What do you call a bad man?

MRS ALLONBY The sort of man who admires innocence.

LORD ILLINGWORTH And a bad woman!

MRS ALLONBY Oh! the sort of woman a man never gets tired of.

☆

MRS ALLONBY We women adore failures. They lean on us.
LORD ILLINGWORTH You worship successes. You cling to them.
MRS ALLONBY We are the laurels to hide their baldness.

☆

LORD ILLINGWORTH I never intend to grow old. The soul is born old but grows young. That is the comedy of life.
MRS ALLONBY And the body is born young and grows old. That is life's tragedy.

☆

LORD ILLINGWORTH One can survive everything now-a-days, except death, and live down anything except a good reputation.
MRS ALLONBY Have you tried a good reputation?
LORD ILLINGWORTH It is one of the many annoyances to which I have never been subjected.

☆

LORD ILLINGWORTH I adore simple pleasures. They are the last refuge of the complex.

★   ★   ★

LADY CAROLINE It's perfectly scandalous the amount of bachelors who are going about society. There should be a law passed to compel them all to marry within twelve months.
LADY STUTFIELD But if they're in love with some one who, perhaps, is tied to another?
LADY CAROLINE In that case, Lady Stutfield, they would be married off in a week to some plain respectable girl, in order to teach them not to meddle with other people's property.
MRS ALLONBY I don't think that we should ever be spoken of as other people's property. All men are married women's property. That is the only true definition of what married women's property really is. But we don't belong to any one.

A Woman of No Importance, Act II

☆

MRS ALLONBY Life, Lady Stutfield, is simply a *mauvais quart d'heure* made up of exquisite moments.

☆

MRS ALLONBY Men always want to be a woman's first love. That is their clumsy vanity. We women have a more subtle instinct about things. What we like is to be a man's last romance.

☆

MRS ALLONBY Man, poor, awkward, reliable, necessary man belongs to a sex that has been rational for millions and millions of years. He can't help himself. It is in his race. The History of Woman is very different. We have always been picturesque protests against the mere existence of common sense. We saw its dangers from the first.

☆

HESTER WORSLEY Oh, your English society seems to me shallow, selfish, foolish. It has blinded its eyes, and stopped its ears. It lies like a leper in purple. It sits like a dead thing smeared with gold. It is all wrong, all wrong.
LADY STUTFIELD I don't think one should know of these things. It is not very, very nice, is it?

☆

HESTER WORSLEY And till you count what is a shame in a woman to be infamy in a man, you will always be unjust, and Right, that pillar of fire, and Wrong, that pillar of cloud, will be made dim to your eyes, or be not seen at all, or if seen, not regarded.
LADY CAROLINE Might I, dear Miss Worsley, as you are standing up, ask you for my cotton that is just behind you? Thank you.

☆

LADY CAROLINE . . . after a good dinner one can forgive anybody, even one's own relations.

☆

LADY HUNSTANTON That would be the last Earl but one. He was a very curious man. He wanted to marry beneath him. Or wouldn't, I believe. There was some scandal about it.

☆

LADY HUNSTANTON And there was also, I remember, a clergyman who wanted to be a lunatic, or a lunatic who wanted to be a clergyman, I forget which, but I know the Court of Chancery investigated the matter, and decided that he was quite sane. And I saw him afterwards at poor Lord Plumstead's with straws in his hair, or something very odd about him. I can't recall what.

☆

LORD ILLINGWORTH All women become like their mothers. That is their tragedy.

MRS ALLONBY No man does. That is his.

☆

LORD ILLINGWORTH I was only twenty-two. I was twenty-one, I believe, when the whole thing began in your father's garden.

MRS ARBUTHNOT When a man is old enough to do wrong he should be old enough to do right also.

LORD ILLINGWORTH My dear Rachel, intellectual generalities are always interesting, but generalities in morals mean absolutely nothing. As for saying I left our child to starve, that, of course, is untrue and silly. My mother offered you six hundred a year. But you wouldn't take anything. You simply disappeared, and carried the child away with you.

MRS ARBUTHNOT I wouldn't have accepted a penny from her. Your father was different. He told you, in my presence, when we were in Paris, that is was your duty to marry me.

LORD ILLINGWORTH Oh, duty is what one expects from others, it is not what one does one's-self.

☆

MRS ARBUTHNOT Gerald cannot separate his future from my past.

LORD ILLINGWORTH That is exactly what he should do. That is exactly what you should help him to do. What a typical woman you are! You talk sentimentally, and you are thoroughly selfish the whole time.

☆

MRS ARBUTHNOT No doubt if I were a man, I would be thoroughly selfish and talk with brutality.

LORD ILLINGWORTH Well, we at any rate have the advantage of being candid.

Not used. Cancelled. Originally followed previous item.

☆

LORD ILLINGWORTH Discontent is the first step in the progress of a man or a nation.

★   ★   ★

LORD ILLINGWORTH There is nothing like youth. The middle-aged are mortgaged to Life. The old are in Life's lumber-room. But youth is the Lord of Life. Youth has a kingdom waiting for it. Every one is born a king, and most people die in exile, like most kings. To win back my youth, Gerald, there is nothing I wouldn't do – except take exercise, get up early, or be a useful member of the community.

A Woman of No Importance, Act III

☆

GERALD It is very curious, my mother never talks to me about my father. I sometimes think she must have married beneath her.
LORD ILLINGWORTH (*winces slightly*) Really?

☆

LORD ILLINGWORTH Oh! talk to every woman as if you loved her, and to every man as if he bored you, and at the end of your first season you will have the reputation of possessing the most perfect social tact.

☆

LORD ILLINGWORTH To get into the best society, now-a-days, one has either to feed people, amuse people, or shock people – that is all!

☆

LORD ILLINGWORTH To be in it is merely a bore. But to be out of it simply a tragedy. Society is a necessary thing. No man has any real success in this world unless he has got women to back him, and women rule society. If you have not got women on your side you are quite over. You might just as well be a barrister, or a stockbroker, or a journalist at once.

☆

LORD ILLINGWORTH Women are pictures. Men are problems. If you want to know what a woman really means – which, by the way, is always a dangerous thing to do – look at her, don't listen to her.

☆

LORD ILLINGWORTH . . . to the philosopher, my dear Gerald, women represent the triumph of matter over mind – just as men represent the triumph of mind over morals.

☆

LORD ILLINGWORTH The history of women is the history of the worst form of tyranny the world has ever known. The tyranny of the weak over the strong. It is the only tyranny that lasts.

☆

LORD ILLINGWORTH Women are a fascinatingly wilful sex. Every woman is a rebel, and usually in wild revolt against herself.

☆

LORD ILLINGWORTH ... the happiness of a married man, my dear Gerald, depends on the people he has not married.

☆

LORD ILLINGWORTH One should always be in love. That is the reason one should never marry.

☆

LORD ILLINGWORTH When one is in love one begins by deceiving one's-self. And one ends by deceiving others. That is what the world calls a romance. But a really *grande passion* is comparatively rare nowadays. It is the privilege of people who have nothing to do. That is the one use of the idle classes in a country ...

☆

LORD ILLINGWORTH You should study the Peerage, Gerald. It is the one book a young man about town should know thoroughly, and it is the best thing in fiction the English have ever done.

☆

LORD ILLINGWORTH ... the world has been made by fools that wise men should live in it!

☆

THE ARCHDEACON ... she has many other amusements. She is very much interested in her own health.
LADY HUNSTANTON Ah! that is always a nice distraction, is it not?

☆

LORD ILLINGWORTH ... the world has always laughed at its own trage-dies, that being the only way in which it has been able to bear them ... consequently, whatever the world has treated seriously belongs to the comedy side of things.
LADY HUNSTANTON Now I am quite out of my depth. I usually am when Lord Illingworth says anything. And the Humane Society is most careless. They never rescue me. I am left to sink. I have a dim idea, dear Lord Illingworth, that you are always on the side of the sinners, and I know I always try to be on the side of the saints, but that is as far as I get. And after all, it may be merely the fancy of a drowning person.
LORD ILLINGWORTH The only difference between the saint and the sin-

ner is that every saint has a past, and every sinner has a future.
A Woman of No Importance, Act III

☆

LADY HUNSTANTON Lady Stutfield is very sympathetic. She is just as sympathetic about one thing as she is about another. A beautfiul nature.

☆

LORD ILLINGWORTH The world is simply divided into two classes – those who believe the incredible, like the public – and those who do the improbable –
MRS ALLONBY Like yourself?
LORD ILLINGWORTH Yes; I am always astonishing myself. It is the only thing that makes life worth living.

☆

LORD ILLINGWORTH I don't intend to grow perfect at all. At least, I hope I shan't. It would be most inconvenient. Women love us for our defects. If we have enough of them, they will forgive us everything, even our gigantic intellects.
MRS ALLONBY It is premature to ask us to forgive analysis. We forgive adoration; that is quite as much as should be expected from us.

☆

LADY HUNSTANTON . . . I think on the whole that the secret of life is to take things very, very easily.
MRS ALLONBY The secret of life is never to have an emotion that is unbecoming.
LADY STUTFIELD The secret of life is to appreciate the pleasure of being terribly, terribly deceived.
KELVIL The secret of life is to resist temptation, Lady Stutfield.
LORD ILLINGWORTH There is no secret of life. Life's aim, if it has one, is simply to be always looking for temptations. There are not nearly enough. I sometimes pass a whole day without coming across a single one. It is quite dreadful. It makes one so nervous about the future.

☆

LORD ILLINGWORTH All thought is immoral. Its very essence is destruction. If you think of anything, you kill it. Nothing survives being thought of.

☆

LORD ILLINGWORTH Moderation is a fatal thing, Lady Hunstanton. Nothing succeeds like excess.

☆

LORD ILLINGWORTH There is something perfectly awful about the memories of most women – they are always exhuming the past and bothering one about the things one has said or done, as if it was any matter what one has said or done.

Not used. Cancelled. Originally preceding the next item

☆

LORD ILLINGWORTH No woman should have a memory. Memory in a woman is the beginning of dowdiness. One can always tell from a woman's bonnet whether she has got a memory or not.

☆

MRS ALLONBY There is a beautiful moon to-night.
LORD ILLINGWORTH Let us go and look at it. To look at anything that is inconstant is charming now-a-days.
MRS ALLONBY You have your looking-glass.
LORD ILLINGWORTH It is unkind. It merely shows me my wrinkles.
MRS ALLONBY Mine is better behaved. It never tells me the truth.
LORD ILLINGWORTH Then it is in love with you.

☆

GERALD My dear mother, it all sounds very tragic, of course. But I dare say the girl was just as much to blame as Lord Illingworth was. – After all, would a really nice girl, a girl with any nice feelings at all, go away from her home with a man to whom she was not married, and live with him as his wife? No nice girl would.
MRS ARBUTHNOT Gerald, I withdraw all my objections. You are at liberty to go away with Lord Illingworth, when and where you choose.

☆

MRS ARBUTHNOT Stop, Gerald, stop! He is your own father!

Curtain, Act III. Cf. N. Coward, *Hay Fever,* Curtain, Act II

★   ★   ★

LADY HUNSTANTON Music makes one feel so romantic – at least it always gets on one's nerves.
MRS ALLONBY It's the same thing, now-a-days.

A Woman of No Importance, Act IV

☆

MRS ALLONBY Lord Illingworth says that all influence is bad, but that a

215

good influence is the worst in the world.

☆

LADY HUNSTANTON Most women in London, now-a-days, seem to furnish their rooms with nothing but orchids, foreigners, and French novels.

☆

LADY HUNSTANTON Well, there *is* a good deal to be said for blushing, if one can do it at the proper moment. Poor dear Hunstanton used to tell me I didn't blush nearly often enough. But then he was so very particular. He wouldn't let me know any of his men friends, except those who were over seventy, like poor Lord Ashton; who afterwards, by the way, was brought into the Divorce Court. A most unfortunate case.

MRS ALLONBY I delight in men over seventy. They always offer one the devotion of a lifetime. I think seventy an ideal age for a man.

☆

MRS ALLONBY I wish Lord Illingworth would ask me to be his secretary. But he says I am not serious enough.
A Woman of No Importance, Act IV

☆

LADY HUNSTANTON It gave quite an atmosphere of respectability to the party.

MRS ALLONBY Ah, that must have been what you thought was thunder in the air.

LADY HUNSTANTON My dear, how can you say that? There is no resemblance between the two things at all.

☆

MRS ALLONBY I hope you don't think you have exhausted life, Mr Arbuthnot. When a man says that, one knows that life has exhausted him.

☆

MRS ALLONBY Lord Illingworth would talk about nothing but Mr Arbuthnot the whole of yesterday afternoon. He looks on him as his most promising disciple: I believe he intends him to be an exact replica of himself for the use of schools.
Not used. Cancelled. Originally preceded second entrance of Alice

☆

MRS ALLONBY Au revoir, Mr Arbuthnot. Mind you bring me back

something nice from your travels – not an Indian shawl – on no account an Indian shawl.

☆

LORD ILLINGWORTH Now, what I propose is this.

MRS ARBUTHNOT Lord Illingworth, no proposition of yours interests me.

☆

LORD ILLINGWORTH According to our ridiculous English laws, I can't legitimise Gerald. But I can leave him my property. Illingworth is entailed, of course, but it is a tedious barrack of a place. He can have Ashby, which is much prettier, Harborough, which has the best shooting in the north of England, and the house in St James's Square. What more can a gentleman desire in this world?

MRS ARBUTHNOT Nothing more, I am quite sure.

☆

LORD ILLINGWORTH As for a title, a title is really rather a nuisance in these democratic days. As George Harford I had everything I wanted. Now I have merely everything that other people want, which isn't nearly so pleasant.

☆

LORD ILLINGWORTH I was very young at the time. We men know life too early.

MRS ARBUTHNOT And we women know life too late. That is the difference between men and women.

☆

1894

... I love superstitions. They are the colour element of thought and
imagination. They are the opponents of common sense. Common
sense is the enemy of romance.

The aim of your society seems to be dreadful. Leave us some unreality. Don't make us too offensively sane.

I love dining out; but with a society with so wicked an object as
yours I cannot dine. I regret it. I am sure you will all be charming; but
I could not come, though thirteen is a lucky number.

> Public Letter to William Harnett Blanch, Founder and President of
> the Thirteen Club, read at its Dinner at Holborn Restaurant,
> 13 January 1894

★   ★   ★

One evening there came into his soul the desire to fashion an image of
The Pleasure that abideth for a Moment. And he went forth into the world
to look for bronze. For he could only think in bronze.

But all the bronze of the whole world had disappeared, nor anywhere in the whole world was there any bronze to be found, save only
the bronze of the image of *The Sorrow that endureth for Ever*.

Now this image he had himself, and with his own hands, fashioned,
and had set it on the tomb of the one thing he had loved in life. On the
tomb of the dead thing he had most loved had he set this image of his
own fashioning, that it might serve as a sign of the love of man that
dieth not, and a symbol of the sorrow of man that endureth for ever.
And in the whole world there was no other bronze save the bronze of
this image.

And he took the image he had fashioned, and set it in a great furnace, and gave it to the fire.

And out of the bronze of the image of *The Sorrow that endureth for Ever*
he fashioned an image of *The Pleasure that abideth for a Moment*.

> 'The Artist'. *Poems in Prose. Fortnightly Review*, July 1894

★   ★   ★

When Narcissus died the pool of his pleasure changed from a cup of
sweet waters into a cup of salt tears, and the Oreads came weeping

through the woodland that they might sing to the pool and give it comfort.

And when they saw that the pool had changed from a cup of sweet waters into a cup of salt tears, they loosened the green tresses of their hair and cried to the pool and said, 'We do not wonder that you should mourn in this manner for Narcissus, so beautiful was he'.

'But was Narcissus beautiful?' said the pool.

'Who should know that better than you?' answered the Oreads. 'Us did he ever pass by, but you he sought for, and would lie on your banks and look down at you, and in the mirror of your waters he would mirror his own beauty.'

And the pool answered, 'But I loved Narcissus because, as he lay on my banks and looked down at me, in the mirror of his eyes I saw ever my own beauty mirrored.'

'The Disciple'. Ibid.

★   ★   ★

It was night-time and He was alone.

And He saw afar-off the walls of a round city and went towards the city.

And when He came near He heard within the city the tread of the feet of joy, and the laughter of the mouth of gladness and the loud noise of many lutes. And He knocked at the gate and certain of the gate-keepers opened to Him.

And He beheld a house that was of marble and had fair pillars of marble before it. The pillars were hung with garlands, and within and without there were torches of cedar. And He entered the house.

And when He had passed through the hall of chalcedony and the hall of jasper, and reached the long hall of feasting, He saw lying on a couch of sea-purple one whose hair was crowned with red roses and whose lips were red with wine.

And He went behind him and touched him on the shoulder and said to him, 'Why do you live like this?'

And the young man turned round and recognised Him, and made answer and said, 'But I was a leper once, and you healed me. How else should I live?'

And He passed out of the house and went again into the street.

And after a little while He saw one whose face and raiment were painted and whose feet were shod with pearls. And behind her came, slowly as a hunter, a young man who wore a cloak of two colours. Now the face of the woman was as the fair face of an idol, and the eyes of the young man were bright with lust.

And He followed swiftly and touched the hand of the young man and said to him, 'Why do you look at this woman and in such wise?'

And the young man turned round and recognised Him and said,

219

'But I was blind once, and you gave me sight. At what else should I look?'

And He ran forward and touched the painted raiment of the woman and said to her, 'Is there no other way in which to walk save the way of sin?'

And the woman turned round and recognised Him, and laughed and said, 'But you forgave me my sins, and the way is a pleasant way.'

And He passed out of the city.

And when He had passed out of the city He saw seated by the road-side a young man who was weeping.

And He went towards him and touched the long locks of his hair and said to him, 'Why are you weeping?'

And the young man looked up and recognised Him and made answer, 'But I was dead once and you raised me from the dead. What else should I do but weep?'

'The Doer of Good'. Ibid.

★ ★ ★

The assistant editor of the *Sunday Sun,* on whom seems to devolve the arduous duty of writing Mr T. P. O'Connor's apologies for him, does not, I observe with regret, place that gentleman's conduct in any more attractive or more honourable light by the attempted explanation that appears in the letter published in your issue of today. For the future it would be much better if Mr O'Connor would always write his own apologies. That he can do so exceedingly well no one is more ready to admit than myself. I happen to possess one from him.

To the Editor, Pall Mall Gazette, printed 25 September 1894

☆

Mr O'Connor's subsequent conduct in accusing me of plagiarism, when it was proved to him on unimpeachable authority that the verses he had vulgarly attributed to me were not by me at all . . . is perhaps best left to the laughter of the gods and the sorrow of men . . . when Mr O'Connor, with the kind help of his assistant editor, states, as a pos-sible excuse for his original sin, that he and the members of his staff 'took refuge' in the belief that the verses in question might conceivably be some very early and youthful work of mine, he and the members of his staff showed a lamentable ignorance of the nature of the artistic temperament. Only mediocrities progress. An artist revolves in a cycle of masterpieces, the first of which is no less perfect than the last.

★ ★ ★

Kindly allow me to contradict, in the most emphatic manner, the sug-gestion, made in your issue of Thursday last, and since then copied into many other newspapers, that I am the author of *The Green*

Carnation.

I invented that magnificent flower. But with the middle-class and mediocre book that usurps its strangely beautiful name I have, I need hardly say, nothing whatsoever to do. The flower is a work of art. The book is not.

To the Editor, *Pall Mall Gazette,* printed 2 October 1894

★　　★　　★

Education is an admirable thing. But it is well to remember from time to time that nothing that is worth knowing can be taught.

'A Few Maxims for the Instruction of the Over-Educated'. *Saturday Review,* 17 November 1894

☆

Public opinion exists only where there are no ideas.

☆

The English are always degrading truths into facts. When a truth becomes a fact it loses all its intellectual value.

☆

It is a very sad thing nowadays that there is so little useless information.

☆

The only link between Literature and the Drama left to us in England at the present moment is the bill of the play.

☆

In old days books were written by men of letters and read by the public. Nowadays books are written by the public and read by nobody.

☆

Most women are so artificial that they have no sense of Art. Most men are so natural that they have no sense of Beauty.

☆

Friendship is far more tragic than love. It lasts longer.

☆

What is abnormal in Life stands in normal relations to Art. It is the only thing in Life that stands in normal relations to Art.

☆

A subject that is beautiful in itself gives no suggestion to the artist. It lacks imperfection.

☆

The only thing that the artist cannot see is the obvious. The only thing that the public can see is the obvious. The result is the Criticism of the Journalist.

'A Few Maxims for the Instruction of the Over-Educated'. *Saturday Review*, 17 November 1894

☆

Art is the only serious thing in the world. And the artist is the only person who is never serious.

☆

To be really mediaeval one should have no body. To be really modern one should have no soul. To be really Greek one should have no clothes.

☆

Dandyism is the assertion of the absolute modernity of Beauty.

☆

The only thing that can console one for being poor is extravagance. The only thing that can console one for being rich is economy.

☆

One should never listen. To listen is a sign of indifference to one's hearers.

☆

Even the disciple has his uses. He stands behind one's throne, and at the moment of one's triumph whispers in one's ear that, after all, one is immortal.

☆

The criminal classes are so close to us that even the policeman can see them. They are so far away from us that only the poet can understand them.

☆

Those whom the gods love grow young.

★   ★   ★

The first duty in life is to be as artificial as possible. What the second duty is no one has as yet discovered.

'Phrases and Philosophies for the Use of the Young.' *Chameleon*, December 1894

☆

Wickedness is a myth invented by good people to account for the curious attractiveness of others.

☆

If the poor only had profiles there would be no difficulty in solving the problem of poverty.

☆

Those who see any difference between soul and body have neither.

☆

A really well-made buttonhole is the only link between Art and Nature.

☆

Religions die when they are proved to be true. Science is the record of dead religions.

☆

The well-bred contradict other people. The wise contradict themselves.

☆

Nothing that actually occurs is of the smallest importance.

☆

Dulness is the coming of age of seriousness.

☆

In all unimportant matters, style, not sincerity, is the essential. In all important matters style, not sincerity, is the essential.

☆

If one tells the truth one is sure, sooner or later, to be found out.

☆

Pleasure is the only thing one should live for. Nothing ages like happiness.

☆

It is only by not paying one's bills that one can hope to live in the memory of the commercial classes.

☆

No crime is vulgar, but all vulgarity is crime. Vulgarity is the conduct of others.

'Phrases and Philosophies for the Use of the Young.' *Chameleon,*
December 1894

☆

Only the shallow know themselves.

☆

Time is waste of money.

☆

One should always be a little improbable.

☆

There is a fatality about all good resolutions. They are invariably made too soon.

☆

The only way to atone for being occasionally a little overdressed is by being always absolutely overeducated.

☆

To be premature is to be perfect.

☆

Any preoccupation with ideas of what is right or wrong in conduct shows an arrested intellectual development.

☆

Ambition is the last refuge of the failure.

☆

A truth ceases to be true when more than one person believes in it.

☆

In examinations the foolish ask questions that the wise cannot answer.

☆

Greek dress was in its essence inartistic. Nothing should reveal the body but the body.

☆

One should either be a work of art, or wear a work of art.

☆

It is only the superficial qualities that last. Man's deeper nature is soon found out.

☆

Industry is the root of all ugliness.

☆

The ages live in history through their anachronisms.

☆

It is only the gods who taste of death. Apollo has passed away, but Hyacinth, whom men say he slew, lives on. Nero and Narcissus are always with us.

☆

The old believe everything: the middle-aged suspect everything: the young know everything.

☆

The condition of perfection is idleness: the aim of perfection is youth.

☆

Only the great masters of style ever succeeded in being obscure.

☆

There is something tragic about the enormous number of young men there are in England at the present moment who start life with perfect profiles, and end by adopting some useful profession.

☆

To love oneself is the beginning of a life-long romance.

★　　　★　　　★

MRS MARCHMONT Going on to the Hartlocks to-night . . .?
LADY BASILDON I suppose so. Are you?
MRS MARCHMONT Yes. Horribly tedious parties they give, don't they?
LADY BASILDON Horribly tedious! Never know why I go. Never know why I go anywhere.
MRS MARCHMONT I come here to be educated.
LADY BASILDON Ah! I hate being educated!
MRS MARCHMONT So do I. It puts one almost on a level with the commercial classes, doesn't it? But dear Gertrude Chiltern is always telling me that I should have some serious purpose in life. So I come here to try to find one.
LADY BASILDON I don't see anybody here to-night whom one could pos-

sibly call a serious purpose. The man who took me in to dinner talked to me about his wife the whole time.

MRS MARCHMONT How very trivial of him!

LADY BASILDON Terribly trivial! What did your man talk about?

MRS MARCHANT About myself.

LADY BASILDON And were you interested?

MRS MARCHANT Not in the smallest degree.

LADY BASILDON What martyrs we are, dear Margaret!

MRS MARCHMONT And how well it becomes us, Olivia!

An Ideal Husband, January 1895. Act I, Overture

☆

LADY MARKBY Dear Duchess, and how is the Duke? Brain still weak, I suppose? Well, that is only to be expected, is it not? His good father was just the same. There is nothing like race, is there?

☆

MRS CHEVELEY Since he has been at the Foreign Office, he has been so much talked of in Vienna. They actually succeed in spelling his name right in the newspapers. That in itself is fame, on the continent.

☆

VICOMTE DE NANJAC And you are younger and more beautiful than ever. How do you manage it?

MRS CHEVELEY By making it a rule only to talk to perfectly charming people like yourself.

VICOMTE DE NANJAC Ah! You flatter me. You butter me as they say here.

MRS CHEVELEY Do they say that here? How dreadful of them!

VICOMTE DE NANJAC Yes, they have a wonderful language. It should be more widely known.

☆

LADY MARKBY Sir John's temper since he has taken seriously to politics has become quite unbearable. Really, now that the House of Commons is trying to become useful, it does a great deal of harm.

☆

LADY MARKBY One of the Dorsetshire Cheveleys, I suppose. But I really don't know. Families are so mixed nowadays. Indeed, as a rule, everybody turns out to be somebody else.

☆

MRS CHEVELEY I don't know that women are always rewarded for being charming. I think they are usually punished for it! Certainly, more women grow old nowadays through the faithfulness of their admirers than through anything else! At least that is the only way I can account for the terribly haggard look of most of your pretty women in London!

☆

MRS CHEVELEY Optimism begins in a broad grin, and Pessimism ends with blue spectacles.

☆

MRS CHEVELEY Ah! the strength of women comes from the fact that psychology cannot explain us. Men can be analysed, women – merely adored.

☆

MRS CHEVELEY Science can never grapple with the irrational. That is why it has no future before it, in this world.

☆

MRS CHEVELEY Questions are never indiscreet. Answers sometimes are.

☆

MRS CHEVELEY Politics are my only pleasure. You see nowadays it is not fashionable to flirt till one is forty, or to be romantic till one is forty-five, so we poor women who are under thirty, or say we are, have nothing open to us but politics or philanthropy. And philanthropy seems to me to have become simply the refuge of people who wish to annoy their fellow-creatures. I prefer politics. I think they are more – becoming!

☆

MRS CHEVELEY Oh! I don't care about the London season! It is too matrimonial. People are either hunting for husbands, or hiding from them.

☆

SIR ROBERT CHILTERN Yes: he knew men and cities well, like the old Greek.
MRS CHEVELEY Without the dreadful disadvantage of having a Penelope waiting at home for him.

☆

LORD GORING I am not at all romantic. I am not old enough. I leave romance to my seniors.

☆

LORD CAVERSHAM Can't make out how you stand London Society. The thing has gone to the dogs, a lot of damned nobodies talking about nothing.

LORD GORING I love talking about nothing, father. It is the only thing I know anything about.

LORD CAVERSHAM You seem to me to be living entirely for pleasure.

LORD GORING What else is there to live for, father? Nothing ages like happiness.

An Ideal Husband, January 1895. Act I

☆

LORD GORING I adore political parties. They are the only place left to us where people don't talk politics.

LADY BASILDON I delight in talking politics. I talk them all day long. But I can't bear listening to them. I don't know how the unfortunate men in the House stand these long debates.

LORD GORING By never listening.

☆

LORD GORING You see, it is a very dangerous thing to listen. If one listens, one may be convinced; and a man who allows himself to be convinced by an argument is a thoroughly unreasonable person.

☆

MRS MARCHMONT I like looking at geniuses, and listening to beautiful people!

LORD GORING Ah, that is morbid of you, Mrs Marchmont!

MRS MARCHMONT I am so glad to hear you say that. Marchmont and I have been married for seven years, and he has never once told me that I was morbid. Men are so painfully unobservant!

☆

VICOMTE DE NANJAC I am so fond of eating! I am very English in all my tastes.

☆

MR MONTFORD Like some supper, Mrs Marchmont?

MRS MARCHMONT Thank you, Mr Montford, I never touch supper. But I will sit beside you, and watch you.

MR MONTFORD I don't know that I like being watched when I am eating!

MRS MARCHMONT Then I will watch some one else.

MR MONTFORD I don't know that I should like that either.

MRS MARCHMONT Pray, Mr Montford, do not make these painful scenes of jealousy in public!

☆

MRS CHEVELEY I can't stand your English house-parties. In England people actually try to be brilliant at breakfast. That is so dreadful of them! Only dull people are brilliant at breakfast. And then the family skeleton is always reading family prayers.

☆

MRS CHEVELEY In modern life nothing produces such an effect as a good platitude. It makes the whole world kin.

☆

MRS CHEVELEY Remember to what a point your Puritanism in England has brought you. In old days nobody pretended to be a bit better than his neighbours. In fact, to be a bit better than one's neighbour was considered excessively vulgar and middle-class. Nowadays, with our modern mania for morality, everyone has to pose as a paragon of purity, incorruptibility, and all the other seven deadly virtues – and what is the result? You all go over like ninepins – one after the other. Not a year passes in England without somebody disappearing. Scandals used to lend charm, or at least interest, to a man – now they crush him. And yours is a very nasty scandal. You couldn't survive it.

☆

MRS CHEVELEY Sir Robert, you know what your English newspapers are like. Suppose that when I leave this house I drive down to some newspaper office, and give them this scandal and the proofs of it! Think of their loathsome joy, of the delight they would have in dragging you down, of the mud and mire they would plunge you in. Think of the hypocrite with his greasy smile penning his leading article, and arranging for the foulness of the public placard.

☆

MRS CHEVELEY Even you are not rich enough, Sir Robert, to buy back your past. No man is.

☆

MRS CHEVELEY One should always play fairly – when one has the winning cards.

☆

SIR ROBERT CHILTERN My God! what brought you into my life?
MRS CHEVELEY Circumstances.
An Ideal Husband, January 1895. Act I

☆

MRS CHEVELEY . . . Englishmen always get romantic after a meal, and
that bores me dreadfully.

☆

LADY MARKBY I have often observed that the Season as it goes on produces a kind of softening of the brain. However, I think anything
is better than high intellectual pressure. That is the most unbecoming thing there is. It makes the noses of the young girls so
particularly large. And there is nothing so difficult to marry as a
large nose . . .

☆

LORD GORING I always pass on good advice. It is the only thing to do
with it. It is never of any use to oneself.

☆

MABEL CHILTERN You can come and sit down if you like, and talk about
anything in the world, except the Royal Academy, Mrs Cheveley,
or novels in Scotch dialect. They are not improving subjects.

☆

SIR ROBERT CHILTERN No one should be entirely judged by their past.
LADY CHILTERN One's past is what one is. It is the only way by which
people should be judged.

☆

SIR ROBERT CHILTERN Put out the lights, Mason, put out the lights!

★   ★   ★

LORD GORING Secrets from other people's wives are a necessary luxury
in modern life. So, at least, I am always told at the club by people
who are bald enough to know better. But no man should have a
secret from his own wife. She invariably finds it out. Women have
a wonderful instinct about things. They can discover everything
except the obvious.
An Ideal Husband, Act II

☆

LORD GORING Everything is dangerous, my dear fellow. If it wasn't so,
life wouldn't be worth living.

☆

SIR ROBERT CHILTERN Private information is practically the source of every large modern fortune.

☆

LORD GORING Life is never fair, Robert. And perhaps it is a good thing for most of us that it is not.

☆

LORD GORING There is more to be said for stupidity than people imagine. Personally I have a great admiration for stupidity. It is a sort of fellow-feeling, I suppose.

☆

SIR ROBERT CHILTERN I remember having read somewhere, in some strange book, that when the gods wish to punish us they answer our prayers.

☆

LORD GORING I am always saying what I shouldn't say. In fact, I usually say what I really think. A great mistake nowadays. It makes one so liable to be misunderstood.

☆

LORD GORING Well, the English can't stand a man who is always saying he is in the right, but they are very fond of a man who admits that he has been in the wrong. It is one of the best things in them.

☆

LORD GORING . . . in England a man who can't talk morality twice a week to a large, popular, immoral audience is quite over as a serious politician. There would be nothing left for him as a professional except Botany or the Church.

☆

SIR ROBERT CHILTERN . . . I feel that public disgrace is in store for me. I feel certain of it. I never knew what terror was before. I know it now. It is as if a hand of ice were laid upon one's heart. It is as if one's heart were beating itself to death in some empty hollow.

☆

LORD GORING . . . everyone has some weak point. There is some flaw in each one of us. My father tells me that even I have faults. Perhaps I have. I don't know.

☆

LORD GORING Oh, I should fancy Mrs Cheveley is one of those very modern women of our time who find a new scandal as becoming as a new bonnet, and air them both in the Park every afternoon at five-thirty. I am sure she adores scandals, and that the sorrow of her life at present is that she can't manage to have enough of them.

An Ideal Husband, Act II

☆

SIR ROBERT CHILTERN Why do you say that?

LORD GORING Well, she wore far too much rouge last night, and not quite enough clothes. That is always a sign of despair in a woman.

☆

LORD GORING It is always worth while asking a question, though it is not always worth while answering one.

☆

LORD GORING . . . there is a fashion in pasts just as there is a fashion in frocks. Perhaps Mrs Cheveley's past is merely a slightly *décolleté* one, and they are excessively popular nowadays. Besides, my dear Robert, I should not build too high hopes on frightening Mrs Cheveley. I should not fancy Mrs Cheveley is a woman who would be easily frightened. She has survived all her creditors, and she shows wonderful presence of mind.

☆

LORD GORING All I do know is that life cannot be understood without much charity; cannot be lived without much charity. It is love, and not German philosophy, that is the true explanation of this world, whatever may be the explanation of the next.

☆

MABEL CHILTERN Musical people are so absurdly unreasonable. They always want one to be perfectly dumb at the very moment when one is longing to be absolutely deaf.

☆

MABEL CHILTERN At luncheon I saw by the glare in his eye that he was going to propose again, and I just managed to check him in time by assuring him that I was a bimetallist. Fortunately I don't know what bimetallism means. And I don't believe anybody else does either. But the observation crushed Tommy for ten minutes. He looked quite shocked.

☆

MABEL CHILTERN If he proposed at the top of his voice, I should not mind so much. That might produce some effect on the public. But he does it in a horrid confidential way. When Tommy wants to be romantic he talks to one just like a doctor.

☆

MABEL CHILTERN I wouldn't marry a man with a future before him for anything under the sun.

☆

MABEL CHILTERN You can stand geniuses . . . As a rule, I think they are quite impossible. Geniuses talk so much, don't they? Such a bad habit! And they are always thinking about themselves, when I want them to be thinking about me.

☆

LADY MARKBY Nothing is so dangerous as being too modern. One is apt to grow old-fashioned quite suddenly. I have known many instances of it.

☆

LADY MARKBY The fact is, we all scrabble and jostle so much nowadays that I wonder we have anything at all left on us at the end of an evening. I know myself that, when I am coming back from the Drawing Room, I always feel as if I hadn't a shred on me, except a small shred of decent reputation, just enough to prevent the lower classes making painful observations through the windows of the carriage.

☆

LADY MARKBY I'm sure I don't know half the people who come to my house. Indeed, from all I hear, I shouldn't like to.

☆

LADY MARKBY I don't think man has much capacity for development. He has got as far as he can, and that is not far, is it?

☆

LADY MARKBY In my time, of course, we were taught not to understand anything. That was the old system, and wonderfully interesting it was. I assure you that the amount of things I and my poor dear sister were taught not to understand was quite extraordinary.

☆

LADY MARKBY . . . modern women understand everything, I am told.

MRS CHEVELEY Except their husbands. That is the one thing the modern woman never understands.

LADY MARKBY And a very good thing too, dear, I dare say. It might break up many a happy home if they did.

An Ideal Husband, Act II

☆

LADY MARKBY . . . since Sir John has taken to attending the debates regularly, which he never used to do in the good old days, his language has become quite impossible. He always seems to think that he is addressing the House, and consequently whenever he discusses the state of the agricultural labourer, or the Welsh Church, or something quite improper of that kind, I am obliged to send all the servants out of the room. It is not pleasant to see one's own butler, who has been with one for twenty-three years, actually blushing at the sideboard, and the footman making contortions in corners like persons in circuses.

☆

LADY MARKBY But in his present state, Sir John is really a great trial. Why, this morning before breakfast was half over, he stood up on the hearth rug, put his hands in his pockets, and appealed to the country at the top of his voice. I left the table as soon as I had my second cup of tea, I need hardly say. But his violent language could be heard all over the house!

☆

LADY MARKBY I can't understand this modern mania for curates. In my time we girls saw them, of course, running about the place like rabbits. But we never took any notice of them, I need hardly say. But I am told that nowadays country society is quite honeycombed with them. I think it most irreligious.

☆

LADY MARKBY And then the eldest son has quarrelled with his father, and it is said that when they meet at the club Lord Brancaster always hides himself behind the money article in *The Times.* However, I believe that is quite a common occurrence nowadays and that they have to take in extra copies of *The Times* at all the clubs in St James's Street; there are so many sons who won't have anything to do with their fathers, and so many fathers who won't speak to their sons.

☆

MRS CHEVELEY The art of living. The only really Fine Art we have produced in modern times.

LADY MARKBY Ah! I am afraid Lord Brancaster knew a good deal about that. More than his poor wife ever did.

☆

LADY MARKBY Well, like all stout women, she looks the very picture of happiness, as no doubt you noticed.

☆

LADY MARKBY Her own sister, Mrs Jekyll, had a most unhappy life; through no fault of her own, I am sorry to say. She ultimately was so broken-hearted that she went into a convent, or on to the oper- atic stage, I forget which. No; I think it was decorative art-needle- work she took up. I know she had lost all sense of pleasure in life.

☆

LADY MARKBY As I intend it to be a visit of condolence, I shan't stay long.

☆

LADY MARKBY Shall I see you at Lady Bonar's to-night? She has dis- covered a wonderful new genius. He does – nothing at all, I believe. That is a great comfort, is it not?

☆

LADY MARKBY Dining at home by yourselves? Is that quite prudent? Ah, I forgot, your husband is an exception. Mine is the general rule, and nothing ages a women so rapidly as having married the general rule.

☆

MRS CHEVELEY Morality is simply the attitude we adopt towards people whom we personally dislike.

☆

SIR ROBERT CHILTERN It is not the perfect, but the imperfect, who have need of love. It is when we are wounded by our own hands, or by the hands of others, that love should come to cure us – else what use is love at all? All sins, except a sin against itself, Love should forgive. All lives, save loveless lives, true Love should pardon.

★   ★   ★

LORD GORING Got my second buttonhole for me, Phipps?
PHIPPS Yes, my lord.
LORD GORING Rather distinguished thing, Phipps. I am the only person

235

of the smallest importance in London at present who wears a buttonhole.

PHIPPS Yes, my lord. I have observed that.

LORD GORING You see, Phipps, Fashion is what one wears oneself.
What is unfashionable is what other people wear.

PHIPPS Yes, my lord.

LORD GORING Just as vulgarity is simply the conduct of other people.

PHIPPS Yes, my lord.

LORD GORING And falsehoods the truths of other people.

PHIPPS Yes, my lord.

LORD GORING Other people are quite dreadful. The only possible
society is oneself.

PHIPPS Yes, my lord.

An Ideal Husband, Act III

☆

LORD GORING Extraordinary thing about the lower classes in England –
they are always losing their relations.

PHIPPS Yes, my lord! They are extremely fortunate in that respect.

☆

LORD GORING It is the growth of the moral sense in women that makes
marriage such a hopeless, one-sided institution.

☆

LORD CAVERSHAM You have got to get married, and at once. Why,
when I was your age, sir, I had been an inconsolable widower for
three months, and was already paying my addresses to your
admirable mother.

☆

LORD CAVERSHAM Bachelors are not fashionable any more. They are a
damaged lot. Too much is known about them. You must get a
wife, sir.

☆

LORD CAVERSHAM At present I make your mother's life miserable on
your account. You are heartless, sir, quite heartless.

☆

LORD GORING If there was less sympathy in the world there would be
less trouble in the world.

LORD CAVERSHAM That is a paradox, sir. I hate paradoxes.

LORD GORING So do I, father. Everybody one meets is a paradox nowadays. It is a great bore. It makes society so obvious.

LORD CAVERSHAM Do you always really understand what you say, sir?
LORD GORING Yes, father, if I listen attentively.
LORD CAVERSHAM If you listen attentively! – Conceited young puppy!

☆

MRS CHEVELEY To expect the unexpected shows a thoroughly modern intellect.

☆

MRS CHEVELEY Who on earth writes to him on pink paper? How silly to write on pink paper! It looks like the beginning of a middle-class romance. Romance should never begin with sentiment. It should begin with science and end with a settlement.

☆

LORD GORING In married life affection comes when people thoroughly dislike each other, father, doesn't it?
LORD CAVERSHAM Certainly, sir. I mean certainly not, sir. You are talking very foolishly to-night. What I say is that marriage is a matter for common sense.
LORD GORING But women who have common sense are so curiously plain, father, aren't they? Of course I only speak from hearsay.
LORD CAVERSHAM No woman, plain or pretty, has any common sense at all, sir. Common sense is the privilege of our sex.
LORD GORING Quite so. And we men are so self-sacrificing that we never use it, do we, father?
LORD CAVERSHAM I use it, sir. I use nothing else.
LORD GORING So my mother tells me.
LORD CAVERSHAM It is the secret of your mother's happiness.

☆

SIR ROBERT CHILTERN Oh! spies are of no use nowadays. Their profession is over. The newspapers do their work instead.

☆

SIR ROBERT CHILTERN I was brutal to her this evening. But I suppose when sinners talk to saints they are brutal always.

☆

MRS CHEVELEY I have a perfect passion for listening through keyholes. One always hears such wonderful things through them.
LORD GORING Doesn't that sound rather like tempting Providence?
MRS CHEVELEY Oh! surely Providence can resist temptation by this time.

☆

LORD GORING I am going to give you some good advice.

MRS CHEVELEY Oh! pray don't. One should never give a woman anything that she can't wear in the evening.

An Ideal Husband, Act III

☆

LORD GORING Pray have a cigarette. Half the pretty women in London smoke cigarettes. Personally I prefer the other half.

MRS CHEVELEY Thanks. I never smoke. My dressmaker wouldn't like it, and a woman's first duty in life is to her dressmaker, isn't it? What the second duty is, no one has as yet discovered.

☆

MRS CHEVELEY The English think that a cheque-book can solve every problem in life.

☆

MRS CHEVELEY Poor old Lord Mortlake, who had only two topics of conversation, his gout and his wife! I never could quite make out which of the two he was talking about. He used the most horrible language about them both.

☆

MRS CHEVELEY I did love you. And you loved me. You know you loved me; and love is a very wonderful thing. I suppose that when a man has once loved a woman, he will do anything for her, except continue to love her?

☆

MRS CHEVELEY If one could only teach the English how to talk, and the Irish how to listen, society here would be quite civilised.

☆

MRS CHEVELEY My dear Arthur, women are never disarmed by compliments. Men always are. That is the difference between the two sexes.

☆

LORD GORING . . . self-sacrifice is a thing that should be put down by law. It is so demoralising to the people for whom one sacrifices oneself. They always go to the bad.

☆

MRS CHEVELEY Oh, there is only one real tragedy in a woman's life.

The fact that her past is always her lover, and her future invariably her husband.

☆

MRS CHEVELEY A woman whose size in gloves is seven and three-quarters never knows much about anything.

☆

LORD GORING The drawback of stealing a thing, Mrs Cheveley, is that one never knows how wonderful the thing that one steals is.

★　　　★　　　★

LORD GORING Fathers should be neither seen nor heard. That is the only proper basis for family life. Mothers are different. Mothers are darlings.

An Ideal Husband, Act IV

☆

LORD GORING My dear father, when one pays a visit it is for the purpose of wasting other people's time, not one's own.

☆

LORD GORING All that one should know about modern life is where the Duchesses are; anything else is quite demoralising.

☆

LORD GORING . . . only people who look dull ever get into the House of Commons, and only people who are dull ever succeed there.

☆

LORD GORING Youth isn't an affectation. Youth is an art.

☆

LORD GORING A thoroughly sensible wife would reduce me to a condition of absolute idiocy in less than six months.

☆

LORD GORING . . . if we men married the women we deserved, we should have a very bad time of it.

☆

MABEL CHILTERN Lord Goring, I never believe a single word that either you or I say to each other.

☆

MABEL CHILTERN I am afraid that he has one of those terribly weak

239

natures that are not susceptible to influences.

An Ideal Husband, Act IV

☆

MABEL CHILTERN It is very good for you to be in the way, and to know what people say of you behind your back.

☆

MABEL CHILTERN Well, my duty is a thing I never do, on principle. It always depresses me.

An Ideal Husband, Act IV

☆

LORD GORING Mabel, do be serious. Please be serious.

MABEL CHILTERN Ah! that is the sort of thing a man always says to a girl before he has been married to her. He never says it afterwards.

1895

'What are your views upon the much-vexed question of subject-matter in art?'

'Everything matters in art, except the subject.'

When I recovered I said, 'Several letters have been written lately that deal with the monstrous injustice of the social code of morality at the present time.'

'Ah', answered Mr Wilde, with an air of earnest conviction, 'it is indeed a burning shame that there should be one law for men and another law for women. I think' – he hesitated, and a smile as swift as Sterne's "hectic of a moment" flitted across his face – 'I think that there should be no law for anybody.'

Gilbert Burgess , '*An Ideal Husband,* at the Haymarket Theatre. A talk with Mr Wilde', *The Sketch,* 9 January 1895

☆

'In writing, do you think that real life or real people should ever give one inspiration?'

'The colour of a flower may suggest to one the plot of a tragedy: a passage in music may give one the sestet of a sonnet; but whatever actually occurs gives the artist no suggestion. Every romance that one has in one's life is a romance lost to one's art. To introduce real people into a novel or a play is a sign of an unimaginative mind, a coarse, untutored observation, and an entire absence of style.'

'I'm afraid I can't agree with you, Mr Wilde. I frequently see types and people who suggest ideas to me.'

'Everything is of use to the artist except an idea.'

☆

'What are the exact relations between literature and the drama?'

'Exquisitely accidental. That is why I think them so necessary.'

'And the exact relations between the actor and the dramatist?'

Mr Wilde looked at me with a serious expression which changed almost immediately into a smile, as he replied, 'Usually a little strained.'

☆

'Do you consider the future outlook of the English stage is hopeful?'

'I think it must be. The critics have ceased to prophesy. That is something. It is in silence that the artist arrives. What is waited for never succeeds; what is heralded is hopeless.'

Gilbert Burgess , 'An Ideal Husband, at the Haymarket Theatre. A talk with Mr Wilde', The Sketch, 9 January 1895

★   ★   ★

ALGERNON Did you hear what I was playing, Lane?

LANE I didn't think it polite to listen, sir.

ALGERNON I'm sorry for that, for your sake. I don't play accurately – any one can play accurately – but I play with wonderful expression. As far as the piano is concerned, sentiment is my forte. I keep science for Life.

LANE Yes, sir.

The Importance of Being Earnest, February 1895. Act I

☆

ALGERNON Why is it that at a bachelor's establishment the servants invariably drink the champagne? I ask merely for information.

LANE I attribute it to the superior quality of the wine, sir. I have often observed that in married households, the champagne is rarely of a first-class brand.

ALGERNON Good heavens! Is marriage so demoralising as that?

LANE I believe it *is* a very pleasant state, sir. I have had very little experience of it myself up to the present. I have only been married once. That was in consequence of a misunderstanding between myself and a young person.

ALGERNON *(languidly)* I don't know that I am much interested in your family life, Lane.

LANE No, sir; it is not a very interesting subject. I never think of it myself.

☆

ALGERNON Lane's views on marriage seem somewhat lax. Really, if the lower orders don't set us a good example, what on earth is the use of them? They seem, as a class, to have absolutely no sense of moral responsibility.

☆

ALGERNON I really don't see anything romantic in proposing. It is very romantic to be in love. But there is nothing romantic about a definite proposal. Why, one may be accepted. One usually is, I believe. Then the excitement is all over. The very essence of

242

romance is uncertainty. If ever I get married, I'll certainly try to forget the fact.

☆

JACK It is a very ungentlemanly thing to read a private cigarette case.

☆

ALGERNON Oh! it is absurd to have a hard-and-fast rule about what one should read and what one shouldn't. More than half of modern culture depends on what one shouldn't read.

☆

ALGERNON The truth is rarely pure and never simple. Modern life would be very tedious if it were either, and modern literature a complete impossibility!

☆

ALGERNON The amount of women in London who flirt with their own husbands is perfectly scandalous. It looks so bad. It is simply washing one's clean linen in public.

☆

ALGERNON You don't seem to realise, that in married life three is company and two is none.
JACK *(sententiously)* That, my dear young friend, is the theory that the corrupt French Drama has been propounding for the last fifty years.
ALGERNON Yes; and that the happy English home has proved in half the time.

☆

ALGERNON I hate people who are not serious about meals. It is so shallow of them.

☆

LADY BRACKNELL I'm sure the programme will be delightful, after a few expurgations. French songs I cannot possibly allow. People always seem to think that they are improper, and either look shocked, which is vulgar, or laugh, which is worse. But German sounds a thoroughly respectable language, and indeed, I believe is so.

☆

LADY BRACKNELL Pardon me, you are not engaged to any one. When you do become engaged, I, or your father, should his health permit him, will inform you of the fact. An engagement should come

on a young girl as a surprise, pleasant or unpleasant, as the case
may be. It is hardly a matter that she could be allowed to arrange
for herself.

The Importance of Being Earnest, February 1895. Act I

☆

LADY BRACKNELL Do you smoke?

JACK Well, yes, I must admit I smoke.

LADY BRACKNELL I am glad to hear it. A man should always have an
occupation of some kind. There are far too many idle men in
London as it is.

☆

LADY BRACKNELL I have always been of opinion that a man who desires
to get married should know either everything or nothing. Which
do you know?

JACK *(after some hesitation)* I know nothing, Lady Bracknell.

LADY BRACKNELL I am pleased to hear it. I do not approve of anything
that tampers with natural ignorance. Ignorance is like a delicate
exotic fruit; touch it and the bloom is gone. The whole theory of
modern education is radically unsound. Fortunately in England,
at any rate, education produces no effect whatsoever. If it did, it
would prove a serious danger to the upper classes, and probably
lead to acts of violence in Grosvenor Square.

☆

LADY BRACKNELL What between the duties expected of one during
one's lifetime, and the duties exacted from one after one's death,
land has ceased to be either a profit or a pleasure. It gives one
position, and prevents one from keeping it up. That's all that can
be said about land.

☆

LADY BRACKNELL Now to minor matters. Are your parents living?

JACK I have lost both my parents.

LADY BRACKNELL To lose one parent, Mr Worthing, may be regarded
as a misfortune; to lose both seems like carelessness. Who was
your father? He was evidently a man of some wealth. Was he born
in what the Radical papers call the purple of commerce, or did he
rise from the ranks of the aristocracy?

☆

LADY BRACKNELL To be born, or at any rate bred, in a hand-bag,
whether it had handles or not, seems to be me to display a contempt for the ordinary decencies of family life that reminds one of

244

the worst excesses of the French Revolution. And I presume you know what that unfortunate movement led to? As for the locality in which the hand-bag was found, a cloak-room at a railway station might serve to conceal a social indiscretion – has probably, indeed, been used for that purpose before now – but it could hardly be regarded as an assured basis for a recognised position in good society.

☆

LADY BRACKNELL You can hardly imagine that I and Lord Bracknell would dream of allowing our only daughter – a girl brought up with the utmost care – to marry into a cloak-room, and form an alliance with a parcel. Good morning, Mr Worthing!

☆

JACK Cecily and Gwendolen are perfectly certain to be extremely great friends. I'll bet you anything you like that half an hour after they have met, they will be calling each other sister.
ALGERNON Women only do that when they have called each other a lot of other things first.

☆

GWENDOLEN Ernest, we may never be married. From the expression on mamma's face I fear we never shall. Few parents now-a-days pay any regard to what their children say to them. The old-fashioned respect for the young is fast dying out. Whatever influence I ever had over mamma, I lost at the age of three. But although she may prevent us from becoming man and wife, and I may marry some one else, and marry often, nothing that she can possibly do can alter my eternal devotion to you.

★   ★   ★

MISS PRISM I am not in favour of this modern mania for turning bad people into good people at a moment's notice. As a man sows so let him reap.

The Importance of Being Earnest, Act II

☆

CECILY I keep a diary in order to enter the wonderful secrets of my life. If I didn't write them down, I should probably forget all about them.
MISS PRISM Memory, my dear Cecily, is the diary that we all carry about with us.
CECILY Yes, but it usually chronicles the things that have never happened, and couldn't possibly have happened. I believe that

Memory is responsible for nearly all the three-volume novels that
Mudie sends us.

MISS PRISM Do not speak slightingly of the three-volume novel, Cecily. I
wrote one myself in earlier days.

CECILY Did you really, Miss Prism? How wonderfully clever you are! I
hope that it did not end happily? I don't like novels that end happily. They depress me so much.

MISS PRISM The good ended happily, and the bad unhappily. That is
what Fiction means.

The Importance of Being Earnest, Act II

☆

MISS PRISM Cecily, you will read your Political Economy in my absence.
The chapter on the Fall of the Rupee you may omit. It is somewhat too sensational. Even these metallic problems have their
melodramatic side.

☆

CECILY I have never met any really wicked person before. I feel rather
frightened. I am so afraid he will look just like every one else.

Enter ALGERNON, *very gay and debonair.*

He does!

☆

CECILY You, I see from your card, are Uncle Jack's brother, my cousin
Ernest, my wicked cousin Ernest.

ALGERNON Oh! I am not really wicked at all, cousin Cecily. You
mustn't think that I am wicked.

CECILY If you are not, then you have certainly been deceiving us all in
a very inexcusable manner. I hope you have not been leading a
double life, pretending to be wicked and being really good all the
time. That would be hypocrisy.

☆

CECILY Well, he said at dinner on Wednesday night, that you would
have to choose between this world, the next world, and Australia.

ALGERNON Oh, well! The accounts I have received of Australia and the
next world, are not particularly encouraging. This world is good
enough for me, cousin Cecily.

☆

CECILY Miss Prism says that all good looks are a snare.

ALGERNON They are a snare that every sensible man would like to be
caught in.

CECILY Oh, I don't think I would care to catch a sensible man. I shouldn't know what to talk to him about.

☆

MISS PRISM You are too much alone, dear Dr Chasuble. You should get married. A misanthrope I can understand – a womanthrope, never!

CHASUBLE *(with a scholar's shudder)* Believe me, I do not deserve so neologistic a phrase. The precept as well as the practice of the Primitive Church was distinctly against matrimony.

MISS PRISM *(sententiously)* That is obviously the reason why the Primitive Church has not lasted up to the present day.

☆

CHASUBLE Your brother Ernest dead?

JACK Quite dead.

MISS PRISM What a lesson for him! I trust he will profit by it. ·

☆

JACK He seems to have expressed a desire to be buried in Paris.

CHASUBLE In Paris! *(Shakes his head.)* I fear that hardly points to any very serious state of mind at the last. You would no doubt wish me to make some slight allusion to this tragic domestic affliction next Sunday. (JACK *presses his hand convulsively.)* My sermon on the meaning of the manna in the wilderness can be adapted to almost any occasion, joyful, or, as in the present case, distressing. *(All sigh.)* I have preached it at harvest celebrations, christenings, confirmations, on days of humiliation and festal days. The last time I delivered it was in the Cathedral, as a charity sermon on behalf of the Society for the Prevention of Discontent among the Upper Orders. The Bishop, who was present, was much struck by some of the analogies I drew.

☆

JACK Ah! that reminds me, you mentioned christenings, I think, Dr Chasuble? I suppose you know how to christen all right? (DR CHASUBLE *looks astounded.)* I mean, of course, you are continually christening, aren't you?

MISS PRISM It is, I regret to say, one of the Rector's most constant duties in this parish. I have often spoken to the poorer classes on the subject. But they don't seem to know what thrift is.

☆

CHASUBLE But surely, Mr Worthing, you have been christened already?

JACK I don't remember anything about it.

CHASUBLE But have you any grave doubts on the subject?
JACK I certainly intend to have.

The Importance of Being Earnest, Act II

☆

ALGERNON Well, I don't like your clothes. You look perfectly ridiculous in them. Why on earth don't you go up and change? It is perfectly childish to be in deep mourning for a man who is actually staying for a whole week with you in your house as a guest. I call it grotesque.

☆

CECILY It is always painful to part from people whom one has known for a very brief space of time. The absence of old friends one can endure with equanimity. But even a momentary separation from any one to whom one has just been introduced is almost unbearable.

☆

ALGERNON I hope, Cecily, I shall not offend you if I state quite frankly and openly that you seem to me to be in every way the visible personification of absolute perfection.
CECILY I think your frankness does you great credit, Ernest. If you will allow me, I will copy your remarks into my diary. *(Goes over to table and begins writing in diary.)*
ALGERNON Do you really keep a diary? I'd give anything to look at it. May I?
CECILY Oh no. *(Puts her hand over it.)* You see, it is simply a very young girl's record of her own thoughts and impressions, and consequently meant for publication. When it appears in volume form I hope you will order a copy. But pray, Ernest, don't stop. I delight in taking down from dictation. I have reached 'absolute perfection'. You can go on. I am quite ready for more.

☆

ALGERNON I love you, Cecily. You will marry me, won't you?
CECILY You silly boy! Of course. Why, we have been engaged for the last three months.

☆

ALGERNON But how did we become engaged?
CECILY Well, ever since dear Uncle Jack first confessed to us that he had a younger brother who was very wicked and bad, you, of course, have formed the chief topic of conversation between myself and Miss Prism. And, of course, a man who is much talked

248

---

about is always very attractive. One feels there must be something in him, after all. I daresay it was foolish of me, but I fell in love with you, Ernest.

ALGERNON Darling. And when was the engagement actually settled?

CECILY On the 14th of February last. Worn out by your entire ignorance of my existence, I determined to end the matter one way or the other, and after a long struggle with myself I accepted you under this dear old tree here. The next day I bought this little ring in your name, and this is the little bangle with the true lover's knot I promised you always to wear.

☆

ALGERNON My letters! But, my own sweet Cecily, I have never written you any letters.

CECILY You need hardly remind me of that, Ernest. I remember only too well that I was forced to write your letters for you . . . The three you wrote me after I had broken off the engagement are so beautiful, and so badly spelled, that even now I can hardly read them without crying a little.

ALGERNON But was our engagement ever broken off?

CECILY Of course it was. On the 22nd of last March. You can see the entry if you like. *(Shows diary.)* 'To-day I broke off my engagement with Ernest. I feel it is better to do so. The weather still continues charming.'

ALGERNON But why on earth did you break it off? What had I done? I had done nothing at all. Cecily, I am very much hurt indeed to hear you broke it off. Particularly when the weather was so charming.

CECILY It would hardly have been a really serious engagement if it hadn't been broken off at least once. But I forgave you before the week was out.

☆

CECILY Dr Chasuble is a most learned man. He has never written a single book, so you can imagine how much he knows.

☆

CECILY Considering that we have been engaged since February the 14th, and that I only met you to-day for the first time, I think it is rather hard that you should leave me for so long a period as half an hour. Couldn't you make it twenty minutes?

☆

GWENDOLEN But even men of the noblest possible moral character are extremely susceptible to the influence of the physical charms of

others. Modern, no less than Ancient History, supplies us with
many most painful examples of what I refer to. If it were not so,
indeed, History would be quite unreadable.

The Importance of Being Earnest, Act II

☆

GWENDOLEN I never travel without my diary. One should always have
something sensational to read in the train.

☆

CECILY This is no time for wearing the shallow mask of manners. When
I see a spade I call it a spade.
GWENDOLEN *(satirically)* I am glad to say that I have never seen a
spade. It is obvious that our social spheres have been widely different.

☆

GWENDOLEN I had no idea there were any flowers in the country.
CECILY Oh, flowers are as common here, Miss Fairfax, as people are in
London.
GWENDOLEN Personally I cannot understand how anybody manages to
exist in the country, if anybody who is anybody does. The country
always bores me to death.
CECILY Ah! This is what the newspapers call agricultural depression, is
it not? I believe the aristocracy are suffering very much from it
just at present. It is almost an epidemic amongst them, I have
been told.

☆

GWENDOLEN From the moment I saw you I distrusted you. I felt that
you were false and deceitful. I am never deceived in such matters.
My first impressions of people are invariably right.
CECILY It seems to me, Miss Fairfax, that I am trespassing on your
valuable time. No doubt you have many other calls of a similar
character to make in the neighbourhood.

☆

JACK Well, that is no business of yours.
ALGERNON If it was my business, I wouldn't talk about it. It is very vulgar to talk about one's business. Only people like stockbrokers do
that, and then merely at dinner parties.

☆

ALGERNON When I am in trouble, eating is the only thing that consoles
me. Indeed, when I am in really great trouble, as any one who

knows me intimately will tell you, I refuse everything except food and drink. At the present moment I am eating muffins because I am unhappy. Besides, I am particularly fond of muffins.

★　　　★　　　★

CECILY They have been eating muffins. That looks like repentance.
The Importance of Being Earnest, Act III

☆

LADY BRACKNELL Come here. Sit down. Sit down immediately. Hesitation of any kind is a sign of mental decay in the young, of physical weakness in the old. *(Turns to* JACK.*)* Apprised, sir, of my daughter's sudden flight by her trusty maid, whose confidence I purchased by means of a small coin, I followed her at once by a baggage train. Her unhappy father is, I am glad to say, under the impression that she is attending a more than unusually lengthy lecture by the University Extension Scheme on the Influence of a permanent income on Thought. I do not propose to undeceive him. Indeed I have never undeceived him on any question. I would consider it wrong. But of course you will clearly understand that all communication between yourself and my daughter must cease immediately from this moment. On this point, as indeed on all points, I am firm.

☆

LADY BRACKNELL I do not know whether there is anything peculiarly exciting in the air of this particular part of Hertfordshire, but the number of engagements that go on seems to me considerably above the proper average that statistics have laid down for our guidance. I think some preliminary inquiry on my part would not be out of place. Mr Worthing, is Miss Cardew at all connected with any of the larger railway stations in London? I merely desire information. Until yesterday I had no idea that there were any families or persons whose origin was a Terminus.

☆

LADY BRACKNELL Three addresses always inspire confidence, even in tradesmen.

☆

JACK I have also in my possession, you will be pleased to hear, certificates of Miss Cardew's birth, baptism, whooping cough, registration, vaccination, confirmation, and the measles; both the German and the English variety.

LADY BRACKNELL Ah! A life crowded with incident, I see; though per-

251

haps somewhat exciting for a young girl. I am not myself in favour of premature experiences.

The Importance of Being Earnest, Act III

☆

LADY BRACKNELL A moment, Mr Worthing. A hundred and thirty thousand pounds! And in the Funds! Miss Cardew seems to me a most attractive young lady, now that I look at her. Few girls of the present day have any really solid qualities, any of the qualities that last, and improve with time. We live, I regret to say, in an age of surfaces. *(To* CECILY.) Come over here, dear. (CECILY *goes across.)* Pretty child! your dress is sadly simple, and your hair seems almost as Nature might have left it. But we can soon alter all that. A thoroughly experienced French maid produces a really marvellous result in a very brief space of time. I remember recommending one to young Lady Lancing, and after three months her own husband did not know her.

JACK And after six months nobody knew her.

☆

LADY BRACKNELL There are distinct social possibilities in your profile. The two weak points in our age are its want of principle and its want of profile. The chin a little higher, dear. Style largely depends on the way the chin is worn. They are worn very high, just at present.

☆

LADY BRACKNELL Never speak disrespectfully of Society, Algernon. Only people who can't get into it do that.

☆

LADY BRACKNELL But I do not approve of mercenary marriages. When I married Lord Bracknell I had no fortune of any kind. But I never dreamed for a moment of allowing that to stand in my way.

☆

LADY BRACKNELL To speak frankly, I am not in favour of long engagements. They give people the opportunity of finding out each other's character before marriage, which I think is never advisable.

☆

LADY BRACKELL Algernon is an extremely, I may almost say an ostentatiously, eligible young man. He has nothing, but he looks everything. What more can one desire?

─ 1895 ─

☆

LADY BRACKNELL Untruthful! My nephew Algernon? Impossible! He is an Oxonian.

☆

LADY BRACKNELL How old are you, dear?

CECILY Well, I am really only eighteen, but I always admit to twenty when I go to evening parties.

LADY BRACKNELL You are perfectly right in making some slight alteration. Indeed, no woman should ever be quite accurate about her age. It looks so calculating.

☆

LADY BRACKNELL Thirty-five is a very attractive age. London society is full of women of the very highest birth who have, of their own free choice, remained thirty-five for years. Lady Dumbleton is an instance in point. To my own knowledge she has been thirty-five ever since she arrived at the age of forty, which was many years ago now.

☆

LADY BRACKNELL Come, dear; (GWENDOLEN *rises*) we have already missed five, if not six, trains. To miss any more might expose us to comment on the platform.

☆

LADY BRACKNELL At their age? The idea is grotesque and irreligious! Algernon, I forbid you to be baptized. I will not hear of such excesses. Lord Bracknell would be highly displeased if he learned that this was the way in which you wasted your time and money.

CHASUBLE Am I to understand then that there are to be no christenings at all this afternoon?

JACK I don't think that, as things are now, it would be of much practical value to either of us, Dr Chasuble.

CHASUBLE I am grieved to hear such sentiments from you, Mr Worthing. They savour of the heretical views of the Anabaptists, views that I have completely refuted in four of my unpublished sermons.

☆

LADY BRACKNELL Is this Miss Prism a female of repellent aspect, remotely connected with education?

CHASUBLE (*somewhat indignantly*) She is the most cultivated of ladies, and the very picture of respectability.

253

LADY BRACKNELL It is obviously the same person.
The Importance of Being Earnest, Act III

☆

LADY BRACKNELL This noise is extremely unpleasant. It sounds as if he
was having an argument. I dislike arguments of any kind. They
are always vulgar, and often convincing.

☆

GWENDOLEN This suspense is terrible. I hope it will last.

☆

MISS PRISM *(calmly)* It seems to be mine. Yes, here is the injury it received through the upsetting of a Gower Street omnibus in
younger and happier days. Here is the stain on the lining caused
by the explosion of a temperance beverage, an incident that
occurred at Leamington. And here, on the lock, are my initials. I
had forgotten that in an extravagant moment I had had them
placed there. The bag is undoubtedly mine. I am delighted to
have it so unexpectedly restored to me. It has been a great incon-
venience being without it all these years.

☆

JACK *(in a pathetic voice)* Miss Prism, more is restored to you than this
hand-bag. I was the baby you placed in it.
MISS PRISM *(amazed)* You?
JACK *(embracing her)* Yes – mother!
MISS PRISM *(recoiling in indignant astonishment)* Mr Worthing, I am un-
married!
JACK Unmarried! I do not deny that is a serious blow. But after all,
who has the right to cast a stone against one who has suffered?
Cannot repentance wipe out an act of folly? Why should there be
one law for men, and another for women? Mother, I forgive you.
(Tries to embrace her again.)
MISS PRISM *(still more indignant)* Mr Worthing, there is some error.
(Pointing to LADY BRACKNELL*)*: There is the lady who can tell you
who you really are.
JACK *(after a pause)* Lady Bracknell, I hate to seem inquisitive, but
would you kindly inform me who I am?

☆

LADY BRACKNELL Every luxury that money could buy, including christening, had been lavished on you by your fond and doting
parents.

☆

LADY BRACKNELL *(meditatively)* I cannot at the present moment recall what the General's Christian name was. But I have no doubt he had one. He was eccentric, I admit. But only in later years. And that was the result of the Indian climate, and marriage, and indigestion, and other things of that kind.

☆   ●

JACK Algy! Can't you recollect what our father's Christian name was?
ALGERNON My dear boy, we were never on speaking terms. He died before I was a year old.

☆

LADY BRACKNELL The General was essentially a man of peace, except in his domestic life. But I have no doubt his name would appear in any military directory.

☆

LADY BRACKNELL Yes, I remember now that the General was called Ernest. I knew I had some particular reason for disliking the name.

☆

JACK Gwendolen, it is a terrible thing for a man to find out suddenly that all his life he has been speaking nothing but the truth. Can you forgive me?
GWENDOLEN I can. For I feel that you are sure to change.

★   ★   ★

MR OSCAR WILDE I do not believe that any book or work of art ever had any effect upon morality.
MR EDWARD CARSON, QC Am I right in saying that you do not consider the effect in creating morality or immorality?
MR OSCAR WILDE Certainly I do not.

Regina (Wilde) v. Queensberry, 3 April 1895

☆

MR EDWARD CARSON, QC 'Religions die when they are proved to be true.' Is that true?
MR OSCAR WILDE Yes; I hold that. It is a suggestion towards a philosophy of the absorption of religions by science, but it is too big a question to go into now.
MR EDWARD CARSON, QC Do you think that was a safe axiom to put forward for the philosophy of the young?
MR OSCAR WILDE Most stimulating.
MR EDWARD CARSON, QC 'If one tells the truth, one is sure, sooner or

later, to be found out;?

MR OSCAR WILDE That is a pleasing paradox, but I do not set very high store on it as an axiom.

MR EDWARD CARSON, QC Is it good for the young?

MR OSCAR WILDE Anything is good that stimulates thought in whatever age.

MR EDWARD CARSON, QC Whether moral or immoral?

MR OSCAR WILDE There is no such thing as morality or immorality in thought. There is immoral emotion.

Regina (Wilde) v. Queensberry, 3 April 1895

☆

MR EDWARD CARSON, QC 'A truth ceases to be true when more than one person believes in it'?

MR OSCAR WILDE Perfectly. That would be my metaphysical definition of truth; something so personal that the same truth could never be appreciated by two minds.

☆

MR EDWARD CARSON, QC 'There is something tragic about the enormous number of young men there are in England at the present moment who start life with perfect profiles, and end by adopting some useful profession'?

MR OSCAR WILDE I should think that the young have enough sense of humour.

MR EDWARD CARSON, QC You think that is humorous?

MR OSCAR WILDE I think it is an amusing paradox, an amusing play on words.

☆

MR EDWARD CARSON, QC This is in your introduction to *Dorian Gray:* 'There is no such thing as a moral or an immoral book. Books are well written, or badly written.' That expresses your view?

MR OSCAR WILDE My view on art, yes.

MR EDWARD CARSON, QC Then, I take it, that no matter how immoral a book may be, if it is well written, it is, in your opinion, a good book?

MR OSCAR WILDE Yes, if it were well written so as to produce a sense of beauty, which is the highest sense of which a human being can be capable. If it were badly written, it would produce a sense of disgust.

MR EDWARD CARSON, QC Then a well-written book putting forward perverted moral views may be a good book?

MR OSCAR WILDE No work of art ever puts forward views. Views belong to people who are not artists.

MR EDWARD CARSON, QC A perverted novel might be a good book?

MR OSCAR WILDE I don't know what you mean by a 'perverted' novel.

MR EDWARD CARSON, QC Then I will suggest *Dorian Gray* is open as to the interpretation of being such a novel?

MR OSCAR WILDE That could only be to brutes and illiterates. The views of Philistines on art are incalculably stupid.

MR EDWARD CARSON, QC An illiterate person reading *Dorian Gray* might consider it such a novel?

MR OSCAR WILDE The views of illiterates on art are unaccountable. I am concerned only with my view of art. I don't care twopence what other people think of it.

MR EDWARD CARSON, QC The majority of persons would come under your definition of Philistines and illiterates?

MR OSCAR WILDE I have found wonderful exceptions.

☆

MR EDWARD CARSON, QC The affection and love of the artist of *Dorian Gray* might lead an ordinary individual to believe that it might have a certain tendency?

MR OSCAR WILDE I have no knowledge of the views of ordinary individuals.

MR EDWARD CARSON, QC You did not prevent the ordinary individual from buying your book?

MR OSCAR WILDE I have never discouraged him.

☆

MR EDWARD CARSON, QC But let us go over it phrase by phrase. 'I quite admit that I adored you madly.' What do you say to that? Have you ever adored a young man madly?

MR OSCAR WILDE No, not madly; I prefer love – that is a higher form.

MR EDWARD CARSON, QC Never mind about that. Let us keep down to the level we are at now?

MR OSCAR WILDE I have never given adoration to anybody except myself. *(Loud laughter.)*

MR EDWARD CARSON, QC I suppose you think that a very smart thing?

MR OSCAR WILDE Not at all.

☆

MR EDWARD CARSON, QC I believe you have written an article to show that Shakespeare's sonnets were suggestive of unnatural vice?

MR OSCAR WILDE On the contrary I have written an article to show that they are not. I objected to such a perversion being put upon Shakespeare.

☆

257

MR EDWARD CARSON, QC 'I wanted to have you all to myself.' Did you ever have that feeling?

MR OSCAR WILDE No; I should consider it an intense nuisance, an intense bore.

MR EDWARD CARSON, QC 'I was afraid that the world would know of my idolatry.' Why should he grow afraid that the world should know of it?

MR OSCAR WILDE Because there are people in the world who cannot understand the intense devotion, affection, and admiration that an artist can feel for a wonderful and beautiful personality. These are the conditions under which we live. I regret them.

Regina (Wilde) v. Queensberry, 3 April 1895

☆

MR EDWARD CARSON, QC In another passage Dorian Gray receives a book. Was the book to which you refer a moral book?

MR OSCAR WILDE Not well written, but it gave me an idea.

MR EDWARD CARSON, QC Was not the book you have in mind of a certain tendency?

MR OSCAR WILDE I decline to be cross-examined upon the work of another artist. It is an impertinence and a vulgarity.

☆

MR EDWARD CARSON, QC Why should a man of your age address a boy [Lord Alfred Douglas] nearly twenty years younger as 'My own boy'?

MR OSCAR WILDE I was fond of him. I have always been fond of him.

MR EDWARD CARSON, QC Do you adore him?

MR OSCAR WILDE No, but I have always liked him. I think it is a beautiful letter. It is a poem. I was not writing an ordinary letter. You might as well cross-examine me as to whether *King Lear* or a sonnet of Shakespeare was proper.

MR EDWARD CARSON, QC Apart from art, Mr Wilde?

MR OSCAR WILDE I cannot answer apart from art.

MR EDWARD CARSON, QC Suppose a man who was not an artist had written this letter, would you say it was a proper letter?

MR OSCAR WILDE A man who was not an artist could not have written that letter.

MR EDWARD CARSON, QC Why?

MR OSCAR WILDE Because nobody but an artist could write it. He certainly could not write the language unless he were a man of letters.

MR EDWARD CARSON, QC I can suggest, for the sake of your reputation, that there is nothing very wonderful in this 'red rose-leaf lips of yours'?

MR OSCAR WILDE A great deal depends on the way it is read.

MR EDWARD CARSON, QC 'Your slim gilt soul walks between passion and poetry.' Is that a beautiful phrase?

MR OSCAR WILDE Not as you read it, Mr Carson. You read it very badly.

MR EDWARD CARSON, QC I do not profess to be an artist; and when I hear you give evidence, I am glad I am not.

☆

MR EDWARD CARSON, QC May I ask why you gave this man, who you knew was a notorious blackmailer, ten shillings?

MR OSCAR WILDE I gave it out of contempt.

MR EDWARD CARSON, QC Then the way you show your contempt is by paying ten shillings?

MR OSCAR WILDE Yes, very often.

☆

MR EDWARD CARSON, QC Was his [Alphonse Conway's] conversation literary?

MR OSCAR WILDE On the contrary, quite simple and easily understood. He had been to school where naturally he had not learned much.

★   ★   ★

MR EDWARD CARSON, QC Did he [Alfred Taylor] use to do his own cooking?

MR OSCAR WILDE I don't know. I don't think he did anything wrong.

MR EDWARD CARSON, QC I have not suggested that he did.

MR OSCAR WILDE Well, cooking is an art.

Ibid. 4 April 1895

☆

MR EDWARD CARSON, QC Did Atkins call you 'Oscar'?

MR OSCAR WILDE Yes. I called him 'Fred', because I always call by their Christian names people whom I like. People whom I dislike I call something else.

☆

MR EDWARD CARSON, QC Did you ask what his [Charles Parker's] previous occupation was?

MR OSCAR WILDE I never inquire about people's pasts.

MR EDWARD CARSON, QC Nor their future?

MR OSCAR WILDE Oh, that is problematical.

☆

MR EDWARD CARSON, QC Do you drink champagne yourself?

MR OSCAR WILDE Yes; iced champagne is a favourite drink of mine –
strongly against my doctor's orders.

MR EDWARD CARSON, QC Never mind your doctor's orders, sir!

MR OSCAR WILDE I never do.

Ibid. 4 April 1895

☆

MR EDWARD CARSON, QC Do I understand that even a young boy you
might pick up in the street would be a pleasing companion?

MR OSCAR WILDE I would talk to a street arab, with pleasure.

MR EDWARD CARSON, QC You would talk to a street arab?

MR OSCAR WILDE If he would talk to me. Yes, with pleasure.

★   ★   ★

MR C. F. GILL During 1893 and 1894 you were a good deal in the company of Lord Alfred Douglas?

WILDE Oh, yes.

MR C. F. GILL Did he read that poem [Douglas's sonnet 'In Praise of
Shame'] to you?

WILDE Yes.

MR C. F. GILL You can, perhaps, understand that such verses as these
would not be acceptable to the reader with an ordinarily balanced
mind?

WILDE I am not prepared to say. It appears to me to be a question of
· taste, temperament and individuality. I should say that one
man's poetry is another man's poison! *(Laughter.)*

MR C. F. GILL I daresay! The next poem is one described as 'Two
Loves'. It contains these lines:

> 'Sweet youth,
> Tell my why, sad and sighing, dost thou rove
> These pleasant realms? I pray thee tell me sooth,
> What is thy name?' He said, 'My name is Love',
> Then straight the first did turn himself to me,
> And cried, 'He lieth, for his name is Shame.
> But I am Love, and I was wont to be
> Alone in this fair garden, till he came
> Unasked by night; I am true Love, I fill
> The hearts of boy and girl with mutual flame.'
> Then sighing said the other, 'Have thy will,
> I am the Love that dare not speak its name.'

Was that poem explained to you?

WILDE I think that is clear.

MR C. F. GILL There is no question as to what it means?

WILDE Most certainly not.

MR C. F. GILL Is it not clear that the love described relates to natural

260

love and unnatural love?

WILDE No.

MR C. F. GILL What is the 'Love that dare not speak its name'?

WILDE 'The Love that dare not speak its name' in this century is such a great affection of an elder for a younger man as there was between David and Jonathan, such as Plato made the very basis of his pilosophy, and such as you will find in the sonnets of Michelangelo and Shakespeare. It is that deep, spiritual affection that is as pure as it is perfect. It dictates and pervades great works of art like those of Shakespeare and Michelangelo, and those two letters of mine, such as they are. It is in this century misunderstood, so much misunderstood that it may be described as the 'Love that dare not speak its name', and on account of it I am placed where I am now. It is beautiful, it is fine, it is the noblest form of affection. There is nothing unnatural about it. It is intellectual, and it repeatedly exists between an elder and a younger man, when the elder man has intellect, and the younger man has all the joy, hope and glamour of life before him. That it should be so the world does not understand. The world mocks at it and sometimes puts one in the pillory for it. *(Loud applause, mingled with some hisses.)*

MR JUSTICE CHARLES If there is the slightest manifestation of feeling I shall have the Court cleared. There must be complete silence preserved.

Regina v. Wilde & Taylor. 30 April 1895

☆

MR JUSTICE WILLS Oscar Wilde and Alfred Taylor, the crime of which you have been convicted is so bad that one has to put stern restraint upon one's self to prevent one's self from describing, in language which I would rather not use, the sentiments which must rise to the breast of every man of honour who has heard the details of these two terrible trials. That the jury have arrived at a correct verdict in this case I cannot persuade myself to entertain the shadow of a doubt; and I hope, at all events, that those who sometimes imagine that a judge is half-hearted in the cause of decency and morality because he takes care no prejudice shall enter into the case, may see that that is consistent at least with the utmost sense of indignation at the horrible charges brought home to both of you.

It is no use for me to address you. People who can do these things must be dead to all sense of shame, and one cannot hope to produce any effect upon them. It is the worst case I have ever tried. That you, Taylor, kept a kind of male brothel it is impossible to doubt. And that you, Wilde, have been the centre of a circle of extensive corruption of the most hideous kind among young men, it is equally impossible to doubt.

I shall, under the circumstances, be expected to pass the severest sentence that the law allows. In my judgment it is totally inadequate for such a case as this. The sentence of the Court is that each of you be imprisoned and kept to hard labour for two years. *(Some cries of 'Oh! Oh!' and 'Shame' were heard in Court.)*

THE CONVICT WILDE And I? May I say nothing, my lord?

Regina v Wilde & Taylor (Second Trial). 25 May 1895

APPENDIX I

*A Russian Realistic Romance**

We wish Vizetelly and Co. had not polluted the fair name of Dostoieff-sky by including *Crime and Punishment* among their series of unclean romances which they borrow from the French. Between the Russian novelist and the obscene brood of pseudo-realists which roosts in the *Cloaca maxima* of France there is a great gulf fixed. The three Russian novelists whose fame is European were men of ideal aims, of a strange sweetness of soul, and of a subtle personal fascination, compared with which the personalities of the so-called realists are but as satyrs to angels. Turgenieff, Tolstoy, and Dostoieffsky were men whose thought is a distinctly purifying, inspiring, ennobling element in European literature. Tolstoy – no longer a novel writer – is now living what he conceives to be the true Christ-life in cobbling shoes; Dostoieffsky died four or five years ago; Turgenieff only the other day; but the works of these three men will not speedily pass into oblivion. They are not so well known as they should be in England, but every year sees an addition to the number of their admirers. There is much in *Crime and Punishment* which reminds the reader of the author's former work, known in this country under the title of *Buried Alive*. The same minute-ness in the description of details and in the analysis of human thought and action, which made the weird story of Russian prison-life so strangely real, characterizes the present volume, although it illumi-nates quite another side of existence. The figures in the grand, gloomy picture are a handful of men and women taken haphazard from the crowd of the Russian capital. They are nearly all poor. The central figure in the novel is one of those impecunious 'students,' the outcomes of whose turbulent brains have often been a curse where they were in-tended to be a blessing to their country. He appears everywhere; is never out of sight in the scenes vibrating between the highest heights and deepest depths of life. Rodia Romanovitch Raskolnikoff has left the St Petersburg University six months before the story begins, being without means to pursue his studies. Since then he has fled the society of men; has brooded over many social questions; has written an article in a social paper on crime, in which he declares that crime, though it is

---

**Crime and Punishment*. A Russian Realistic Novel. By Feodor Dostoieffsky. Vizetelly and Co.

punishable in ordinary men and women, is permitted to extraordinary beings. This idea has become morbidly attractive, and in order to experiment whether he belongs to the 'extraordinary' party, he kills an old female usurer and her half-idiotic sister. Circumstances favour him; in semi-delirium, which shortly after grows into a dangerous brain fever, he commits the deed without being discovered, but his punishment begins at once. He returns to his stifling little back room, effacing every trace of the murder, and to his friends – young men of the party of Progress, although harmless enough and endowed with thoroughly Russian unselfishness and fidelity. Raskolnikoff's mother is one of the devoted, weak-minded women to whom much senselessness must be forgiven because they have loved much. She starves herself in order that her son may have plenty; she consents to the marriage of her beautiful daughter to a cold-hearted, scheming official, that her Rodia may have the chance of a good career; and Rodia, the son, haunted by the spectre of the dead usurer, flees from his mother's and sister's presence when they come from their quiet village to seal by the daughter's marriage the sacrifice made for Rodia's sake. Chance wills, meanwhile, that Raskolnikoff becomes the friend of a poverty-striken family. He meets the drunken father at the public-house, and hears that his consumptive wife and little children are at home, crying for bread. Still worse, he learns that his eldest daughter, when yet on the threshold of childhood, has prostituted herself to keep her relatives from starving; the father is killed, and on the days between the death and burial, the ravings of the widow and the moans of the orphans for the first time distract his thought for a moment from the bloody shadow which ever follows him. In the interval he sees the fallen girl, Sonia, for the first time. Timid, with tearful child-eyes she looks up to him as her benefactor and her only friend. Her character is drawn with consummate skill. She is a figure of tragic pathos. A strange fascination attracts him to seek her out in her own lodgings, a bare little room in an obscure street of St Petersburg; and there, in the haunt of impurity and sin, the harlot and the assassin meet together to read the story of Lazarus and Dives. In that same den Rodia confesses his crime, and, in anguish almost too deep for words, the outcast girl implores the criminal, for God's sake, to confess his crime and make atonement. His torture becoming ever more intense, he is suspected, and endeavours to fly to America. But doomed, like a lost ghost, to haunt the place of his crime, he is at last, by Sonia's pleas, persuaded to give himself up to justice, and is sentenced to seven years' penal servitude in Siberia. By a waste Siberian river we meet Raskolnikoff again, moody and stubborn, with nothing but glowering looks for his fellow-convicts and hardly a word for Sonia who has followed him and patiently waits for the dawn of love in the criminal's eye. At last it comes: he has been ill; Sonia has also been ill, and again they meet by the lonely riverside, early on a bright summer morning. Then the spell is broken; the light of love gleams in his eye, he looks up into her face from where he sits on a log by the water-side, and 'she saw it, and did not doubt that he loved her – loved her at last!' and with that the story ends.

Round this meagre skeleton of a plot are grouped a number of figures, beautiful among whom is the criminal's sister – pure, innocent, and unarmed like the heavenly Una; and the subtle skill with which their various characters are delineated makes *Crime and Punishment* one of the most interesting and curious psychological studies of modern fiction. Sometimes a beautiful poem in prose, in the shape of a dream that is told, lightens up the scene with a golden brightness of sunlight that now and then recalls the best passages in the novels of Turgenieff. A small defect on the translator's part, which somewhat mars the enjoyment of the reader who is without a clue to the mysteries of Russian nomenclature, is the confusion of names; thus, for instance, is Raskolnikoff's sister often in almost the same breath mentioned as Dounia, Dounetchka, and Eudoxia Romanovna; while her brother figures as Rodka, Rodia, Rodion Romanovitch, and M. Raskolnikoff. Also would it add to the lucidity of the story if the otherwise able translator had deemed it advisable (since the mere fact of a word being written in italics does not enlighten the reader as to its meaning) to explain that the Russian word *tchin* signifies a Government office, that a *tchinovnik* is an official in the same, that a *traltir* is a public-house and a *khalat* a dressing-gown.

Pall Mall Gazette
28 May 1886

APPENDIX 2

A Fire at Sea[*]

In the month of May of the year eighteen hundred and thirty-eight I happened to be crossing from St Petersburg to Lubeck on the steamship *Nicholas the First*. As at that time there was very little railway communication, every tourist took the sea-route, and for the same reason many people brought their travelling carriages with them, so as to be able to continue their tour through Germany, France, and other countries. We had with us, I remember, twenty-eight private conveyances, and were in all two-hundred and eighty passengers, including twenty children. I was very young at the time, and as I did not suffer at all from seasickness I enjoyed my new experiences immensely. Some of the ladies on board were extremely pretty, and a few quite beautiful; most of them, alas! are long since dead.

It was the first time that my mother had ever allowed me to go away by myself, and before I left she made me promise to be on my best behaviour, and, above all things, never to touch a card. As it happened, it was this last promise that was the first to be broken.

One particular evening there was a great gathering of the passengers in the saloon, where some well-known Russian bankers were gambling. They used to play a kind of lansquenet, and the jingle of the gold pieces, which were much more common then than they are now, was quite deafening. Suddenly one of the players, seeing that I did not join in, and not understanding why, asked me to take a hand, and when in my boyish simplicity I told him my reason, he went into a fit of laughter, and called out to his friends that he had made a real find, a young man who had never played cards in his life, and who consequently was quite certain to have the most extraordinary luck, fool's luck in fact! . . . I don't know how it came about, but ten minutes later I was sitting at the gambling-table with a lot of cards in my hand, as bold as brass, and playing, playing like a madman!

I must acknowledge that in my case the old proverb turned out true; money kept coming to me in waves; and beneath my trembling perspiring hands the gold piled itself up in heaps. The banker who had in-

[*]In a posthumous volume, ('Œuvres Dernières de I. Tourgueneff,' Hetzel et Cie, Paris) this is said to have been a real incident in the novelist's life, dictated by him in French three months before he died.

Ross, Robert Baldwin, creative art critic and Wilde's literary executor 18-20, 24, 37
Rossetti, Dante Gabriel, deficient in soul-marketing enthusiasm 70
Rossetti, William Michael, excessive in life-curriculum regurgitation 80
Rousseau, Jean Jacques, confessor 126
Rubempré, Lucien de, his death a grief incurable for Vivian 103
Ruskin, John, seminal and later nostalgic influence on Wilde 11-15, 32, 76, 88, 96-97, 102, 131

St James's Gazette, Tory periodical (ed. S. J. Low) hostile to Wilde 167-69, 196
St James's Theatre performs Shakespeare, and subsequently Wilde 59, 189-95, 242-55
St Mary Magdalen, her shame may be the protector of modern Lucretias 130
St Stephen, his martyrdom receives additional horrific complications 69
St Thomas the Apostle, his scepticism enlarges his venerability beyond his merits 107, 120
La Sainte Courtesane (Wilde) unfinished play left by author in cab 14
Salomé (Wilde), written in French and probably untranslatable 32-34, 197-204
Salt a pitfall and a pillar for the British cook 56
Samuel, a prophet in his infancy inspiring use of second-generation models 99
Sappho, a pillar of flame to antiquity, a pillar of shadow to us 96
San Francisco, as a form of celestial revelation 46-47, 165
Sand, George (Amandine Aurore Lucie Dupin, Baronne Dudevant) 89-90
Saturday Review, edited by W. H. Pollock and (from 1894) Frank Harris 79, 221-22
Schopenhauer, Artur, an analyst of Hamlet's invention 105
Schroeder, Horst (*Oscar Wilde, the Portrait of Mr W. H. – Its Composition, Publication and Reception* (1984)) 36
Scots Observer, edited by W. E. Henley, hostile to Wilde in various identities 169-70
Scott, Sir Walter, his indebtedness to Maria Edgeworth 82-83
Selected Letters of Oscar Wilde (1979), ed. Hart-Davis 35
'The Selfish Giant' (Wilde), a story of misanthropic discovery of love 91-92
Sévigné, Madame de (*née* Marie de Rabutin-Chantal), serves French prose 97, 126
Shakespeare, William, an unknown playwright 14, 16, 58-60, 62, 69, 82, 87, 105, 120-23, 126, 132, 137, 152, 176, 178-179
'Shakespeare and Stage Costume' (Wilde), *see* 'The Truth of Masks'
Shaw, George Bernard, Wilde's heir in Irish dramatic composition 17, 21, 31, 32
Shelley, Percy Bysshe, a signer who realised his soul 176
Sheridan, Richard Brinsley, Wilde's precursor in Irish dramatic composition 81
Shylock, Wilde taken by Ruskin to see Irving's performance 13
Simile, the worst Wilde had seen by 1888, even in poetry 89
Smouse, its unintended zoölogical kinship to Snark 116
Socialism, Wilde's, otherwise Anarchism or Individualism 112-13
Son of Oscar Wilde (Holland), autobiography of a victim of tragedy 17-18
'The Soul of Man Under Socialism' (Wilde), a cry and a creed 37, 172-83
South Africa, its poets on the whole depress Wilde 116
Spade, called a spade by Wilkinson, Wordsworth, Cecily but not Gwendolen or Lord Henry Wotton 103, 162, 250
Speaker, a radical periodical in which Wilde reviewed and was reviewed 124-25, 187-88
Spectacles, blue, essential for critics and pessimists 93, 227
Sphinx, Art not one in search of its Oedipus 132
'The Star-Child' (Wilde), a story of a foundling's pride and penitence 187
Stendhal (*pseud., i.e.* Marie Henry Beyle), French novelist and soul-tracker 141
Stevenson, Robert Louis, a humane artist of excessively scientific scholarship 96, 101
Story of the Kings of Rome in Verse (Denman), a judicial murder or infanticide 115-116
Sun, Sunday, displeases Wilde by its brazen persistence in sluggish malice 220
Swimming, a necessity in correct aristocratic response to class struggle 42
Swinburne, Algernon Charles, a vacuum absorbed by Nature 119

Talking, desirability of its being taught, save to Irish 75-76, 238
Talma, François Joseph, enduring legacy of costume accuracy on French acting 87
Tartuffe, an immigrant to English business, indignant at his exposure by Zola 102, 163
Taylor, Alfred, proprietor of male brothel who refused to testify against Wilde and was sentenced with him 261
Taylor, Tom, opponent of Whistler, playwright and *Times* art critic 18, 44
Teaching, now-a-days performed by all those incapable of learning 100
'Ten O'Clock Lecture' (Whistler), reviewed protractedly by Wilde 14, 23, 53-55
Tennyson, Alfred, Lord, Arthur unable to approach Celtic original 82, 110
Terry, (Dame) Ellen, 'Our Lady of the Lyceum' 13
Thackeray, William Makepeace, his gifts find no echoes? 88, 167-68
Theatre stage preferable for legal than for floral arrangements 48, 57-58
Thebes, a very dull city indeed despite musical construction, and corpses 113, 123
Thirteen Club, an institution ceremonially defying superstition at dinner 35
'Thyrsis' (Matthew Arnold), optimistic prediction of its popularity 113
The Times (London), Wilde writes to 183, 204
Timon of Athens, colleague in our rage against the world 122
Tomi, in Dacia, analogous to Australia for disposal of poet 115
'To the Spade of a Friend (an Agriculturalist), Composed while we were Labouring Together in his Pleasure-Ground' (Wordsworth) 104
Transactions of the Psychical Society the limit of Vivian's depressing reading 106-7
Trains as a subject of greater concern to Lady Bracknell than to Romeo 35, 45, 253